CHICKEN SOUP FOR THE AMERICAN IDOL SOUL

CHICKEN SOUP FOR THE AMERICAN IDOL SOUL

Jack Canfield
Mark Victor Hansen
Debra Halperin Poneman

Health Communications, Inc.
Deerfield Beach, Florida

www.hcibooks.com
www.chickensoup.com

We would like to acknowledge the following publishers and individuals for permission to reprint the following material.

Foreword. Reprinted by permission of Paula Abdul. ©2007 Paula Abdul.

Without God, I'm Tone Deaf. Reprinted by permission of Melinda Doolittle. ©2007 Melinda Doolittle.

Thousands Shouting My Name. Reprinted by permission of Carmen Rasmusen. ©2007 Carmen Rasmusen.

The Impossible Dream. Reprinted by permission of Jim Verraros. ©2007 Jim Verraros.

Something to Talk About. Reprinted by permission of Cecile Frot-Coutaz. ©2007 Cecile Frot-Coutaz.

The Only Thing We Knew for Sure. Reprinted by permission of Kimberley Locke. ©2007 Kimberley Locke.

(Continued on page 303)

Library of Congress Cataloging-in-Publication Data

Chicken soup for the American idol soul / [compiled by] Jack Canfield, Mark Victor Hansen, and Debra Poneman.
    p. cm.
    ISBN-13: 978-0-7573-0645-7 (trade paper)
    ISBN-10: 0-7573-0645-4 (trade paper)
    1. Success—Anecdotes. 2. American idol (Television program)—Biography. 3. Entertainers—Religious life. 4. Success—Religious aspects. I. Canfield, Jack, 1944-   II. Hansen, Mark Victor.
III. Poneman, Debra.
    BF637.S8C4725 2007
    158.1'28—dc22

                               2007032436

Publisher: Health Communications, Inc.
           3201 S.W. 15th Street
           Deerfield Beach, FL 33442-8190

Cover design by Larissa Hise Henoch
Interior formatting by Lawna Patterson Oldfield

We dedicate this
book to everyone
who believes in
a dream.

Contents

1. DON'T STOP THINKING ABOUT TOMORROW:
THE DREAM COME TRUE

2. WE ARE FAMILY: THE POWER OF THOSE WE LOVE

3. AIN'T NO MOUNTAIN HIGH ENOUGH:
STORIES OF OVERCOMING OBSTACLES

4. YOU LIFT ME UP: STORIES BY IDOLS
TOUCHED BY OTHERS

7. I GOTTA BE ME: STORIES OF STAYING TRUE TO YOURSELF

8. WITH A LITTLE HELP FROM MY FRIENDS: STORIES OF THOSE WHO HELP US THROUGH

Foreword

When I first heard about *Chicken Soup for the American Idol Soul,* I thought how exciting it was that the #1 show in television history and the #1 bestselling nonfiction series in publishing history should come together, so I felt honored when I was asked to be part of it.

As I've worked on this project and read some of the stories, I've seen that there is more to this marriage than just the merging of two great twenty-first-century *tours de force.* The stories in the Chicken Soup books are all about overcoming odds and going through adversity while staying true to yourself. They are about hope and love, and letting your light shine and sharing it with the world. And, of course, they are about living your dreams—and there is no more perfect illustration of that than an *American Idol* story.

My greatest joy in being part of *American Idol* has been to see kids show up at their first auditions—some shy, some cocky, some nervous, some overconfident—but each with a dream and a background almost always filled with adversity and obstacles that had to be overcome in order for them to be standing in front of us that day. And then, over the course of the season and the years following, I get to watch them blossom into poised, confident, successful young adults.

While it may seem at times that I'm being too positive, as a performer I know how important it is to be acknowledged and supported through encouraging feedback. When you get to know these kids and what they've lived through, you'll see why I find it difficult to step on their dreams. In this book, you'll read their amazing stories—stories of courage and optimism from the *Idols* themselves, as well as from the people who have inspired them, and the people they have inspired. And when you read this book, you'll see what I've seen, and you'll know why I'm always in their corner.

Through my own career, I have also experienced many ups and downs, but I've never let go of my biggest dream, which is to help bring out the best in others. May reading the stories in this book inspire that best in all of you.

Paula Abdul
November 2007

Acknowledgments

We wish to express our heartfelt gratitude to the following people who helped make this book possible.

To Jack's family: Inga, Travis, Riley, Christopher, Oran, and Kyle, for all their love and support.

To Mark's daughter, Elisabeth Del Gesso and her son Seth (Mark's grandson!), and his daughter, Melanie Hansen, for once again sharing and lovingly supporting us in creating yet another book.

From Debra: To my husband, Fred, for his unconditional love and support, unwavering patience, and brilliant insights for this book. You are a gift to me beyond compare. To my daughter, Deanna, for her inspired writing, her impeccable transcriptions, and her pure heart. To my son, Daniel, for his uncomplaining acceptance of my time constraints and invaluable editorial input. And to all three of them for being the finest human beings I have the honor to know. To my mom, Celia Halperin, for a lifetime of selfless giving from her pure heart—and the great food that appeared in our refrigerator. To my other family members and friends for being there with love through this demanding time: Ben Gasbarra; Larry, Diane, and Garrett Halperin; Barbara and Eric Bourdette; Jonathan Poneman; Uncle Herb; Doneen; Barbara DeAngelis;

Marcia Brainin; Kiki Bussell; Judi Bornstein; Radhika Schwartz; Janet Attwood; Rhanda Salameh; Emily Green; Mary Pat Knight; Jill Press; Marci and Ross Quattrochi; Robin Tennant; Pam Dell; Jeanie and Kim up in heaven; Nandu Menon and Harsha Michel; Michael Laughrin; Bill Farber; Thomas Gates; Amsheva Mallani; Karin Chesley; all the divine Mothers and Masters; my magnificent Melaleuca business partners (thank you for your patience and understanding!); and my precious godchildren—I love you all so very much. And, last but not least, to the amazing Lise Hintze—you know I couldn't have done this without you. Our many laughs and occasional tears are what got me through.

To the incomparable Marci Shimoff, whose combination of competence, brilliance, and innocence of heart continues to leave us speechless. Thank you for conceiving of this book and for your vital collaborative input.

To our publisher and friend, Peter Vegso, for his continuous support and allegiance to all of us and to the *Chicken Soup for the Soul* brand.

To Russ Kamalski—your exceptional insight, patience, and genuine loving support meant the world to us. Your enthusiasm got this book off the ground, and your steady guidance kept it on track. You have the extraordinary gift of keeping everyone happy!

To Patty Hansen—we deeply appreciate your thorough and competent handling of the legal aspects of this book, your gift as a brilliant editor, and your wise judgment as an exceptional liaison. Thank you for going far beyond the call of duty in helping us.

To D'ette Corona, our co-author liaison, what can we say—you are incredible. We felt you completely supporting this book and us with a smile all along the way. We love you!

To Patty Aubery, for being there on every step of the journey.

To Jennie Cote and Maggie Carlyle, for always being willing to go the extra mile for us. You made the difficult parts of our job easy.

Thank you to FremantleMedia and 19 Entertainment for making this book happen. For FremantleMedia: Cecile Frot-Coutaz, Wylleen May, Nigel Lythgoe, Ken Warwick, Patrick Lynn, Reilly Oliver, Manfred Westphal, Keith Hindle, Olivier Gers, Rebecca Morris, David Luner, James Ngo, Anna Nettle, and the amazing Nora Wong. Nora, you are not only a brilliant and competent businesswoman, but also a magnificent human being. For 19 Entertainment: Simon Fuller, Robert Dodds, Iain Piria, Ann Edelblute, Allison Carpenter, Martha Brass, Mark Brittain, Maya Maraj, and Sarah Farrow.

To our wonderful writers and editors, Cindy Buck, Lise Hintze, Carol Rehme, Josh Murray, Brian Aubrey, Deanna Poneman, Cynthia Lane, and Carol Kline. This book would not be what it is without your thoughtful input and extraordinary skill.

To Sergio Baroni, Bill Levacy, Gayatri Schriefer, and Katina Griffin for their loving support.

To Veronica Romero, Barbara LoMonaco, Lisa Williams, Teresa Collett, Robin Yerian, Jesse Ianniello, Lauren Edelstein, Lauren Bray, Laurie Hartman, Patti Clement, Michelle Statti, Debbie Lefever, Connie Simoni, Karen Schoenfeld, Marty Robinson, Patti Coffey, Pat Burns, Kristi Waite, and Blake Arce who support Jack's and Mark's businesses with skill and love.

To Michele Matrisciani, Carol Rosenberg, Andrea Gold, Allison Janse, and Katheline St. Fort, our editors at Health Communications, Inc., for their devotion to excellence.

To Lori Golden, Kelly Maragni, Sean Geary, Patricia McConnell, Kim Weiss, Paola Fernandez-Rana, Christine Zambrano, and Jaron Hunter, for doing such an incredible job supporting our books.

To Tom Sand, Claude Choquette, and Luc Jutras, who manage year after year to get our books translated into thirty-six languages around the world.

To Larissa Hise Henoch, Lawna Patterson Oldfied, Andrea Perrine Brower, Anthony Clausi, Peter Quintal and Dawn Von Strolley Grove for their talent, creativity, and unrelenting patience while producing book covers and inside designs that capture the essence of Chicken Soup for the Soul.

To all the *Idols* and behind-the-scenes crew—you were a delight to meet and work with, and are all so beautiful inside and out. We now know even more profoundly why you deserve all the success you have.

And to all the fans who submitted a story, we deeply appreciate your sharing your experiences with us. While it wasn't possible to use everything everyone sent, we were deeply moved by your stories and your generosity in sharing them with us. Don't stop writing!

Because of the size of this project, we may have left out the names of some people who helped along the way. Please know that we really do love and appreciate all of you.

Introduction

Since the day we began to write this book, we've had people tell us that we have the best job in the world. We couldn't agree more. What *Idol* lover wouldn't want to spend his or her days sitting and recalling memories with Ruben Studdard or Jordin Sparks? We knew that meeting with the *Idols*, the behind-the-scenes crew, and the *Idol* fans would be fun and exciting—and allow us to be the envy of the neighborhood—but we didn't suspect that writing this book would be the fulfillment of our own dreams.

It's no secret that *American Idol* is a show like no other. What was at first thought by many to be a simple talent competition has turned into a cultural phenomenon unprecedented in entertainment history. There is not a corner of our country where people aren't discussing *Idol*—even if they are busy justifying why they *don't* watch it! And in writing this book, we've learned that it's not only the top *Idols* from each season who have had their lives dramatically altered by this show; it's also countless people from all walks of life, all across America.

When we began soliciting stories, we started with the fans. As anticipated, we received many stories from people who, inspired by the *Idols*, had found the courage to go out and achieve their own dreams. But we also received stories we never anticipated. There was the story from the couple who, because of *American Idol,* chose to keep their marriage together, from the military wife who found the show to be the one thing that took her mind off the daily apprehension she lived with while her husband was overseas defending our country, and from the parents of a terminally ill child whose dying wish was fulfilled by an *Idol.* We received stories from literally hundreds of others who shared that, because of *Idol,* they were able to forget their physical, financial, and emotional pain, and instead enjoy, for at least a few brief hours each week, happiness, excitement, pins-and-needles anticipation, elation, and even love.

Yes, these fans love their *Idols.* Just walk by the water fountain or coffee machine and listen to what people are saying at any school or office in America on a Wednesday or Thursday morning.

While working on stories with the behind-the-scenes crew—the stylists, musicians, vocal coaches, producers, stage manager, and director—we found that they, too, had been touched and inspired by the *Idols.* We also discovered that they each had their own unique story of overcoming tremendous odds, and felt that through *Idol,* they were now living their American dream. We found these professionals, all of whom were now at the pinnacle of success in their respective fields, to be exceedingly gracious and humble—and grateful to be a part of the *Idol* family. As you'll see in their stories, they share not only a passion for the show, but a deep respect for one another and a genuine desire to support the contestants in any way they can.

It was Simon Fuller, CEO of 19 Entertainment, who, in 2001, following the success of *American Idol's* precursor, England's *Pop Idol,* had the idea to export his smash hit to America. Although it seemed that everyone doubted the show would succeed—it was turned down by almost every major network—Fuller was undaunted. Finally, FOX's Vice President of Alternative Programming, Mike Darnell, went to bat for the Brits and convinced FOX to commit to at least eight shows. Because of Fuller's vision and FOX's willingness to take a chance, *American Idol* was introduced to the American public and has become the stuff of which television history is made.

Everyone has an opinion about why *American Idol* is such an enormous success. Some think it's because the viewers vote to decide who stays and who goes. Some think it's the acerbic critiques of judge Simon Cowell. Some think it's the thrill of watching the American dream come true before our eyes. Fuller believes credit goes to the amazing team he's assembled, including judges Paula Abdul, Randy Jackson, and Simon Cowell; host Ryan Seacrest; and Executive Producers Nigel Lythgoe, Ken Warwick, and Cecile Frot-Coutaz.

After having spent the greater part of the last year working on this book, we believe that all of those things are true, but there is another reason for the show's success.

We believe that the success of *American Idol* lies in that it is not just a talent competition, but a real-life human drama. Yes, it pulls us in because we love the singing, the judges' comments, and the nail-biting anticipation. But, even more significantly, it pulls us in because we become intimately involved in the lives of these charming, talented young dreamers, many of whom came from the most challenging of circumstances. As the competition unfolds, we not only root for them, but we *care* about them. We not only love their performances, but we love *them* and what they represent—and we want to know more about their stories. In the process of bringing their stories to you, we have discovered what most have suspected—these are not just talented singers, but extraordinary human beings. They touch our lives with the beauty of their voices because it reflects the beauty of their souls.

We are honored and grateful to be a part of the marriage of Chicken Soup for the Soul and *American Idol*, since through writing this book we have been given the opportunity to achieve our own American dream—which has always been to inspire, uplift, and bring happiness and hope into people's lives.

We trust that these stories will bring you happiness and hope and inspire you to achieve your American dream.

Share with Us

We would like to invite you to send us stories you would like to see published in future editions of Chicken Soup for the Soul.

We would also love to hear your reactions to the stories in this book. Please let us know what your favorite stories are and how they affected you.

Please submit your stories through our website:

www.chickensoup.com

or write to us at:

Chicken Soup for the Soul
PO Box 30880
Santa Barbara, CA 93130
fax: 805-563-2945

We hope you enjoy reading this book as much as we enjoyed compiling and editing it.

1

DON'T STOP THINKING ABOUT TOMORROW:
THE DREAM COME TRUE

There are some people who live in a dream world, and there are some who face reality— and then there are those who turn one into the other.

Douglas Everett

Without God, I'm Tone Deaf

Melinda Doolittle
Top 10, Season 6

I was six years old the night my mom and I walked into our apartment, switched on the lights, and nothing happened. She said to me, "Baby, this is going to be such a special night for us. We're going to do everything by candlelight! We're going to eat by candlelight and talk by candlelight—it will be so much fun."

I helped my mom gather up all the candles we could find, and I just loved our candlelit evening together—until I decided I wanted to read. I found it hard to do by candlelight and told my mom I wasn't having fun anymore. I was ready for the lights to be back on.

"Well, baby," she explained, "we won't be able to do that until tomorrow when we get some money and give it to the man at the electric company."

But I wanted the lights back on right then. So as my mom continued to explain the mechanics of bill-paying, I told her that I was going to pray to God to turn the lights back on. I said I knew he would do it because he knows how much I love to read. So I prayed, and then I went over to the switch—and on came the lights.

My mom taught me that with God all things are possible if your heart is in the right place. She never dissuaded me from trying anything, even if my success was unlikely. Like the time I tried to be a gymnast, which I was terrible at. Or when I started to play the saxophone, which was a disaster. Or when I took up the flute, which was only a little bit better.

But what I really wanted to do was sing. There was only one problem: I was completely tone deaf.

In fact, it was so bad that when I auditioned for the grammar-school choir, they let me in because they said I had charisma, but they asked me just to lip-synch. So there was little Melinda, smack in the middle, singing her heart out. But, in fact, I was lip-synching. I really didn't mind because I loved music, and I loved being able to smile and make the audience happy. It never even dawned on me to be upset about being asked not to sing.

One day during my lip-synching career—I must have been about twelve at the time—I was in a shoe store with my mom. When Whitney Houston came on the music system, everyone stopped and listened. *How cool would it be if I could sing like that?* I thought. *Just grab people's hearts so that they stop and listen to me sing.* So I told my mom that since I'm not good at anything else, I would like to be good at singing. She replied, "Baby, you are *really* going to have to pray *very* hard."

When we got home, I told her that I was going to sing in the youth talent show at our church, which was one month away. Although my mom was supportive, she was also honest. She told me that would be a great faith project for me. So I prayed, "Lord, I want to be able to sing in the talent show." My mom also told me I would have to practice *really, really, really* hard.

Every day, I tried to hit those notes, and they wouldn't come out right. My mom kept saying, "You've got to keep working at it. You're not there yet, but just keep trying and praying."

The day of the talent show arrived, and I wasn't yet confident that I could sing, but I was confident in the fact that up until then God had always answered my prayers. I saw no reason why he wouldn't this time.

So I strode onto the stage, dressed in my new dress and the shoes I had bought at that shoe store just one month before, and I opened my mouth. Amazingly, out came this beautiful tone! It was like night and day. And not only could I sing, but I could hear harmonies. My mom cried.

After the show, people called the pastor and said, "It wasn't fair to let Melinda lip-synch for the talent show." It was hard for them to believe the pastor when he replied, "She didn't—that was really her."

After that day, I got asked to join the worship team and the all-state choir, and I've been singing ever since.

One of the other things I loved to do was dance. It was something else I did badly, but that never stopped me before. When I was in college, I was practicing a dance number for a school show when my friend's mom walked up to me at rehearsal and said, "I don't know if you even sing, but I looked up at you and I got this message that I have to have you sing background for a recording session we're doing tomorrow. It must be a God thing."

Her name was Roz Thompson, and her husband was Chester Thompson. He'd played with greats like Phil Collins and John Fogerty, and she was not only a well-known worship leader but had sung with everyone from CeCe Winans to Donna Summer. They were recording a tribute to Rich Mullins called *My Deliverer*.

Roz drove me to the session, where I sang background for one song. When I was done, the producer handed me a check. I said to him, "I only did one song." He said, "I know." And I said, "Are you serious?" It was more money than I made at my part-time job in a month.

From that one session, my phone started ringing, and my career as a background singer began. To me it was just about the best thing in the world—to get paid to sing.

Nearly seven years later, I decided to audition for *Idol*. Although I'm sure my success story is similar to other's, I think each of us has a different moment when everything changes, when everything comes together. For me, it was the night that Diana Ross was the guest mentor.

Until that night, I still thought of myself as a background singer, even when the judges tried to tell me I was more. But that night, when I sang "Home," and I looked out and everybody was standing on their feet and clapping for me—that was the moment it all came full circle. The lyrics tell about being in a different place, a different time, and a different world—and there I was, little Melinda Doolittle, living the dream that I had in the shoe store so many years ago—the dream of people stopping and wanting to hear what I had to sing. I knew it was now truly a different world.

God had turned on the lights when I wanted to read, and had given me a voice when I wanted to sing. It was now up to me to be the best representative of him that I could be. On Diana Ross night, I knew it would never be hard to do. For it was on that night, when the people wouldn't stop clapping and they thought they were clapping for me, I knew the truth—and I will always know the truth—that without God . . . I'm tone deaf.

Thousands Shouting My Name

Carmen Rasmusen
Top 10, Season 2

My mom has always told me to visualize. "Anything you want to have happen, Carmen, you just have to see it first in your mind. . . ." I knew that she was right, but honestly, there are just so many times that you can hear the visualization lecture without wanting to run screaming from the room—or at least change the subject.

When I was a freshman in high school, my mom and dad took me to see the Dixie Chicks at the Delta Center in Salt Lake City. During the concert, the Dixie Chicks said, "We want to tell all of you out there to never give up on your dreams. Just see yourself doing whatever it is you dream about, and one day that dream will be yours." I turned to my mom and told her that one day I'd be singing in that same place, and thousands of people would be shouting my name. True to style, my mom told me that I had to visualize it, and that's what I started to do every night before I went to bed.

When we heard about the *American Idol* auditions, my mom immediately said, "You're meant to do this." So I participated in a contest that was held in Salt Lake City at the FOX 13 studios for a guaranteed audition for *Idol* with all expenses paid to Los Angeles. It didn't mean that the winner of the local contest would even get past the first judge at the *Idol* audition, but it did mean that he or she wouldn't have to camp out in line.

"I'm so nervous!" I said, as we pulled up to the FOX studio.

"Carmen," my mom said, as we got out of the car, "you're going to win this contest, and you're going to L.A. I know it's your destiny."

One hour later, I was announced as the winner out of 200 contenders of the "Salt Lake City *Idol*" contest, and was on my way home to pack and hop on a plane.

I sailed through my first audition in front of a senior producer, and my next in front of Executive Producer Ken Warwick. Then it was on to the Big 3—which turned out to be the Big 2 because Randy was away filming a commercial. That day, I got my golden ticket to Hollywood.

Hollywood Week was intense. Since I was only seventeen, my mom had to be there. I was happy about that since she was always positive that I was going all the way. Not an ounce of doubt in her mind! Imagine her surprise when I was cut on my third audition, the day before they decided on the Final 32.

My mom put her arm around me as I was going in for that fateful audition and whispered, "I'll be visualizing for you." They had us in lines of twenty and said, "Will everyone in the first line step forward, please? Congratulations, you are going through! Second line, step forward, please . . . "

When I looked at my line, I was with everyone who had forgotten their words or had messed up in some other way. I knew it was over—and I was right.

"Congratulations for making it this far, but unfortunately . . ." And that was that. It was November 2002.

"I don't get it!" I cried, back in our hotel room while we packed—this time for home.

"Did you visualize yourself making it?" my mom asked.

"Yes, and obviously, it doesn't work. I don't want to talk about it."

I think my mom was actually kind of in shock. For her, it was like knowing every day of your life that your hair is blonde, and then waking up one morning and it's blue.

So, "Miss FOX 13 Salt Lake *Idol*" came home, applied to BYU, and started planning a different life. My mom, however, picked herself up from her blue-hair moment and told me she still believed that I was going to be in the Top 12. She believed it so much that every time a FedEx truck passed our house, she fully expected that it was going to stop and deliver a letter from the producers apologizing for having made a horrible mistake and begging me to come back.

Three months passed, and that familiar sound of the *American Idol* theme song began to fill our house every Tuesday and Wednesday night. I couldn't stand it—whenever I heard that music, I felt like *I* was supposed to be on the show. So I would walk out and go sulk in my room, while my nine-year-old sister was busy calling in and voting for Kimberly Caldwell.

Soon there were only a few weeks left until the Top 12 were chosen. I forced myself to sit down one night and watch as the contestants screamed and jumped up and down when they were told that they had made it into the finals. My mother's words rang in my ears: "One of the most powerful forms of visualization is 'acting as if.' See the images, hear the sounds, act out what it would *feel* like if you achieved your dream—and see what happens."

Getting up from the couch, I walked into my parents' bathroom. I stood in front of the mirror for a while, staring at my disappointed reflection. Then, I started to smile—

bigger and bigger. I clapped my hands in excitement. Then I started to scream, jump up and down, and shout, "I made it into the Top 12! I'm going to sing on TV in front of millions of people!" I felt the excitement in every fiber, and I swear, although I was just acting, I knew something had shifted. I can't explain what it was, but I was so elated— for no real reason whatsoever!

Two weeks later, my mom was going out when the phone rang. She was on for longer than usual, so I went in to see who she was talking to. She was grinning from ear to ear and kept saying, "Okay. All right." I could almost taste her excitement. Finally, she hung up the phone.

"Who was *that*?" I asked.

"Guess," she said, with the cutest Cheshire Cat grin on her face.

"Who, Mom?! Come on!"

"Guess," she repeated, doing a little jumping-up-and-down thing and grabbing my hands.

"Who, Mom, who?!"

Now I was jumping up and down with her and squealing, as she just kept on repeating, "You have to guess."

I knew it had to be someone amazing, because even for my mom, this was no normal amount of excitement!

Finally, she shouted, "It was Ken Warwick, the producer from *American Idol*. They want you back! You've been picked to be on the Wild Card show. You leave for Los Angeles in the morning." It was February 2003.

I slowly turned to look at myself in the mirror. I started screaming and clapping and jumping up and down, *exactly* as I had acted it out just two weeks before . . . only now, I wasn't acting. I was really, truly going to be on the show and singing in front of millions.

And one week later, I sat on the bench during the results show and heard Simon Cowell say, "The person I've chosen for the Top 12 . . . is Carmen."

It was one of the most exhilarating moments of my life when I stood up and joined the other eleven contestants. And as I looked over at my mom, something passed between us.

After I came in at #6, and the famous Clay vs. Ruben Finale ended with Ruben taking the crown, we began our forty-city *American Idols Live!* tour. And I know I will never forget the night when I took the stage at the Delta Center in Salt Lake City . . . and thousands of people were shouting my name.

The Impossible Dream

Jim Verraros
Top 10, Season 1

I've loved to sing from the time I discovered my vocal cords.

I sang while I played. I sang in the tub. I sang to break the silence. I had no idea that I had any kind of exceptional voice until one day when I was seven. I sang "One Moment in Time" for my music teacher at school, and she went nuts.

"You blow my mind!" she said. She couldn't believe my parents hadn't entered me in *Star Search*—or at least had me audition for *The Mickey Mouse Club*. But my parents had no way of knowing their son had singing talent.

Both of my parents are deaf.

People think that must have been hard for me, but growing up in my home had some real advantages. At a young age, I was comfortable around adults and mature topics since I often interpreted for my parents at appointments with doctors, attorneys, and other professionals. By the time I was six, I knew more about real estate than most adults.

Watching closed-captioned TV allowed me to excel in reading, writing, and spelling. When I was fourteen, I placed seventh in the state of Illinois for the Scripps National Spelling Bee.

And I attended college on an acting scholarship. I truly believe my acting ability emerged out of necessity. Since my parents couldn't hear my tone of voice, I couldn't express anger, frustration, or excitement in words; I had to do it with my body language and facial expressions.

But there are disadvantages, too. No matter how much success I achieve, no matter how many fans cheer for me, my two most important fans can't hear me sing.

I remember the moment it really hit me that my mom would never be able to hear my voice the way everyone else does. We were driving down the road, and one of my favorite songs came on the radio, so I cranked it up and began to sing along. She looked at me and put her hand on my throat to feel the vibration. I realized that was the closest she would ever get. She says it's enough for her; I wish it were enough for me.

After my appearance on *Idol*, I released a CD. I had written seven of the eleven songs myself, and I really wanted my dad to understand what I had accomplished. The case contained a liner with all the lyrics so he could read the words, but I wanted him to *feel* it. I turned up the bass as loud as I could so he could feel the beat, and I signed each song as I sang it to him. He let me know which ones were his favorites.

When I auditioned for *American Idol*, the judges asked me what one thing I wanted people to know about me.

"I grew up in a house with deaf parents," I answered.

"Would you sign your song as you sing?" they asked. I was more than happy to.

When my audition aired, the TTY at my mom's house rang off the hook. And when we did our *American Idols Live!*

tour, deaf fans showed up at the concerts and gave me the "I love you" sign from the audience. They connected with me; they embraced me. And I felt honored to help bring the deaf community into the world of music.

My parents flew out to the last city on the tour. It was so wonderful for my group of *Idols* to see where I came from. I introduced my parents to everyone, and they all hugged. My mother is in love with Justin Guarini, and she couldn't believe she was meeting him. He's truly one of the warmest, most genuine people in the world.

When it came time for my solo that night, I remember looking out at the audience and seeing my mom. She was watching other people's reactions, and I could see how proud she was that they loved me.

My mom and dad support me and believe in me so much, even though they'll never be able to hear me sing. I wouldn't trade them for all the hearing parents in the world, but sometimes I dream that one day, by some miracle, I could pick up the phone and say "I love you" without an interpreter in the middle.

Who knows? Maybe I will. Impossible things happen every day. After all, a boy who grew up with two deaf parents made it into the Top 10, didn't he?

Something to Talk About

Cecile Frot-Coutaz
CEO, FremantleMedia North America
and Executive Producer

"Dude, you have a hit on your hands." Nigel and I had to agree with Randy. It was June 11, 2002. *American Idol* had just launched that night, and we were celebrating at Hollywood Billiards. Up until then, no one was at all sure this show would make it in the United States, although its precursor, *Pop Idol,* had been a big hit in the United Kingdom.

The first person I hired to work on *American Idol* was Wylleen May. Together, we created the initial budget while sitting in an International House of Pancakes on Ventura Boulevard. She confessed to me later, "You know, when you first called me and we met to do that budget, I really didn't think the show was going to work."

Nor did Susan Slammer, the music director who worked on the show for the first three seasons. Part of her job was to get us clearance for all the music on the show, and we had to figure out how to do all these deals because nothing had ever been done on this scale before.

I'll never forget how, when I had finished explaining the details to her, she gave me a puzzled look that said, "Are you completely crazy?"

Now, six seasons later, we all say to one another, "We'll probably never be associated with something so big ever again in our lives. This is the biggest show in the history of this country—the kind of show people will be writing books about in the future." And in that sense, the show's success has been especially gratifying for me.

I was born in France, and I came from a family of academics and scientists. We had a TV in our home, but it wasn't a priority, and my parents were very judicious with what and when we were allowed to watch. For them, *Benny Hill* was considered "suitable" programming and not much else! Hence, I was not as well-versed as my fellow schoolmates when it came to the popular shows of the day. I also happened to be a bit of a nerd, which is not a good thing for a young schoolgirl. The one topic everyone seemed to relate to was the latest, greatest TV show. I, unfortunately, had almost nothing to talk about with my classmates.

After graduating from business school, I started working for the Pearson Media Group. My parents couldn't have been more embarrassed. Not only was this a media company, but it was an *English* media company! According to the worldview of my relatives, one of the worst things you could possibly do if you were French was to go work in England. I don't know if I accepted the position to defy my dad or because it was a first step toward what has continued to be my destiny.

After I had been with Pearson for some time, they hired a man named Greg Dyke to oversee their TV business. Greg, who eventually went on to run the BBC, became my mentor. I worked for him for four years doing mergers and acquisitions in the television industry.

At one point he told me he was going to have me handle all the production business for several countries, specifically Spain, Portugal, Italy, and France. I balked, saying that I had only done mergers and acquisitions up to that point and had never done anything like running a territory.

Greg asked, "What's the worst that can happen?" Then, without waiting for my reply, he answered his own question, "The worst thing is that you screw it up. The secret about management is that it's not all that hard. It's just about making decisions, and as long as you make more good ones than bad ones, you'll be okay. And as long as you're constantly taking action and you're not stupid, you'll get it right more often than not."

I took his words to heart. He gave me tremendous confidence. I learned from Greg that as long as you apply yourself, act with integrity, and put everything you've got into what you're doing, you have a fair chance of succeeding.

This was a very liberating moment for me. Not coming from an entertainment background, I had thought that I had less of a chance of succeeding than others. Greg helped me to get over that notion. I've learned not to be afraid and to just follow my instincts.

The first test of my mettle came up shortly after I took the position. I traveled to France to meet with the major French network, TF 1, where we had two shows—one that had gone very well and another that had gone badly. I went in to meet with the five most senior executives from that network. I had gone on my own, and I'm certain they thought it would be an absolute cakewalk to bully this woman in her early thirties. There were banana peels all over the place.

They wanted to get out of the deal on one of the shows, and I wouldn't give in. I held my ground—partly because I didn't know any better and partly because I was determined to do what I thought was right. Although I was petrified, I won the fight. It was a pivotal moment in my career that taught me to fight for what I believe in.

To this day, I tell people that if you believe in something, never, ever give up, as cliché as it sounds. I don't think *American Idol* would be as big as it is now if, on creative issues, people in charge hadn't stuck to their guns. That's the reason the show is so edgy and hard-hitting, especially in its early stages. We don't shy away from controversy, even if we get criticized for it.

But the people I no longer receive criticism from are my parents. Four years ago, they came to the States to visit me for the first time since I came here. It happened to be at the time of the Season 2 Finale at the Kodak Theater, so I got them a couple of tickets. At the end of the show, my dad came over and gave me what he thought was a great compliment.

"You did pretty well tonight," he said. "You filled the whole auditorium." He was very proud, but I had to let him know that that wasn't the point.

Those of us who are a part of *Idol* are very blessed because something this big may never happen again. And I know we should enjoy it and remember more often how very fortunate we are.

If you had asked me four years ago, I would have said, "This will probably go on for another couple of years." But I don't think any of us in our wildest dreams thought it would do this well for this long. Maybe it was timing. Maybe it was luck. Maybe it was craft. But everything just lined up in the right way. And this one-time nerd now has something just about everyone wants to talk about.

The Only Thing We Knew for Sure

Kimberley Locke
Top 10, Season 2

When I was in fifth grade, reporters interviewed kids from my school for an article in the newspaper. My mom saved the article. In it, I said, "One day there's going to be a woman president, and I'm going to be a singer and a lawyer."

At the beginning of my junior year in college, I had to make a decision: get serious about my singing or get serious about my schooling. Although I was an artist, I was also a realist and knew I needed something to support myself. And one thing was for sure—I didn't want to end up being a forty-year-old woman singing in a club.

Singing was my gift, but I decided to quit my band and throw myself into my studies. I made the Dean's List my last four semesters of college and was accepted to law school. With my part-time job, I paid in advance for the first semester and purchased a closet full of books.

And then, out of nowhere, came the onslaught of friends convinced I was destined to be the next *American Idol*—or, at least, that I should try to be.

First, my ex-fiancé called. Don was casual. He was like, "What's up, and how ya doin', and by the way, have you ever watched this show *American Idol*?" I told him I don't watch TV, and even if I did, I wouldn't be watching it now because I was living in the library, thank you very much.

Next, on my way to Bible Study not more than a week later, I stopped to see my friend Pam. She insisted I sit down and watch *American Idol*.

"I'm missing Bible Study."

"I'm sorry, but you have to watch this show."

She did that for two weeks in a row.

Knowing better than to stop at Pam's again, the next week I stopped to visit my sister-in-law, Angie. She was also playing it cool . . .

"Hey, Kim, what's doin'?" And then, when I turned to go, she said, "I hate to make you miss Bible Study, but you have to stay and watch this show called *American Idol*."

"Pam already made me watch it. Twice."

"I don't care, you're watching it again. I could so see you on this show."

"Thanks, but I'm going to Bible Study." This time I managed to escape.

Then Don phoned again. "Guess what? You are *not* going to believe this. *American Idol* is holding auditions in Nashville!" My silence must have given away my minimal excitement because he added, "And if I have to come and take you, you're going." This was more significant than it sounds because he lives two hours away, and the auditions were within walking distance of my apartment.

But when my mind is made up, I stick to it. And I'd already chosen law school over singing. That was my final answer.

When the week leading up to the audition rolled around, Mike, one of my coworkers, collared me in the hallway. "You know, Kimberly, I've never heard you sing, but if your friends are so insistent that you do this, I think you should." Mike followed me right into my office. "Why don't you sing for me, and I'll give you my opinion?"

"Right here? Now?"

"Sure."

As the last notes faded away, he joined my chorus of supporters. "You have nothing to lose," he pointed out, "and everything to gain."

But I did have something to lose. Applying to law school hadn't been a cakewalk, and I didn't want to have to start over again and risk not being reaccepted.

When the morning of the audition arrived, I woke at 6:30 and stared at the ceiling, mulling over why I should do it . . . and why I shouldn't. A loud voice in my head reminded me, *You've been on a thousand auditions, and this is probably going to be just as unsuccessful. You'll be wasting your time.*

But something urged me get out of bed. I threw on some clothes. I had to pull them out of the dirty laundry basket since I *really* was *not* planning on doing this, and I headed outside into the pouring rain.

"Lord," I said out loud, "I am not waiting in this downpour. If this is meant to be, then it's got to be easy."

Thousands of people huddled, wet and cold, outside the auditorium doors. Some had camped there all night. I was assigned number 1,800. Right after they handed me my number, they shut down the line, opened the doors, and let us in.

Not knowing how long the audition might take, I'd told my boss I might be a couple of hours late for work. I ended up being four days late.

When they announced, "You're going to Hollywood!" I was thrilled beyond words. Then when I learned that Hollywood Week started the exact same day as law school, I knew that I couldn't play it both ways anymore.

The dean might not be supportive if I said I had to miss the first week of classes in order to audition for a talent show.

I cried a lot. I prayed a lot. I asked for friends' advice, and I talked endlessly to my mother. Finally, I knew what I had to do.

"I'm going to do this, Mom. It's a risk I'm willing to take, and if it's meant to be, it will be. If not, I'll reapply to law school next year."

The dean asked me to submit a letter stating my intent to withdraw. I held on to it until the very last moment. I remember my final hesitation as I slowly pulled down the handle of the ominous blue mailbox on the corner. Then I opened my shaking hand and let it go. Once the letter was gone, I knew there was no turning back.

The moment it slid through that mail slot and the door slammed shut, that's when the magic really began. I have not had one moment of regret. Not ever.

In Hollywood, Clay, Ruben, and I immediately formed a bond. I don't know if it was our spirituality or that we were all from the South. We just sensed something in each other, and we became this inseparable little tripod. Immediately, we made a pact that we were going to be together in the Top 12. After many rounds in Hollywood, they put us in groups of twenty-four, and only two out of each group went through. The three of us were put in the same group, and I remember realizing that meant one of us wasn't going to make it. Our hearts were pounding when they announced that Ruben and I would be the two going on, but we still never doubted that the three of us would be together.

Ruben just turned to Clay and said, "Don't worry, you'll be coming back as the Wild Card."

Then we went into the Coke room and prayed. And sure enough, Clay was chosen as the Wild Card, and we all ended up together in the Top 12. Then we prayed that we would be together in the Final 3!

And that was how it was.

But to be honest, that night, huddled together on the corner of the red couch, holding each other's hands in our little circle, we really didn't know exactly what to pray for because we weren't quite sure what we were getting ourselves into. We had no idea that because of this experience, our lives would dramatically change, and our long-cherished dreams of touching millions with our music were about to come true. The only thing we knew for sure that night was that we were happy to be there—together.

Now There's Enough for Everybody

Ruben Studdard
American Idol, Season 2

My whole life, I never wanted to do anything but be a singer. But before *Idol*, it just didn't seem to work my way.

In the fall of 1999, I left college during my junior year to pursue a career in music. This was not welcomed by my mother because both my parents are educators. There were four of us friends in different colleges in the South, and we all decided to leave school. I promised my mom if I didn't make it in five years, I'd go back.

Our group was called God's Gift, and we practiced every day. We practiced, practiced, practiced, but we never seemed to get anywhere. We shopped demos, went out to find deals—we tried just about everything.

Sometimes, it got us down. I remember a minister saying, "Everything happens in God's time, so be patient." I was pretty much the only guy in the group who had already been doing this for years, so my thought was, *How much more patient can I be?*

Eventually, the group gave up because it just wasn't happening. I joined a jazz band called Just a Few Cats. By that point, I wasn't even concerned with making it; I just wanted to have fun. Soon, we became the most popular group in Birmingham. We started playing 500–600 seat venues that sold out almost immediately.

One day, a background singer in our band said she was going to try out for *American Idol* and asked me to go with her.

"I'm not doing that," I said.

I thought I was everything the *American Idol* wasn't. I mean, I wasn't exactly Kelly Clarkson. I was this big guy in a jazz band who in college had been pursuing a degree in operatic performance. I just envisioned going up there and embarrassing myself on national television. All the odds were against me.

But I told my friend I'd go to give her support and to cheer when she made it through. We drove to Nashville and spent all night waiting outside. Fortunately, she brought pillows and blankets because we had to sleep on the ground.

In the morning, one of the producers woke us and asked if we were there to audition.

"Yeah," I said, still half-asleep. Maybe I meant, "Yeah," as in, "Yeah, she's here to audition and I'm with her," but next thing I knew, I was singing in front of the assistant producers. I made it through, and my friend didn't.

From that moment on, I had to believe there was a master plan because it all just flowed, one thing after the other.

I was told to come back the following day for the next audition, but I sure didn't want to sleep outside again. Then I found out a friend was in Nashville for an engineering conference and just happened to have an extra hotel room.

When I met the show's producer, Nigel Lythgoe, he said, "You don't look like an *American Idol*, but I bet you can sing."

I sang Stevie Wonder's "Ribbon in the Sky," and Nigel said, "Man, you are going on."

I was flying high when I went home to Birmingham, but I had to return to Nashville the next week to sing for Randy, Simon, and Paula. I didn't know what to do because my car wouldn't make it.

My brother Kevin offered to take me. This was really something because I always drove him nuts when I sang. He would beg me to stop singing, *please*. When we were kids and walked to the store, he punched me out for singing all the way down the street. But now he was driving me to Nashville?

When I sang for the judges, all three said, "Absolutely, yes!"

I just knew something great was going to happen. I didn't think I was going to win the show by any means, but I did feel like it just might give me the opportunity to somehow live my dreams.

American Idol helped me accomplish more than I could have dreamed in a million years on my own. I sang at the American Music Awards. I was nominated for a GRAMMY®. I went to South Africa and sang in soccer stadiums. I've done concerts for hundreds of thousands of people. I've had a platinum album and Billboard #1 songs. I never would have imagined that I'd sing for the President, but I did that, too—twice. I've done so much since *Idol*—and I would have been happy just making one album!

When people ask me for advice, I'm always willing to share it: always be prepared. I know that might sound funny since I sure didn't seem prepared for the audition that morning in Nashville, but I can honestly say I've studied my craft since I was ten years old. I went to school to be a classical musician. I took every class I could on music theory. If your opportunity shows up and you're not prepared, you might lose it . . . and it might not come back again.

Last weekend, I sang at Ella Fitzgerald's ninetieth

Birthday Benefit with Natalie Cole, Quincy Jones, and Nancy Wilson. When I do a gig, I'm always prepared. I tell people, "Don't wing it." You know when someone's winging it, and it's not going to get you where you want to go.

And the other advice I give is to always have a pleasing attitude. The one thing everyone always says about me is I have a good attitude. I believe that will take you further than a great voice or loads of talent.

Needless to say, my life has changed since *Idol*. But I'm the same guy, the same Ruben—the same son, the same friend, the same brother. Kevin and I still love—and fight with—each other. When people ask if we still fight over the last sandwich in the refrigerator, like I talked about on the show, I tell them that's another thing that's changed since *Idol*: now there's always enough of everything for all of us.

And don't think I'm not grateful. I'm one of those people who lives life based on gratitude. I believe the more grateful you are, the more good things will come to you. I will always be grateful to *American Idol*—I will never forget what it has done to help me make my dreams come true.

Don't Dream in Black and White

Nigel Lythgoe
Executive Producer

I always wanted to be in "show business." Even as a kid,
I was a show-off. At eleven years of age, I started dancing.
I came from a very tough background. My father worked
on the Liverpool docks, and in those days boys just didn't
dance. I had to prove my masculinity to my dad by going
into boxing. I guess I was the original Billy Elliot. For your
son to be a dancer, even a tap dancer, was just not all right
on Merseyside. Unfortunately, my boxing was pitiful, so
my dad couldn't even take pride in that.

When I became a choreographer and started choreo-
graphing the television show of one of the greatest British
divas, Shirley Bassey, my dad's friends said, "I saw your
kid's show on television." At that point, it wasn't *The
Shirley Bassey Show* anymore; it was "your kid's show."
Finally, he could take pride in me.

From the beginning, I was always one of those kids who
would say, "I can do that."

Direct? "I can do that."

Produce a show? "I can do that."

But then you have to follow through. As I became bigger in the business and became the executive rather than the producer, I heard a lot of people say what they could do, but then not follow through. I've given many people opportunities, and they haven't taken them. That's rather sad as the opportunity won't necessarily be there again.

American Idol is the American dream. How ironic is it that the Brits have brought back the American dream to America? And it's not just promising the American dream; it's actually delivering it. Every time a Kelly Clarkson or a Carrie Underwood receives another award from their peers, it's validating what this program is all about, which is allowing these kids to become household names. You don't even have to win to share the dream. Jennifer Hudson and Chris Daughtry have proven that.

But, first of all, you have to have the talent. Contestants are wasting my time and their own if they haven't. I don't believe in shilly-shallying around, so I certainly don't mind telling them if I believe their talent is nonexistent. But I don't think I help anybody when I just say, "You suck," so I try to give constructive criticism. However, I do think that for some people, their dreams will only come true when they're asleep.

And wasted dreams can become nightmares. . . .

Some of the kids that I see throughout the country have this "You owe me" attitude, like, "Life owes me. I deserve to be a star, and you need to make me a star." They don't realize that it doesn't just happen because you think you deserve it.

Then again, a lot of people think it will happen with hard work. No matter how hard you work, if you haven't got the talent, you're still not going to make it.

Even when you've got the talent, there is no guarantee the door of opportunity will open for you. If you're fortunate enough and a door does open, I tell people, "March boldly through it. Don't be hesitant. Move across that threshold because not many doors open, and just as often doors are slammed in your face. You have to go through with guts, and if you make a fool of yourself, well, maybe next time a door is open, you'll be a little more thoughtful about what you've got and what you're going to do with it."

We audition hundreds of thousands of people every season, which no one has ever done before. We find them and give them the platform on which to perform. We don't create stars; America does that. We're supporting these kids, but then their talent will justify them being chosen— or not. This show has grown not only in popularity but in validity in the industry, and that's very important. It's not just another TV talent show.

I never want to stop anybody's dream. Really, I don't. I never want to stop the scale of their dream. But we all need a reality check every now and then. Being judged at an audition provides that check and brings a few deluded individuals back down to Earth.

However, if you're going to dream, dream in the biggest scale possible. I would much prefer you aim at a million and only get 999,999 than aim at 100 and achieve it. In one case, you've achieved your goal, but in the other, although you may not have quite achieved everything you wanted, you've achieved a whole lot more than a hundred!

So, if you're going to dream, dream in Technicolor. Don't dream in black and white.

The Coolest Thing in the World

Patrick Lynn
Senior Producer

When I was a kid, my dad would take us to Dodgers games in Los Angeles, and on the way home he would drive us past the studios. Gazing out the window from the back seat of my dad's 1970 Ford Torino station wagon, I was mesmerized by the mystery of those huge buildings called Paramount, Fox, and MGM that took up city blocks.

I dreamed about what it would be like to actually walk into one of those places and be able to say I had a job there. I thought, *It would be the coolest thing in the world to work there, and then go home and watch the shows I'd made.*

When I was eighteen, I got my first gig at a studio. I was just out of high school, and I volunteered for a job as a tour guide on the 20th Century Fox lot. We were given a short tour ourselves, and then we became tour guides. I remember they gave us these silly hats to wear. Between tours, we had a lot of downtime, so I would just wander around and find out about different parts of the stage. My most vivid memory was seeing these big murals on the wall from some of the most famous Fox films. My favorite was the mural depicting John Ford directing.

It's been a long journey from there to here, with a lot of lessons learned. I moved on from tour guide to work as a production assistant for a computer graphics company. It was an amazing second job because the company worked on so many huge films, like *Hunt for Red October* and the original *Die Hard*.

After that, I took a job where I learned about the politics of the business. I quit one day, on principle, because of a personality conflict. Later, I learned that, for me that was a stupid thing to do.

But as one door closes, another always opens, and next I worked for the production coordinator and line producer at the Samuel Goldwyn Company. That's where I learned how to be a production coordinator. I worked my way up the ladder and eventually made it to director of acquisitions. Shortly after that, the company was sold, and I had to move on.

Literally, almost a day after I left Goldwyn, a young filmmaker named Joe Carnahan asked if I wanted to be the producer's rep on a film he had just made. It was a great move for me, and Joe has gone on to do great things in the film industry. It was empowering to have his confidence and the confidence of others. So, for about three years I repped and helped other young filmmakers with their films.

Things were changing in the industry, and reality TV was taking off. A buddy of mine named Billy Cooper called and asked if I wanted to work on this new television show about "top-gun reality." It was going to be called *American Fighter Pilot*. How could I not? And when that run came to an end, I got an offer to work on a show based on England's huge hit *Pop Idol*. Here, it was going to be called *American Idol*.

I accepted the offer.

A few days later, a couple of others from *Fighter Pilot* and I were in a conference room watching the tapes from *Pop Idol*. We were all enthralled—especially by this guy named Simon Cowell and his way of telling people how bad or good their singing was. He was completely honest with a wicked side. We knew the show could be huge. There was no reason why it wouldn't work. I was excited.

Early on, one of my jobs was coordinating the auditions in some of the cities. I started making calls to venues where we wanted to hold them. It was difficult at first. I'd make one call after another and explain that we wanted to hold auditions in their concert hall or hotel ballroom for a TV show called *American Idol,* and then I'd be like, "Hello? Hello?" They'd hung up on me.

Eventually, we found suitable locations, and we hit the road. We had pretty good turnouts the first season due to the promos FOX ran after *The Simpsons.* But people couldn't believe we were going to put bad singers on TV. America was just starting to try and figure this whole show out, but enough people showed up to audition that we had a great first season.

Season 2 was another story, since we were already a huge hit. I remember being in Detroit where we had set up auditions in a downtown hotel, and thousands of people started showing up. It was just crazy because we didn't want to turn anyone away, but they just kept coming. We had a limited amount of wristbands and time. It was then that we realized we would have to get bigger venues. Stadiums were in our future.

Each year, everything about this show gets bigger and bigger. It's just a show, of course, but it's also a phenomenon. *Idol* premiered about a year after 9/11, a time when our country needed something to believe in. People loved it because it took their minds off the news. It didn't have anything to do with terrorists or politics. It was something that people could rely on from week to week, and even if they themselves couldn't sing or would never audition for anything, identifying with the contestants made them feel like they were a part of something big.

The greatest thing about the show is that, right before your eyes, you see dreams come true for people. People believe in *Idol*. They wouldn't show up at the auditions if they didn't believe. And for many, even if they don't make it through, the excitement of just being a part of something so big is a dream come true.

As for me, I still drive past the studios, but now, I also get to drive in. And at the end of the day, I go home and watch the shows I'm a part of—and it is the coolest thing in the world. Hey, *American Idol* is about achieving the American dream—and no one said that was just for the contestants.

Letting Go

Chris Sligh
Top 10, Season 6

As everyone knows, life has its ups and downs. And sometimes, you have to go through a lot of downs— frustrating times when things don't work out, and your dreams seem to be slipping through your fingers— before the up phase begins. Then you can be swept up higher than you ever imagined, and life somehow fulfills its promise.

That's what happened to me.

About four years ago, I had great hopes for the future. I had just gotten married to an amazing woman. I was a musician, and my band looked like it was heading for success. I wasn't in a great position financially—I was a pizza delivery driver—yet I was optimistic. But when that job didn't last, I was out of work for months.

During those months, things started slipping downhill. For a while, I worked at a small church as a worship leader, but the church folded. Then I was negotiating to buy a roofing company, but it turned out they had financial problems, and the company collapsed while we were still negotiating. The job market in my area was really bad, and I had another four months out of work, trying to make ends meet by doing odd jobs in the neighborhood.

By this time I was pretty discouraged, and I questioned God a lot. I didn't care about being rich, but I wanted to be able to earn a decent living so that my wife and I could have kids down the road. Eventually, I landed a job at an automobile manufacturing company. It was the worst job of my life. I spent ten- to twelve-hour workdays underneath cars, putting on exhausts. I am normally a very happy person, but for the first time in my life I was depressed. When I came home, I would be so tired and sore that I could hardly move. I was having problems with my hands, and then I developed carpal tunnel syndrome. Since I am a guitar player, that freaked me out.

Besides my great wife, the only other bright spot in my life was my band. I really believed in it, and even put $6,000, which I didn't really have, into making a CD in Nashville. We were working with a record company, and we were right on the verge of securing a deal. We'd had other offers that had fallen through, but this one was looking good.

Just as things were starting to really look up again—I was even able to leave the manufacturing job and begin working with a marketing firm leasing houses nationwide—the deal didn't happen, and my band broke up. We'd been together for three and a half years, but everyone was fed up with all the promises that never panned out. The hardest thing for me was that right after we split up, we didn't even talk to each other—and relationships are really important to me.

I sank to my lowest point.

I felt like quitting music altogether. I just didn't know what I was going to do. I had been a drama minor in college, and I remember saying to my wife, "I just don't think I can do music anymore. Maybe I can do some acting or something like that."

Sarah replied, "Chris, you are a great singer and an amazing songwriter. I think you just need to take some time off and let go. Work at your leasing job, write some songs—just be easy and see what happens."

Her words and support allowed me to stop pushing, and when I did, I had a realization: *I don't have to be a rock star in order to be successful. The only thing I have to do is love my wife, appreciate what I do have, love the people around me, and live as the best person I can be.*

So I just let go. That's when I found that when you let go, that's when the best things happen.

Over the next couple of months, everything opened up for me. I wrote over forty songs, just out of nowhere. It was good stuff, too. Then I met another guitar player; he and I meshed really well. Soon after that, I reconnected with a bass player I'd known. Then we got a drummer, and we had ourselves a band. Everything just fell into place. In March, only a month after we got together, we won a really big Battle of the Bands contest and got to open for a major-label group at a huge concert.

Later that year, I tried out for *American Idol.* This wasn't my first time; I had tried two years in a row, but had never made it past the first round. But this year, one of my friends said that since I seemed to be on a roll, I should just go down to *Idol* and see what happens.

So that's what I did.

I didn't really expect to make it past Randy, Simon, and Paula—or even *to* Randy, Simon, and Paula. But I auditioned, and this time I got that ticket to Hollywood. My luck really had turned.

Sarah and I made the commitment to pursue the *Idol* dream wherever it might lead. This involved a lot of sacrifices, financial and otherwise, but I never regretted a moment or a dime of it. My life has changed completely. It's been amazing, exciting, and totally unexpected.

Looking back, I could see that this had all come from that talk I had with Sarah and the way my thinking had changed. I still knew what was important to me, but I didn't feel so desperate to make it work. And by letting go, the guy who hadn't gotten past the first round for two years was now in the Top 10.

When the day came that I was voted off and went home, it was easy for me to accept because eventually everyone goes home—except for just one person. I was satisfied that I had gone further than I ever dreamed I would. And I was going home to a beautiful wife who loved me and a great band to play with.

I'll call guys back at my church now, and they say in awe, "Why in the world would you call me?" And I tell them, "This doesn't change me." I hope it never changes me.

It's not everyone's lot in life to be on *American Idol*, but I tell people to persist in their dreams, whatever they may be. There will be setbacks and disappointments along the road, but if you get clear on what's really important to you, commit to that, and keep going—you can't lose.

Just let go of things having to be a certain way, stay true to the highest, and you'll eventually turn the corner. Amazing things will start to happen.

I know.

I've been there.

The American Dream Still Lives

Radhika Schwartz
American Idol Fan

In my entire adult life, I've never owned a television set. What I know about pop culture, I hear on the streets or read in the headlines of the tabloids while I'm checking out at the local Hy-Vee.

I'm a reader. My escape of choice is a good book. Although there may not be many of us left, my friends and I still go to book-club meetings and haunt libraries. So when my intelligent, well-educated, middle-aged contemporaries started spending Tuesday and Wednesday nights glued to *American Idol,* I could only shake my head in disbelief and think that the world had finally gone insane.

That is, until the night I "got it."

When I called and asked my friend if I could stay in her guest room while visiting my father in Chicago, she graciously agreed. However, she warned that if I were to arrive as expected on *American Idol* night, I could look forward to being ignored. Furthermore, I was told that I would not even get a hug unless I arrived during the commercial, but I was welcome to come in and sit down with the family and watch until the show was over—if I did so quietly.

Tuesday night arrived and, just my luck, I pulled into the driveway of her Chicago lakefront home right at the beginning of the show. Without ringing the bell, I tiptoed in, whispered hello to her purebred dogs, and slid into the soft leather recliner angled precisely toward the television in the well-appointed family room. My friend took her eyes from the screen just long enough to shoot me a smile.

With my cynicism as a barrier between me and the action on the screen, it's amazing I saw what I saw. It didn't take me long to realize why the show was so wildly popular: it is the cultural phenomenon our country so desperately needs during these years when the mass consciousness has become cynical and devoid of hope.

I watched young people from all walks of life sing with their whole hearts in the innocent belief that they could be the next *American Idol*. These were kids who hadn't listened when they were told they weren't supposed to be able to become stars. No one had let them in on the secret that stardom was only for the children of hotel magnates, or those groomed for success before they were out of diapers.

My friend narrated as the contestants sang.

"He's in the U.S. Navy."

"She's a bank teller and a single mom."

"He's half-Filipino and half-Portuguese."

"She's only seventeen. Her father is black; her mother is white."

"His parents emigrated from Venezuela when he was three."

These kids were not model-thin or movie-star gorgeous. They were short and tall, chic and nondescript, squeaky clean and tattooed. They were black, white, Latino, and East Indian. They were us!

And, at that moment, I got it: this show is about reigniting the American dream, the dream on which our nation was founded, the dream for which our parents and grandparents gave up everything to come to this country. Our ancestors came to America with the belief that anything was possible here. Generations later, on *American Idol,* we're witnessing the same fearless, naïve, and innocent idealism that allowed impossible dreams to be realized being played out every week right before our eyes.

People watch *American Idol* because they, too, have hopes and dreams inside of them. Each week when these kids win, people watching feel like they have won as well. We're tired of hearing about fear. We'd rather hear about hope. And hope is what this show is all about. *American Idol* has reignited the American dream.

As for me, I can't honestly say I'm rushing out to buy a television set, but I will say I've been humbled. How was I to know that what I had labeled a B-level talent show could actually be such a moving force reigniting the hopes of millions of people across our country?

I can't wait to hear who wins.

Taylor Made

Heather Cook Lindsay
American Idol Fan

At 6:30 PM, I navigated the small station wagon into a spot for the handicapped on the second floor of the parking garage, directly adjacent to the concert facility. After putting on my coat, I patted the pockets, checking once again for the presence of both tickets. I looked over at my seventy-year-old mother and watched her step carefully from the car. She looked a bit uncomfortable, her arthritis most likely rearing its ugly head. Concert-going hadn't been her thing for at least two decades.

Back in the eighties, long before her arthritis settled in and necessitated a complete knee replacement, she had loved going to concerts. Our entire family loved music of all kinds. However, as health concerns developed and funds became less plentiful, such luxuries were few and far between.

As I locked the car, I wondered how this night was going to turn out. *Was coming to the show really a smart thing to do?* Glancing over at my mother, I sensed her resolve. We were both determined to go forward with our plan. I knew we couldn't turn back now.

For both of us, the previous few years had brought a great deal of hardship. Aside from her arthritis and knee replacement, she found herself living alone for the first time ever. Barely able to make ends meet, she had accepted a job at a store that sold every type of lighthouse-themed object you could imagine. She enjoyed the work, but the physical demands were becoming increasingly difficult. Her physical and financial concerns were many, and I worried about her constantly.

I had recently moved to Maine from North Carolina, not only to spend more time with my mother, but also because I needed her care, as well. Four years earlier, I had awoken one morning covered with skin lesions and unable to move. My flesh was literally burning off, and I couldn't use my arms and legs. After many months of doctors and hospitals, I was diagnosed with a rare virus. At the age of thirty, I was staring down the barrel of a life beset by chronic pain, fevers, memory loss, and endless fatigue. The teaching career I had worked so hard to establish would now be just a memory; my illness was so severe that I had become unable to work.

Thankfully, both my mother and I were firm believers in the power of gratitude and positive thinking. We knew that joy and happiness could be found at almost any time, and in the most unexpected places.

We never expected that joy to come in the form of an *American Idol*.

Walking slowly, we reached the facility, showed our tickets, and were directed to our seating area.

We had heard on the radio that the Cumberland Civic Center was completely sold out. *The American Idols Live!* Season 5 tour was the fastest sell-out the center had seen in years. On the day the tickets went on sale, I had spent the entire morning on the computer, hoping to score them through the web. I was one of the lucky ones. My purchase ultimately went through. But as soon as I bought them, I began to doubt. *Would my mother and I even be able to make it?*

Ten days before the concert date, my mother urged me to sell the tickets, but I held firm. I knew who we were going to see, and I knew how much it meant to both of us.

Now, with those tickets in hand, we found our seats in the middle of a row. I bit my lip and tried to stay calm. Directly in front of us, I noticed an elderly man who was struggling to stay awake. Next to him sat his wife, who was breathing with the assistance of an oxygen tank, which she had tucked under her seat. Thinking I had found two people worse off than we were, also scrunched in the middle of the row, I wanted to ask them what had brought them to the show.

Just then, a little girl in pink ran down the aisle and jumped on the elderly man's lap. I watched his initial grimace turn into a smile as he hugged his granddaughter. The rest of the family filed in and took up the entire row of seats in front of us. There were three generations of that family together at the concert. *What an unusual event,* I thought to myself. *How rare it is these days that an entire family, aged five through eighty-five, can happily attend the same show!*

As the lights grew dim, I glanced around the Civic Center and smiled. I was amazed not by the number of people, but at the differences among them. I had never seen such a diverse group of people assembled under the same roof. It was good to be a part of something that felt so special.

All the performers gave it their all, singing the songs they had sung on *Idol* and mixing in some new selections. I watched the grandfather in front of me tap his fingers and nod his head to an Aerosmith tune. I watched a teenage boy cheer when the first notes of a Stevie Wonder song began. My mom was completely comfortable, enjoying the event with light glowing from her eyes.

Suddenly, from the back of the house, a spotlight scanned the audience and then hovered over one spot on the floor. The reigning *American Idol,* Taylor Hicks, appeared and brought down the house.

Over the past few months, my mother and I had flashed hundreds of smiles as we watched Taylor's odd brand of dancing, listened to his whiskey tenor soar, and felt his incredible passion for music. I grabbed my mother's hand, and we both screamed like schoolgirls. Tears fell down my face. I couldn't remember the last time I felt so grateful for just being alive.

For those few moments, my aches and pains and financial worries were forgotten in favor of something more life-giving. Along with thousands of other Americans who, just like us, had countless worries and pains, we let the *Idols* and their music lift and nourish us.

As the music swelled to a close, and the *Idols* finished their last encore, we gathered our things and made our way through the happy crowd back to our car. Once inside, our ears still ringing, we each took a deep breath, glad that we had stuck by our plan to make it to the concert.

As I turned the key in the ignition, I asked my mother what her favorite part of the evening had been, expecting her to say when Taylor first appeared or when he sang one of her favorite songs.

Instead, she turned to me and with a loving smile said, "I'll never forget the glow that fell across your face as the lights grew dim and the music began. But my favorite part of the night was to see your suffering disappear and be replaced by happiness, excitement, and love for life—even if only for a few brief, magic hours."

2

WE ARE FAMILY:
THE POWER OF THOSE WE LOVE

In family life, love is the oil that eases friction, the cement that binds closer together, and the music that brings harmony.

Eva Burrows

Something's Gonna Happen

Natalie Burge
Top 24, Season 1

I grew up in a small farming town in central Illinois, so when I was working on a production deal in Los Angeles, no one could relate when I told them how much I missed the wave of the corn and the smell of the cows. But they did relate when I told them how much I missed my dad.

My mom was my constant traveling companion during my *Idol* days. Since I was sixteen at the time, she had to be with me 24/7 while my dad stayed home and held down the fort.

My dad is a dentist and has always worked long hours to support his family. He's a brilliant man who loves what he does and is also a gentle giant. He has the biggest hands you've ever seen and a heart that's even bigger.

Although I've been in literally hundreds or probably even thousands of performances during my life, my dad has only been able to attend a few dozen. It's not that he doesn't want to be there; it's just that he's dedicated to his practice and doesn't travel much. Although I've performed from coast to coast, not many of my performances have been in Morton, Illinois! When I look out over the audience, my mom's beautiful face is always out there shining its support, while my dad is at home, working in people's mouths so that his little girl can live her dream.

Just days after I returned home from working in Los Angeles in the spring of 2001, I got a call from a producer I had worked with when I was thirteen. He was very excited about this new show called *American Idol* and told me that they were holding auditions in Chicago the next day. He was absolutely convinced that I had to be there.

It sounded like a dream-come-true opportunity, but I had just gotten my license, and driving alone in the big city was not a consideration. My dad was booked with patients, and my mom was recovering from a horrible car accident. It seemed like my dream was dead in the water before it had even begun. But at the eleventh hour a dear family friend named Carol offered to drive me, so we packed the car and hurriedly left for the big city.

Auditioning for *American Idol* was unlike anything I'd ever experienced in all my years of auditions. To get a place in line you had to stay out all night—and it was cold! Carol, bless her heart, offered to stand in line so I could go back to the hotel and get my "beauty sleep." We ended up taking turns of four-hour shifts.

Finally, after everyone's cold hands and stiff vocal cords were herded into the Congress Hotel banquet room, the moment came when I went before the producers of what would soon become an American phenomenon. I was ecstatic to be invited back for the next audition, which was being held one week later.

But, as fate would have it, my mom, who had never missed any of the excitement of my show-biz life, was still recovering. Carol wasn't available either, so it was my dad or bust. I like to think of myself as one of those people who goes with the flow and accepts things as they are without being overly pushy, but I was very driven to go to this second audition.

My parents had instilled in me the philosophy that if you want something badly enough, you find a way to get it. And my dad knew that he was my only logical option at that point. So he rescheduled his patients, put on his big-city clothes, and off we went to the audition that would decide if I was going to Hollywood.

I don't think my dad ever really understood how much I love music. When I was ten years old, my mom and I moved to Branson, Missouri, where I did twelve performances each week at a variety theater on Branson's famous Route 76. My dad was willing to be alone in Morton without us for almost two years—which is more than any husband and father should have to do for his child. But even so, I never felt that he got who I was when I performed, or understood the honor and privilege I felt when I shared my music with the world.

When my dad and I arrived at the audition venue in Chicago, we were once again ushered into a holding room, crammed with all the *Idol* wannabes and their traveling companions. Hours went by as I sat with my dad and waited for my number to be called. I watched one of the TV camera crews interviewing contestants in the lobby before they went into the audition room and as they came out. Another camera crew was filming random contestants and their families, but I didn't want to leave my dad alone because I knew the whole experience was completely foreign to a show-biz first-timer!

All of a sudden, one of the producers walked straight up to me and asked if I would mind singing for the camera.

"Not at all," I said.

My dad watched as they set up the cameras and the lights. When they said, "Action," and I began to sing, my dad was overwhelmed. Out of the corner of my eye, I could see him choking back tears. I'll never forget the look on his face—like his heart was seeing the music in me for the first time. I think that moment, when he saw his little girl in lights, being filmed for a FOX TV show and singing her heart out, made all of his years of sacrifice worthwhile.

And a half-hour later, when I was called in to audition for Randy, Simon, and Paula, and they said, "Welcome to Hollywood," I flew from the room and jumped into my dad's arms. Crying into his fuzzy shirt with my head resting on his heart made all my years of performing worthwhile. To me, making music is about touching another person's soul. That night the soul I touched was the most precious one in the world to me.

Afterward, my dad and I walked to the car in silence. As we drove away, leaving the lights of the city behind us, my dad turned to me and said, "You know, Babycakes, I think something's gonna happen from this *American Idol* thing."

And as I gazed back at this man I loved so much, I thought, *It already has.*

Dedication Night

Matt Rohde
Vocal Coach and Accompanist

"Just don't turn around," we told the contestants. If these kids were going to make it through Dedication Night, it was our only hope.

The show was going live in a few hours. This was the night of the competition that the contestants pick someone they love, someone who has been an inspiration in their lives—usually a parent, grandparent, or spouse—and dedicate their song to them. The producers put together a montage of photos and videos of that loved one and add a voice-over of the contestant talking about why that person means so much to them. Before the kids sing their song, the montage is shown.

All of us were worried that the show might turn into a cry-fest. During dress rehearsal, when the kids were doing their run-throughs with the band, only one or two made it to the end of their song without tears. We thought maybe if they just didn't turn around and watch the montage as it played, they'd have a better chance of making it through.

Our biggest concern was Jordin Sparks. Her dedication was to her little brother, PJ, and she kept breaking down in the middle of her song. Her love for her brother really touched all of us. When a typical seventeen-year-old girl has a fourteen-year-old brother, she usually looks at him mainly as an annoyance, but here was Jordin, on Dedication Night, choosing her brother and weeping whenever she started to sing.

"I don't know what to do. I love him so much," she said.

And as Jordin was struggling to hold it together, I was struggling, too.

I have a baby sister, so I understand that love. She's three years younger than I am, too, and Jordin's dedication made me look back on when I was seventeen and my sister was fourteen. Growing up, there were only the two of us kids. I always looked out for her and felt very protective. Now she's a grown woman in her thirties with a successful career in advertising, but to me she's still my baby sister. So every time Jordin started to cry, I teared up as well.

I believe one of the reasons for this show's remarkable success is the way it touches people's hearts. I've been a musical director for years and have traveled with some of the biggest names in the industry, including J. Lo, Alanis Morissette, and Isaac Hayes. They have all been really great and genuine people, but I've never been touched the way I am here at *Idol.*

Most of these singers aren't professional musicians; they're kids. Their emotions are completely authentic. They're still innocent and haven't learned how to work the audience or turn it on for effect. America can feel that authenticity, and it touches us all so deeply.

So Ryan introduces each contestant on Dedication Night, and their montage is shown and they begin, I know the emotions they're experiencing as they sing for

America. I hold my breath, hoping they'll make it through.

But I'm also hoping they'll never lose those simple, authentic emotions that bring them to tears in the first place—or that innocent generosity of spirit that makes us love them and brings us to tears when each of them goes home.

Her *American Idol*

Sallie A. Rodman
American Idol Fan

The phone always rings right at 9:00 PM on the dot.

"It's time for *Idol*, Mom. Are you ready?" It's my oldest daughter, Jennifer.

"Sure am, and I'm crossin' my fingers for Melinda and Jordin. I heard Jennifer Lopez is coaching them this week!"

"That is so cool!" she replies. "I'm saying a little prayer that Jordin stays, too. Catch you in a little." And with that she hangs up.

Thus starts our weekly journey into an hour of time that is all ours—just me and my daughter, who lives a thousand miles away.

Jennifer is a military wife. She lives with my two grandchildren in Washington state, a long way from her hometown of Los Alamitos. She moved there in the middle of last year and is slowly making friends, but it's not easy being alone. Her husband, Ed, is in the Navy serving in the North Arabian Sea, supporting the troops on the ground in Afghanistan in Operation Enduring Freedom. Ed will be gone on sea duty for another nine months. Watching

American Idol together is one of my ways of reaching out to her so that she doesn't feel so alone.

She grabs a Coke and I grab my tea, and we each settle down in front of our respective TV sets. Her kids are in bed at last, and she can have a little time to herself. We call back and forth on our cell phones between contestants. She's voting for Jordin Sparks, and I was voting for Gina Glocksen until she was voted off last week. We both cried when Gina left. So now we're both voting for Jordin, but we also like Melinda a lot—and Chris, Lakisha, and Blake.

Whoops, there goes my phone again.

"Can you believe that Sanjaya?" she says before I even get a chance to say hello. "What does everyone see in him?"

"I don't know, hon, but they must see something. I know the teenyboppers who work part-time in my office just love him to death."

"Oh," she giggles, "I forgot about them. Haley's up, gotta run. Catch you after," and she's gone again.

And so it goes, week after week.

When the show is over, we recap what Haley wore, how long Melinda held her notes, how rude Simon's remarks were, and who we think might get the boot tomorrow night.

For the contestants, *American Idol* is the dream of a lifetime. For me, *American Idol* is a time to connect with my daughter during these difficult days in her life and hopefully help keep her spirits afloat. For Jennifer, *American Idol* is her little hour of fun where she can escape into a world of feuding judges, beat-boxers and rockers, celebrity coaches, and songs gone awry, while her real American Idol is on the other side of the world, defending our freedom. And Jennifer has a dream, too—to have her idol come back safe and sound to her and her two sleeping children.

My Dream Come True

Scott Savol
Top 10, Season 4

When I think about my upbringing, it's amazing I made it to Number 5 in *American Idol*'s Season 4.

Sometimes it seems like a dream. Did I really get put through in all those rounds? Did I really spend months in Hollywood and meet Hall & Oates, Tony Orlando, and LL Cool J? Did I really tour the U.S. and perform in front of hundreds of thousands of screaming fans shouting my name?

I know it was real, because *American Idol* made my life-long dream come true.

When I was younger, I made a lot of poor choices. I wasn't exactly a bad kid, but I wasn't a poster child for "Boy of the Year," either. All I ever really wanted was for my dad to love me and be proud of me. I wanted to be good enough in his eyes. I never blamed my dad for the way he was; I knew he'd had a tough childhood with his father leaving and all.

What I regret most is that I hung out with friends instead of doing schoolwork. I notice that a lot of the kids who studied hard and went to college are making six figures now, and the kids who didn't pay attention to their grades are serving those guys burgers when they cruise into the drive-through with their nice wheels.

I always figured I'd be a burger flipper because, for as long as I can remember, I was told that I would never amount to anything. After a while I started to believe it, and it really pulled me down.

When I was ten, I loved Bon Jovi and would put on his music and sing by myself in my room. It was my Aunt Janet who encouraged me to sing with her in church. I loved to sing for the same reason most singers do: to make people happy. My dad said that I'd never be good enough to do more than sing in my bedroom.

When I decided to audition for *Idol* in Cleveland, I didn't tell anyone I was going. If I didn't make it through, I didn't want "I-told-you-so" thrown in my face.

Even though I knew I wasn't the typical *American Idol* type, I had nothing to lose. I just told myself that no one could stop me from living my dreams but me. And in my deepest heart of hearts, I believed it would happen for me one day. I made it through the first three rounds and headed to Hollywood.

Next thing I knew, I went from the hundreds in Hollywood to the Top 24 to the Final 12, and kept getting voted back week after week. I was eventually voted off at Number 5 and went home for a few weeks between that night and the Finale.

The day I landed in Cleveland will remain in my mind forever. As I stepped off the plane and walked through the airport, I was met by hundreds of screaming fans—girls crying, people reaching out to touch me, and all these banners and signs saying, "Scotty, We Love You." Of course, my mom was there as well. She had never stopped cheering for me and had buffered the negative media—something all *Idols* have to deal with.

But all I saw was my dad, sitting in a wheelchair because of his knee surgery, at the end of the concourse. I walked straight over and hugged him. He cried and squeezed me hard. Then I heard the words I'd been waiting twenty-eight years for: "I missed you, Scott. I love you, son. I'm really proud of you."

I might have lived my whole life until my dad passed, never doing anything spectacular or making him proud of me. But now my dad saw that I was someone people looked up to as a singer and admired as a role model.

It might have taken twenty-eight years and millions of people voting for me week after week, but I say, "Better late than never." If it took *American Idol* to make it happen, so be it. But I did it—I got the one vote that meant more to me than all the others combined. I got my dad's vote, and made my lifelong dream come true.

The Great Coin Caper

Nikko Smith
Top 10, Season 4

I scrambled around trying to get my things together. I couldn't believe I was going. The call had come that *American Idol* wanted me in Hollywood, and I was racing around my room as fast as I could, trying hard not to forget anything. My head felt like it was going to spin off, but I pushed on, talking to myself. *Okay, where's my list? Should I bring these? No, I don't need those. Do I have everything?*

My father walked into my bedroom and watched as I slam-dunked a pair of socks into my duffel.

"Nikko, I have something for you."

I tossed an extra pair of shorts over his head and into my bag.

I continued to race around him as he stood in the middle of the messy room. My father reached into his pocket and pulled out a gold coin. He stopped me, opened my hand, and placed the coin in my palm.

"Nikko, this coin means a lot to me. Every time I went onto the ball field, it brought me good luck. I'm hoping it will do for you what it did for me."

"Wow, Dad . . . thanks. This means so much to me." I hugged him and thought I was the luckiest guy in the world, not just because Ozzie Smith, the great Baseball Hall of Fame shortstop, was my dad, but because now I held his lucky gold coin. I tucked it safely into my wallet and thought to myself, *I'm going places now!*

As I turned to leave, he put his hand on my shoulder. "You're going to be fine, son. Just do what you do. Stay focused and always remember to keep God first."

I flew out to Los Angeles for the first round of the auditions and was thrown right into the fire with a solo performance. When my knees knocked on stage, I held the coin tightly in my right hand and forged on with my first song. I squeezed it and kept thinking, *God, please get me through this.* I stumbled through some of the words and knew mistakes could cost me. I bit my lip waiting for the verdict.

"You're through!"

Wow! The coin really works!

I forgot some lyrics, but I was still in. Amazing.

Round Two, and it was time for the group performances. I was with Bo Bice, and man, did we rock that one. Oh, yeah—I had my lucky coin. I couldn't help but exclaim, "This thing is truly The Bomb. No doubt about it."

Round Three, and this time I was in trouble. My voice was hoarse, and I had to sing *a cappella*. I took the stage again with my father's precious gift in hand. "Please, God, get me through this," I uttered under my breath. I waited for the decision.

"Nikko . . . you're through!"

Say what? I couldn't believe it. I kissed my gold coin, looked up at the heavens, and said, "Thank you."

The big day came when we would find out if we had made it into the Top 24. I knew I was going to have to enter the elevator and take the long walk to the lone chair in front of the judges to hear my fate. I was scared to death.

One by one, the other contestants exited the elevator, and it seemed like no one was getting through. *This is not good,* I thought.

My name was called, and as the elevator descended, I whispered to my coin, "Please be with me through this. Don't let me down. Don't fail me now."

I sat in the chair and squeezed the coin so hard my fingers hurt. The judges talked about me, but I didn't even hear them. I was shaking so badly my hand throbbed.

"Nikko, you're through!"

I jumped up, kissed the coin, and raced back to the elevator. "I made it!" I yelled. "Yes!" I was moving forward with my dreams, thanks to my dad's coin.

The next day, I had a big interview. I knew what I was going to say as I took the coin out of my wallet and again held it tightly. When the interviewer asked if I had a lucky charm, I said, "Yes, as a matter of fact, I *do*. My father gave me this very special coin he always carried when he played major league baseball."

I explained that he retired in 1996 and kept this rare coin until he passed it down to me.

"That's awesome," she said. "Hold it up for the camera."

As I held it up, I told about the great role it had played in both my father's and my own success. Then I noticed her staring at the coin with a puzzled look on her face. I wondered, *Why is she looking like that?*

The interview ended, but that look on her face still bothered me. So, for the first time, I really *looked* at my coin. *Wait a minute! This can't be!* I thought, and immediately called home.

"Dad, I have a question for you. Why did you tell me you carried this coin every time you went onto the ball field?"

"Because I did, son."

"Dad, I just did an interview, and I held up your coin, and they looked at me like I was crazy."

"They did?"

"Yeah, Dad, they did. You retired in 1996. This coin is a gold Sacagawea, and they weren't made until 2000! It says 2000 right on it!

"Oh."

"Oh?"

He had just been busted! There was a moment of silence, and then we both burst out laughing.

Having the coin had helped me feel my father was with me through it all, and that meant a lot to me. Because I believed it played a part in his success, I believed it was doing the same for me. It gave me that little extra boost of confidence.

Inadvertently, my dad had taught me one of the greatest lessons of my life: it wasn't the coin that had brought me my success; it was my *belief* in the coin. And without the coin to believe in, for the rest of my *Idol* experience, I had only the second part of what my dad had shared with me on the day I left for Hollywood: "Stay focused and remember to keep God first."

So with no lucky charm in my pocket, but those words in my heart, I made it into the Top 10, participated in the Finale, and toured the country in front of hundreds of thousands of fans.

Through the Great Coin Caper, my dad taught me that staying focused and keeping God first are the only lucky charms I'll ever need.

My Superstar

Tamyra Gray
Top 10, Season 1

The moment I decided that I wanted to devote my life to singing, my mother—without a second of hesitation—became my greatest cheerleader. To this day, it means so much to her to be my cheerleader because she has never had much to cheer about in her own life.

As a child, I didn't idolize a superstar. I didn't idolize Mariah Carey or Whitney Houston, although I admired them. My only idol has been my "Mommy."

I grew up in a chaotic household. My mother hid it all so well and bore no evidence of the turmoil she endured. The world around her saw a goddess—a gorgeous beauty who was a little bit shy, demure, and at times, conservative. As a child, she had survived mental anguish and poverty so severe that her family had been forced to live in a school bus for awhile. Still, her spirit was strong.

"Things will be better," she promised, as she brushed my hair gently. "Just believe."

Despite her own longing for acceptance, my mother always made me feel adored. When she smiled at me, I knew I was cherished. She encouraged anything and everything my brothers, sisters, and I dreamed of doing, and she always pushed me to excel. If I came home with a C on my report card, I was grounded until the next semester. When I ask her about it now, she says, "I always knew you had the potential to achieve great things and, if I let you get away with a C, it would mean I was accepting you being average. *I* knew you were exceptional."

Mommy loved music and encouraged us to learn an instrument. As a child, I took up guitar, then quit. Next I tried piano, then quit. I did the same with the flute. I was never denied the opportunity to try something else, nor was I ever forced to continue if it was against my wishes. So my mother let me quit everything except my own instrument—my voice—even though my incessant singing when I was little was more of a nuisance than a joy to my parents!

Apparently, my voice took a while to develop. As a child, when I sang along to songs on the radio, my parents would ask, "Who sings that song?" and I'd answer with the artist's name. "Well, then, let them," they'd tease.

Mommy was my first favorite singer. As she crooned "Loving You," her voice was so pure and beautiful that I sat entranced. As she effortlessly hit those high whistle tones, I melted into the moment and treasured the experience.

"I want to sing like that when I grow up," I announced.

I mimicked the way she threw her head back slightly and tapped her foot gently. I memorized her every nuance, flourish, and move.

Music was my mother's peace and inspiration. It was something glorious for her to turn to when the realities of life were simply too much to handle. As young as I was, I sensed that music was her escape.

It quickly became mine, as well. I sang with the radio. I sang in the shower. I sang when I was bored, when I was happy, and when I was sad. I saw the joy it gave my mother, and soon it began to bring more joy to me than anything else.

My joy soon became my passion.

At the end of seventh grade at Montgomery Village Junior High School there was an annual talent show, and I was determined to go out with a bang. I decided to participate in every category: dancing, singing, and modeling. My parents accepted the dancing and modeling, but when I said I was going to sing, they were shocked. But after all those years of being my mom's audience-of-one, I was ready to use her inspiration and stand on the stage on my own. I was ready to take the stage for her.

In front of hundreds of parents and students, friends and teachers, I stood: a skinny little girl who made up for the space she failed to claim on stage with enough ambition to fill the room. I started to sail through "Just Can't Stay Away" by En Vogue when, just for a moment, I doubted myself. I had been hoarse all day and worried about whether I'd be able to make that high, money note. But then I looked into the audience and saw my mom, who for so long had believed when there wasn't much to believe in, sitting proudly and watching intently. I pictured her in the kitchen, singing effortlessly, hitting notes I could only dream of—and I went for it.

I hit the note. The crowd cheered, and I received my first standing ovation.

I knew that was a pivotal moment in my life, and my parents recognized it as well. From that day on, they got me—and my sister—in front of producers and into the studio. After school, we raced to vocal lessons, and then did our homework. After that we were at the studio until midnight, even later on weekends.

After working with several managers, I knew there was only one person for the job. I needed my "mom-ager," a person who not only understood the business, but who also possessed the talent and grace that was still my daily inspiration—and who believed in me 100 percent.

One evening, while working on a Coca-Cola project in New York, I saw an *American Idol* commercial. "Who wants to be a superstar?" it asked.

It rang in my ears like an alarm clock, telling me to wake up. *Who wants to be a superstar?* Well, *me,* of course!

Breathless with excitement, I approached my mother.

"Mommy, there's this TV show that's about to be filmed called *American Idol: The Search for a Superstar,* and I'd like to do it, but the rules say that you can't have a manager. If you don't want me to do it, and would like the chance to pursue my deals on your own as my manager, I will stick by you." I gulped for air.

"No, I want you to do this," she said, without skipping a beat. "This is the moment you've been waiting for. This is your chance to shine. You have and always will be my superstar, but now it's time for you to be the world's superstar."

My mother had given me life and the gift of song. At that moment, she gave me the strength and courage to pursue a new dream.

I learned incredible, personal lessons on *American Idol.* I learned to be true to my art and to sing with conviction. I learned to accept the judges' criticism as constructive feedback. I learned that however things turn out, it's always for the best.

But it was Mommy who taught me the most important lesson. It was she who taught me to believe even when it seemed there was nothing to believe in. She is *my* superstar.

And because *she* believes, so do I.

I Have to Make This Worth It

Phil Stacey
Top 10, Season 6

I love my family more than you can imagine. I also love my country, so when the tragedy of September 11 occurred, I knew that I didn't want to be a bystander. Several of my buddies and I went to enlist—I wanted to be a Marine officer. When people heard I had joined the military, they couldn't believe it. I'm the last person you would ever think of as a disciplined soldier.

The Marine recruiter noticed I had a vocal degree and asked if I would be a singer with the Navy band. I had pictured myself fighting a war overseas, but my wife Kendra stepped in and said, "Yes, he would."

Just after I enlisted, Kendra found out she was pregnant. My recruiter assured me I could go home from boot camp when the baby came. When the Red Cross found me, my division commander said, "Your wife called, and it looks like she's ready to have that baby." I said, "Great, how do I make arrangements to leave immediately?" He looked at me like, *Yeah, right.* Disappointed doesn't come close to describing how I felt. Kendra was, as always, comforting and understanding.

After nearly nine years of marriage, I can honestly say that Kendra is the perfect wife. She's the one who would always say how well I would do on *American Idol*. I'd been a big fan of the show since the beginning, but never once did I think about auditioning. She was the one who found out when and where the auditions were being held for Season 6.

It turned out that the closest audition site to Florida was in Memphis on September 2, which was perfect because Kendra was pregnant with our second child, and if the auditions were any nearer to the October 17 due date, I would never have gone.

When I made it through the first round, I was pumped, only to find out that we didn't go back the next day to sing in front of the judges. We were supposed to go back the next *month*. I called Kendra and told her I made it through but I wasn't going back. There was no way I would risk missing this baby's birth.

So October 2 rolled around, and Kendra pushed me out the door, assuring me I'd only be gone for two days and she hadn't had one contraction yet, so I shouldn't worry. Everything would be fine. So I flew out of Jacksonville with my dad and brother, landed in Nashville, and drove to Memphis for my audition the next morning.

At 3:00 AM, the phone in my hotel room woke me up. I picked it up and heard a baby crying in the background. I fell into a chair. I didn't know what to do. I was thinking, *What am I doing here? American Idol is a really cool thing, but this is my baby.* Kendra had gone into labor, and less than four hours later, the baby was born. She hadn't called me because she didn't want to distract me and wanted me to get my sleep—which is so like her—but my heart was broken.

My brother and my dad both consoled me, but I just wanted to leave. They kept saying, "Phil, it's going to be worth it in the long run. You're doing this for your kids and your wife." They were trying so hard to make me feel better, but you hear about all these guys who sacrifice their families for their careers, and I just didn't want to be one of those guys.

I was up the rest of the night, and I left for the audition at 6:30 AM. For this round, if I made it through, I would go to Hollywood. I found out that they had me auditioning second to last. I told the producer that my wife had just had a baby, and if they couldn't move me up, I would have to leave. They actually made me call the hospital for them to confirm that it was true because apparently people say stuff like that all the time so that they can be moved up.

So I went in front of the judges, and Randy's like, "Where's the cigar, dawg?"

But I was completely disconnected from my audition at this point.

And then Simon asked, "What's more important to you, Phil, going to Hollywood so you can have a big career—or your baby?"

Boy, that was an easy question. "Baby totally wins."

When they aired the show, they made it seem like Simon rolled his eyes, but he was so supportive. They were all like, "Right answer. You got your priorities straight, man."

When they said, "You're going to Hollywood," it was supposed to be this incredible moment, but all I wanted to do was to get home to my family. And then I found out that there are all these required meetings, and I was freaking out. Finally, we raced to Nashville to get the plane for home—and we missed the flight.

Again, no words could describe how I felt. I told my dad, "I don't care that it's a ten-hour drive. I've gotta get home tonight." So, we started driving. The only problem was that we were all falling asleep, so we turned around and took the first flight out in the morning.

At the hospital, all these people wanted to talk to me about *Idol,* but I was like, "Just let me through."

Finally, I made it to the room. There was my wife, my mom, my daughter Chloe—and my new baby, just laying there in her little bed. All of a sudden, I was in a different place. I was with my family. Then my wife looked at me and said, "Congratulations," as if I was the one who deserved the congratulations. I just went and held her. *American Idol* is about chasing your dream, but my dream at that moment was to be right there with my family.

I had to let go of my desire to be a Marine officer because the military wanted me to be a part of the Navy Band. Now I know that it was worth it because with *Idol* I've represented the military in front of 30 million people twice a week.

Similarly, I gave up being at my daughter's birth to be on *Idol,* and I can never get that back, so I have to make this worth it. Fame and fortune don't interest me, but if when my baby is old enough to understand, she is going to be proud of me—and it will have been worth it.

Kendra says if we had to do it over again, we would have done the exact same thing. And it does feel amazing to find her in the audience and see the pride in her eyes. Do you know what it's like to have someone who never stops believing in you?

I love *American Idol*—the people, the excitement, the applause, and thinking that maybe I'm an inspiration—not only because of my singing, but because I'm a family man and a military man. But if Simon were to ask me again what's more important, my family would still win—hands down.

I just want them to be happy, and from what I hear, my little Chloe is pretty happy every week when she gets to point at the TV and tell anyone who will listen, "That's my daddy."

That's Life

John Stevens
Top 10, Season 3

I loved being at my grandparents' little house. My grandmother was from Scotland, and she had black-and-white photos of her family displayed on the shelves, and pictures of Scotland hanging on all of the walls. Everything was very neat and tidy, and the wallpaper had tiny flowers all over it. My grandmother was always cooking, cleaning, and gardening. Everything was just perfect.

It was a good thing I enjoyed being there. Since my mother often traveled with my older brother's hockey team and my dad had to work, I spent a lot of time at my grandparents' house.

One rainy New York afternoon when I was four years old, I was looking through the vast collection of CDs and records that my grandfather had stacked proudly next to their huge CD player in the corner of their living room. Looking at them was one of my favorite activities.

"Who's this?" I asked my grandfather. When he saw what I had in my hand, his eyes glowed. He took the CD from me, carefully opened the case, and, making sure he held it by the edges, slipped it into the CD player. As he did so, he told me that the man smiling from the CD cover was his favorite artist of all time. The album was called *Frank Sinatra's Greatest Hits*.

He put on song number eight called "That's Life," and he started snapping his fingers and bobbing his head back and forth to the music, so I did the same. He told me all about the "big bands" of the '40s and '50s, and that everyone called Sinatra "Ol' Blue Eyes" and considered him to be the greatest of the greats from that era. I got so excited that he gave me the CD to keep.

Even though I was only four, I told my grandfather, "I'm going to sing like him one day." From then on, I knew what I wanted to do for the rest of my life.

My grandparents have always been my biggest inspirations. My grandmother is a classically trained pianist. Before she married my grandfather and moved to America, she trained at the Royal Academy in London. She was my first piano teacher and introduced me to classical music. Once every month, I would get all dressed up, and she and I would go out together to hear the Buffalo Philharmonic Orchestra. She introduced me to different composers, and I was entranced by every one. While most kids my age were listening to *Sesame Street* and *Barney* songs, I was listening to Bach and Beethoven.

But my favorite activity of all was playing Tripoley or Pinochle with my grandparents, while listening to Frank or watching him perform with Dean Martin on PBS.

Just as everything in her home was perfect, my grandmother was a perfectionist with music as well. The first time I sang in front of an audience was during a chorus concert in the seventh grade. I had a solo. Being on stage and singing for an audience gave me a feeling like nothing else I'd ever experienced. But after my performance, my grandmother gave me quite a critique.

Though she never praised me, I didn't doubt that she loved me or was proud of me. If I had a solo at school or was in a chorus performance or musical, she never said, "Great job! You nailed it." It was always, "You were good, but you can do better."

I took piano lessons for seven years, and every time my grandmother came over she would ask me to play for her. When I was done, she would tell me what I needed to work on. Her critiques prepared me for the *Idol* judges; it's why their criticism never bothered me. I was used to it.

Looking back, I'm grateful that she kept pushing me to do better because she wanted me to reach my full potential. Still, I would have loved to have heard a little praise from her. But she never said, "You were amazing tonight," or "I am so proud of you."

Until *Idol*.

It was Motown Night, and I was set to sing "My Girl." I was nervous and excited because my grandparents had come all the way from upstate New York to Los Angeles to be in the live audience that night. With just hours to go before the show, I came down with an excruciating migraine headache. In the entire history of *Idol*, not one contestant had ever missed a performance because of illness, and I certainly didn't want to be the first. But as show time drew nearer, my migraine got worse. Lying in the green room with my head pounding, I didn't think I was going to make it.

This is my chance to make my grandparents really proud, I thought with despair. Then I told myself, *You just have to get up, go out there, and keep it together for one hour—just one hour.* So I picked myself up, joined the other *Idols*, and performed with a migraine.

When it was over, I knew it wasn't my best performance, and I was criticizing myself and beating myself up. I felt that I had let everybody down. That's when my grandparents walked backstage. I braced myself, expecting my grandmother to say the same words I'd been thinking. Instead, she gave me a huge hug, looked me in the eyes, and said, "Johnny B, you were *fantastic*. I am *so* proud of you."

I don't know if she really thought I had been that great or if she was just proud that I had performed with a migraine. Or maybe she was proud of me because I had a nice connection with Simon Cowell. Simon and I shared a love of Sinatra, and when I told him that my grandfather, who had introduced me to Sinatra's music, was there, Simon went right over to meet my grandparents. He made them feel very special.

But it didn't matter to me why my grandmother and grandfather were proud; all that mattered is that they were and they told me.

Now that my grandmother is gone, I look back on all those years and realize that she only pushed me because she had so much faith in me. If she hadn't thought I could do amazing things, she would have let me settle and not encouraged me to do better. But because she expected great things from me, I expected great things from myself.

I miss my grandmother a lot. No matter where I go with my music career, I'll always have the memory of being on *American Idol* and going all the way to Number 6. But most important, I'll have the memory of Motown night, and the moment my grandmother told me that I had made her proud.

I Will Never Forget

Chris Richardson
Top 10, Season 6

Family has always been everything to me.

No matter what's going on in my life, when I walk into my home I feel happy and safe. There's always that same clean-house smell—a candle burning, seasonal music or Nat King Cole playing, and my mom in the kitchen. I love everything my mom cooks, but my favorite is chicken and dumplings.

She's decorated the kitchen with an apple theme. There's an apple border around the top and apple knick-knacks and lots of baskets—even baskets hanging from the ceiling. She really likes all that kind of stuff. There's an island in the middle of the kitchen where I sit and talk to her about anything. She never tells me what to do. She just says to stay humble and always be true to myself. I took a break from college because I'd gotten this independent record label deal. Even though I know my mom was disappointed, she supports my decisions and knows that if I make a mistake, I'll learn and grow from it.

I can't even explain my dad. He's my vision of everything the perfect father should be. When you're my age and want to live your dream of being a musician or a performer, some dads tell you to get real—or even to get out and get a job. Not my dad. He's my biggest fan. Not only is he always there for me, but he's there for everyone. He's everyone's favorite uncle, cousin, and friend.

My sister, Michelle, is my best friend. As kids, we followed my dad like two little shadows everywhere his band performed. There's never been one moment that Michelle hasn't been there for me. I'm lucky to have her.

I also have an English bulldog named Tommy. He's family, too. I talk to him, and I know he listens. I missed him so much when I was away all those weeks on *Idol*, and I know he missed me.

But the one who really steals my heart is my grandma. I call her Big Momma. I chose her on *American Idol*'s Dedication Night because she's sacrificed so much for us. It's been real lonely for her since my granddad died. Sometimes she just sits and looks out the window and sees faces in the trees.

A few months ago, Big Momma heard about a society for ladies that she wanted to join. She called my mom and sister ten times, asking questions about which dress and hat to wear, and if she should wear gloves, and what about the purse and shoes. She couldn't wait for the day of the meeting and was ready an hour before her ride came.

When she walked in the restaurant all decked out in her outfit, they told her they were sorry but the chapter wasn't open to new members. She was so crushed. It breaks my heart to think how she must have felt. When I make it big, I'm going to buy Big Momma her own society for her own ladies, and she can accept whoever she wants. If I know her, she'll let everyone in.

Big Momma tells anyone who will listen about me being

on TV. She was in the hospital last week and said to the nurse who was taking care of her, "Do you know whose leg it is you're washing?"

And the nurse said, "No, I do not."

Then Big Momma started in with, "Do you watch *American Idol*?" I just love her to pieces.

I value the principles of love and family above anything else. No matter how successful I become, that will never change. When I auditioned for *American Idol,* I was like any of the other 100,000 people waiting in line. I just happened to make it further. But I'm still the same guy. No matter where this *American Idol* experience takes me, I'll always be able to go back home. I'll never forget where I came from.

Under Dawg

Dena Harris
American Idol Fan

American Idol is not just about talent. It's about chasing the dream. Although Americans love to laugh along with Simon, Paula, and Randy at the *Idol*-hopefuls who—bless their hearts—can't carry a tune, I cheer for the underrated underdogs. Why? Because I know what it's like to hold tight to a dream that, if viewed from a realistic perspective, has little chance of being realized.

Let's get one thing straight. My dream is not to sing on national TV. Please. My lack of pitch could give William Hung a run for his money. Dancing? Fuggedaboutit. My dance skills make my singing seem strong in comparison. No, my dream is simpler. My dream, my ultimate goal, is to cook a decent meal for my husband.

I know. It's pathetic, right? But there it is. My mom's idea of cooking was to heat water for instant oatmeal. I inherited that gene. It's not my fault my pot roasts smoke, my soufflés fall, and my burgers are prized by neighbor kids as hockey pucks. I follow the recipes. Really. Things just go wrong. Wrong enough that we have the local fire department on speed dial, and the chief asked me to advise them on days I'll be cooking.

So I'm no Rachael Ray. Hey, it's not like *American Idol* contestants begin their stints as Mariah Carey. It takes months of practice, makeup, and styling to turn contestants from humdrum nobodies into potential superstars. That's all I need, too. With just a little patience, TLC, and a fire extinguisher, I may prove to be the Katharine McPhee of the Food Network.

It was during the first season of *American Idol* that I really put my cooking skills to the test. Eager to play the role of wife-with-hot-and-hearty-dinner-waiting-for-her-man, I attempted meal after meal with no success. My husband, patient guy that he is, faced chicken tenders burnt to a crisp, fish broiled to nothingness, and vegetable medleys that looked like massacres-in-a-bowl.

At the time, my husband was a huge fan of *American Idol*. I had yet to catch the fever, which explains the mix-up that follows.

One night, I served a simple meal of ginger-baked chicken and instant mashed potatoes accompanied by a wild rice and berry side dish. I set the plates in front of us and twisted my hands under the table as my husband took his first bite. He didn't immediately spit it back out, which held promise.

I couldn't stand the suspense. "So? What do you think?"

He chewed thoughtfully, set down his fork, and looked at me. Then my husband, a suit-wearing CPA and—if we're being honest—the whitest man on the planet, said this: "Yo! Okay, let me say it. You did your thing, dawg, you did your thing. I mean, it's not the greatest thing I've ever eaten, but you know, 's awright. I'm proud of you, dawg, proud of you. You worked it. Just keepin' it real. Yeah, baby."

He picked up his fork and continued eating.

"Ah, excuse me," I said after a moment's silence, "but did you just call me a dog?"

"Not dog." He chewed another bite of chicken. "Dawg." He pounded his heart with a fist closed over in a peace sign. "You're a dawg."

"Riii-ght."

Then he introduced me to *American Idol* and the glorious Randy Jackson, and all was forgiven. Forgiven, but not forgotten.

One night, after a breathless romantic interlude, my beloved looked at me with a smug smile. "How was that?"

"Yo, dawg," I drawled, "you did your thing."

My husband's smile wavered as he pondered my meaning.

"Just keepin' it real, dawg," I told him. "Just keepin' it real."

That will teach him to disrespect my cooking.

The Ace of Hearts

Ace Young
Top 10, Season 5

Growing up with four older brothers, footballs were everywhere in our house. We spent a lot of time talking while throwing them around. We also worked out our share of brotherly battles and solved many of life's mysteries while running for passes in our back yard. Being offered a football scholarship really posed a dilemma for me because I had to make a very difficult decision—one that would change my life forever.

I headed out the back door, picked up the pigskin, and asked my father if he wouldn't mind throwing a few. He never minded. I was lucky—my parents were always there for my brothers and me, even if they had just come home from a ten-hour day.

The air was crisp and clear that morning in Colorado—the only fog was in my own mind. I knew throwing the ball around would help as it always did. My father stepped back, cocked his arm, and sent a spiraling pass high up into Denver's crystal-blue sky. It spun perfectly as I went deeper and deeper toward our back-yard end zone with my arms reaching as far as they could go. My father's voice echoed around it, "Run! Faster! You got it, Ace! You got it!" I jumped into the air, and as my hands wrapped around the weathered brown leather, we both shouted, "Touchdown!"

"You sure can catch a ball, son," my father yelled out to me. Yep, I sure could, and I was fast, too. It was *this* blessing that presented both the opportunity and the dilemma that haunted me day and night.

I walked back to my father as he stood proudly with his hands on his hips. He always had words of encouragement to share with his sons. He and my mom taught the five of us to fight for our dreams and reach high until we achieved our goals. They always spoke positively, and this day was no different. "You're a great athlete, Ace." I nodded as he tousled my long hair, while giving me a gentle push. I tossed the ball back to him, and we leaned against the battered wooden fence to catch our breath.

It was then that I shared with him what seemed to be on my mind every waking minute of the day.

"I just can't decide what to do, Dad. I don't know if I'm supposed to play college football or go into music. I love both so much."

My father took the football from my hands, wiped his brow, looked at me intently, and spoke quietly, "Son, I know you love them both, but you'll never be able to figure it out by thinking so much. Let your heart lead you."

With that, he gave me a pat on my back, handed me the ball, smiled, and walked toward the house.

From the time I was very young, I found great comfort sitting alone in my room listening to song lyrics. I would feel every one of them. Sometimes my father or mother would peek in and ask, "Why are you listening to that song, Ace?" My answer would always be the same. I'd put my hand to my chest and say, "Because I feel it." I always felt the pain and joy from a song, and it would stay with me for a very long time.

I stared at the blue sky thinking about my father's words. Suddenly, I knew there was no choice. Sure, I loved it when the crowd cheered as I made a touchdown, and there's no feeling in the world like being the MVP of the big game, but I took my father's advice and let my heart lead my way. I knew what I had to do, and it wasn't scoring touchdowns on the field. It was touching people's hearts from the stage with my music—the same way music had touched me ever since I was a little boy.

Although he hadn't pushed me one way or another, I think my dad was happy with my decision. And I've never looked back. My dad's advice not only helped me make that decision, but gave me the road map for the rest of my life. His words made me realize who I really was and what made me happy. It could have been a hard choice, but when I looked inside my heart, I had no choice. That day opened a new world for me.

Since I was a nine-year-old performing in shopping malls, my mom and dad never missed a show. They've been my biggest fans. They carried my spotlights, speakers, and microphones, and they made sure everything was done just right.

They were so proud of me when I made it on *American Idol* and again when I went on the *American Idols Live!* tour. I'll never forget when the two of them arrived at the arena the first time they came to see me on tour. They were filled with excitement and were more nervous than I was. They walked up the ramp, into the immense coliseum, and looked out into the darkened theater that held thousands of seats. My mom just stood there taking it all in, her eyes filling up with tears. My father put his arm around her shoulder, and they stood together silently.

My father uttered the first words, "Wow, Ace . . . that is a *big* stage!"

I stepped closer, hugged them tightly, and said, "And you know what, Dad? This time you don't have to carry my speakers." My mom laughed out loud as we all wiped tears from our cheeks.

My father wrapped his other arm around my shoulder and said, "I'm so proud of you, son. Just never forget what I told you. Go with your heart, Ace. It will never fail you."

Every step of the way, I have lived by my father's advice and followed my heart. Every decision I've made is based on that. I never think, *How does this look? What will people think? Is this a good strategy?* I don't think; I feel. And even when, from the outside it might look like I should have chosen a different path or made a different choice, I know that if my heart's leading me there, I'll always end up in the right place.

Never Over

Anthony Fedorov
Top 10, Season 4

*You are the only one controlling your own des-
tiny. Keep holding on, don't be afraid, just let
your tears fade with the rain, it's never over . . .*
Anthony Fedorov and Daniel Freiberg

My brother was always there for me, despite the seven
years between us. I always looked up to Denis and was
happy to be the little blond shadow that followed him
around twelve hours a day. We went to the same school in
the Ukraine, and every time he'd turn around in the hallways, there I'd be with a big grin on my face. I was in awe
of him. He hung out with the prettiest girls in school and
was always strumming the coolest songs on his guitar. I
was so proud to say, "That's my big brother."

Denis was my hero, so, of course, I always did what he
said. Growing up, we'd take turns cleaning the house. One
week I'd clean, and the next week he'd clean—that was the
rule. But, being a teenager, he had better things to do than

mop and dust. He'd say, "Anthony, it's your turn to clean *again*," while giving me a wink and a knock on the arm. Sometimes I'd get stuck cleaning three or four weeks in a row! My parents never knew, and I never told on him. I was a good sport, and Denis could do no wrong in my eyes.

I didn't always know that Denis was watching over me, yet he'd pop up unexpectedly at times and share great words of wisdom. One time when I was eight years old, I was picking cigarette butts up off the streets with my friends. We thought it might be daring to try and smoke them. My brother got wind of it and almost knocked me into the neighboring town! I remember him yelling at me, "Anthony! These things can kill you! Don't let me catch you trying this again!" He put the fear of God in me while stuffing my mouth full of bubble gum so my mom wouldn't smell the tobacco on my breath. Denis always had my back.

We came to the United States when I was nine years old because my parents wanted a better life for their two sons. Getting here wasn't so easy. My mother and I were sent back at the border because of improper paperwork. Watching my father and brother go through those giant iron gates without us was one of the most terrifying moments in my life. To be separated from Denis was just incomprehensible to me. I thought about him every day and prayed we would be together again soon. Thankfully, months later, my mother and I were able to leave, and life started anew when our plane touched down in America.

As I grew up and began to sing more, Denis always encouraged me.

"Anthony," he'd say, "you can do this. You were meant to sing. No matter how hard it gets out there, push through it because you have the gift."

Denis's words meant everything to me. If he said it, it had to be true. He believed that I should be a singer, and he never let me lose sight of it. And gradually, as I started to accomplish more, our roles changed. Over time, my brother started to look at me more as an equal—not like a little kid anymore. And we went everywhere together. We were inseparable.

When *American Idol* happened, my whole life changed, but not my relationship with Denis. He'd call me up while I was on the show and tell me how proud he was of me. "You're doing great, little brother. Keep it up!" His words kept me moving forward with unstoppable focus and desire. I knew in my heart I was accomplishing a huge goal, but hearing it from Denis made it real for me. As my dreams were coming true, all I could hear was his voice saying, "You can do this, Anthony. Keep pushing. . . ."

Denis was right—all the hard work and effort did pay off. I made it all the way to Number 4, and I was finally on my way. Even after I was voted off, I was on top of the world.

But my happiness turned to despair when I realized that my family had been keeping something from me while I was in Hollywood. Now the time had come for me to know. The phone rang. My mother's words left me numb.

"Anthony, Denis is very sick."

"How sick?" I asked.

"Denis has cancer, Anthony."

I didn't understand. I didn't know anything about the disease. As my mother told me more, I felt my heart break and my soul rip in half. My big brother was fighting for his life.

Denis fought with every ounce of energy he had. And I kept pushing him because I didn't want him to give in— ever. His strength gave me strength. I wanted to be a part of my brother's battle every step of the way. I was by his side as much as I could be, but I also wanted to give him another reason to keep fighting. I knew that if I kept singing and moving forward, it would give him hope.

He wanted so much to be at my first sold-out concert. He wanted to see me on that stage—that was his dream. His selfless words never stopped, "Anthony, keep singing. You have goals to reach. Keep going . . ." Because he was my big brother, I listened once again.

During his last days, Denis came out to the Binghamton Balloon Festival in upstate New York where I was performing. Soon after he arrived, we shared a moment that will stay with me forever. We climbed into the basket of a balloon together and gently rose up 3,000 feet into the clear blue sky. We stood looking out at the rolling hills and fields stretching to the horizon, our arms around each other's shoulders. Then he turned to me, and for the first time in a very long time, Denis smiled. As I smiled back, I knew our souls would always be together. Nothing could ever pull us apart.

Shortly after, Denis's battle ended.

When Denis passed away, it made me see what was really important. Now I feel I have to succeed not just for myself, but also for my parents. I want them to think about something else. I want them to be happy and enjoy their lives. Losing their son was unimaginably painful for them. I want to help them to smile again. I want to hear their laughter.

Denis was an angel long before he left this Earth. He was a great son and husband, and the greatest older brother and best friend a guy could have. Every good thing a person can be, he was, and he touched many lives. I learned from his passing that nothing and no one should ever be taken for granted. If you love someone, tell them—every day. Cherish those you love and what you have together. And push for what you believe in as if it's the last chance you'll ever get.

As the curtain goes up on Broadway, and I'm standing there for the very first time, I know my big brother and best friend will be looking down on me, saying, "You did it, little brother, and I am here watching over you. You are in control of your own destiny. Our bond will go on forever and ever. It's never over."

3

AIN'T NO MOUNTAIN HIGH ENOUGH:
STORIES OF OVERCOMING OBSTACLES

Success takes determination, persistence, and sometimes camping out on a sidewalk for a few days with tens of thousands of strangers.

Shanna Keller

My Guardian Angel

Constantine Maroulis
Top 10, Season 4

If I went back to my high school and walked the halls, I'd probably still hear my teacher's voice calling out to me, "Constantine! You have such talent; don't waste it!" For some, a teacher like that comes along once in a lifetime. For many, not even once. I now look back and see how lucky I was that she cared about me. Not too many teachers did.

When I was a teenager, I had a lousy attitude and topped it off with bad grades. Deep down, I thought I probably was a good singer, but I didn't have an ounce of confidence in my bones. I'd look in the mirror and see a shy, ugly, geeky kid staring back. And I'd be flat-out terrified if somebody asked me to sing. In fact, I was so scared, there were times when I'd open my mouth and nothing would come out.

I remember the rainy February morning that I walked into her music class. I sat in my chair, half slumped over, thinking that this was gonna be bad. I was chewing gum, figuring I could probably sing and chew at the same time. I mean, I wasn't serious about this singing thing.

The old wooden door opened slowly, and into the classroom walked Mrs. Carol Birdsill. She looked right at me and smiled. I instantly knew that she connected to something inside of me. What it was, I didn't know, but that something whispered, *Sit up, shut up, and put out your hand, Constantine. She is holding the missing puzzle piece you're looking for.* I threw out my gum.

She was a round, jolly woman with big white hair. I loved to watch her sit at her piano and sing her heart out. She was the kindest, sweetest, and probably the most talented woman I had ever met. I loved everything about her, but more importantly, she loved everything about *me.*

For the first time in my life, someone believed in my talent. With Mrs. Birdsill, I didn't have to say a word—she knew how much I struggled to let my inner voice out. She saw my anguish, and she never gave up on me. Her goal was not only to get me to sing, but more importantly, to get me to *believe* I could sing. She also happened to be the musical director for our high-school plays and wanted me to be in them.

One day, she took me aside, looked me in the eye, and said, "You have real talent. Just stop the nonsense and focus! First of all, you have to start doing better in school. Secondly, I know this is something you could pursue professionally some day. I believe in you, Constantine." She gave it to me straight, but it just didn't sink in fast enough. She tried so hard to get to me, but I remained slightly out of her reach. It was just a lot easier hanging out with my friends than facing my fears.

The surprise of my life came when Mrs. Birdsill picked me to be the music teacher for the day. It might not sound like a big deal, but it was. In fact, it was considered a school honor—my first. I was so proud and excited.

The day before my big teaching day dawned, the principal called me down to his office during music class. I thought he probably needed to talk to me about the procedures for the next day. I walked in and he said, "Sit down, Constantine."

My knees knocked as I tried to center myself in the enormous mahogany chair in front of his desk.

"Constantine," he said, "you've done very well in Mrs. Birdsill's class, and it's a great privilege to be chosen as the music teacher for the day. Unfortunately, your other grades are not worthy, and I can't allow you to accept this honor." I sat there motionless as his words went through me like a blade of ice. I was devastated. I had failed again, and I took it out on the one person who meant the most to me.

I fought back my tears as I went to her class, picked up my books, and walked out, never looking back. I had made my decision: *I'm not going to try out for her shows. They're for losers.*

I remember the day before the school's big show—the show I belonged in, and the one I knew Mrs. Birdsill wanted me in so badly. I peeked into the auditorium and saw her hard at work with actors, singers, and band members. I walked home slowly that day with an awful, empty feeling inside.

When I got to my house, I went into the kitchen and threw my books across the floor just as the phone rang. I didn't feel much like talking to anyone, but I picked up the phone and unenthusiastically said hello. The chilling words that came across the phone line left me frozen. "Constantine?! Oh, my God, Constantine, Mrs. Birdsill just died!"

I threw the phone and, as it smashed into the wall, I screamed, "Nooooo! Please, come back. Please!" I wept—my God, I wept. I felt like I had lost my guardian angel, the one who had been sent to help me believe in myself.

My pain was so great that I thought it would never leave. But my lack of will to turn my life around was greater . . . until exactly one year to the day after Mrs. Birdsill's death.

The opening day of our school's annual play was upon us once again—and, once again, I wasn't a part of it. Just as I had done the year before, I peeked into the auditorium, and this time the absence of the jolly woman with the big white hair was painfully obvious.

But a strange thing happened later that day. A huge, round, fluffy white owl perched itself on a telephone pole outside and just sat there, motionless, staring at the school. No one knew where it came from. We had never seen an owl in our neighborhood before—and didn't they just come out in the dark of night?

I went outside and watched that bird for hours. Everyone was talking about it, asking, "Why is it staying there?"

I knew why. That owl had come for me. As I stared at the creature, it stared back, looking right through me, and I felt just like I did when I first walked into Mrs. Birdsill's music room twelve months earlier. The owl took no pity. I fell to my knees and wept—and it just watched me weep. That owl had a message, and in the quiet evening air, I finally heard it, loud and clear.

The next school play was *West Side Story*, and although I was terrified, I auditioned. I found the strength to overcome my fear when I heard Mrs. Birdsill's voice inside me, saying, *I believe in you, Constantine. You can do this.*

I got the part.

I worked harder than I had ever worked at anything in my life, and when the curtain went up on opening night, I sang my best, knowing my guardian angel was right by my side. As I struggled to find that first note, the missing puzzle piece was finally in place. I not only heard her voice saying, *I believe in you,* but for the first time ever, I heard my *own* voice saying, *I believe in me.* And that's how it all began.

Hold On to Love

George Huff with Lise Hintze
Top 10, Season 3

Through the storm, through the rain,
I know higher ground I'll gain,
if I keep holding on to love.

George Huff

"Oh, my God! Oh, my God! My church! That's my church on TV!"

I remember the day as if it were yesterday. The image from 2005 remains so clear. The interview was going along beautifully, effortlessly capturing the beacon of light and warmth that is George Huff—until that moment. At that moment, everything turned dark.

"Ohhh, dear God!"

"What? What is it, George?" I asked.

"Lise, Lise . . . my God, my church! My church is washing away! It's where it all began for me. Oh, my God, Lise . . . my church is floating in pieces. It's on the TV. Oh, Lord! I just can't believe it. I have to say a special prayer for everybody there."

"George, let's stop," I told him. "I don't think we should go on with this interview . . . George?"

Silence. A deafening stillness filled the room. Hurricane Katrina had just hit, and in a tiny apartment in Dallas, Texas, George Huff and his family huddled together and watched in horror while rain and floodwater submerged their city. The unrelenting winds and flooding spared no one as they tore through the French Quarter, the place George Huff had once called home. Heartbroken, he could find no more words as the storm ripped away structures and left only battered memories behind.

At that moment, time stood still for the man who had captivated millions with his radiant smile, soulful voice, and signature bounce during Season 3. Unable to help in any other way, George bowed his head to pray for families torn apart, lives lost, and a community splintered to its core. He desperately tried to understand the meaning of it all and why so many lives were taken. He searched for the essence of what such devastation meant for his own life. George believed that eventually he would find a personal meaning in these events far greater than he could comprehend at this frightening and tumultuous time.

To sing gospel music, and to be able to reach others through that music, meant the world to George Huff. Growing up in poverty, he had sought refuge and peace on the strong, unshakeable steps of his church. George's faith eventually guided him to a path that led to a higher ground—a place of great success and fulfillment.

It was not until two years later that I was able to finish the interview with George.

"I was supposed to be filled with so much joy at that time, Lise. Everything I had prayed for and dreamed of was finally happening for me. It was a feeling of elation like no other. Then, in an instant, I felt like all I had achieved was in vain. There were so many unanswered questions. How could this have happened? I was so happy, yet lives were shattered around me. My plans were big. I was going to return to my roots in New Orleans and share my blessings, but now there wasn't a New Orleans to go home to. Everything was destroyed. My hometown was gone. My city was obliterated. I was heartbroken.

"I searched. Oh, Lord, did I search! Feeling helpless and lost, I turned to my own music, seeking solace and comfort. Surprisingly, my own words inspired me. At this time of great pain, I didn't know my lyrics would minister to my own soul the way they did to others. While searching for answers, I went back and listened to 'Hold On to Love,' and the words jumped right out at me. The message was so simple and yet so powerful.

"You see, in the projects, everyday life was a struggle; it was hard. But we focused and kept our faith strong by letting love carry us. We believed in each other, and we still do. And never do we ever lose sight of that—never. It was the love we shared that brought us through such severe times. It was the love that made things right. Love goes a long, long way in overcoming adversity. And when I watched my church crumble in the storm, I realized something so incredibly powerful: my church wasn't a structure; my church was the people.

"So many who survived were left with feelings of despair. They wanted to feel loved, like they belonged somewhere. They needed to hear words of encouragement. The rebuilding of the church would come with nails and mortar, but the people needed to rebuild their souls with love and understanding. They needed to find hope and a voice that would say, 'I will stand strong with you.'

"New Orleans was a ghost town, and so many people were isolated for such a very long time. So many cried out for help and for a friend. I believed in my heart that they were looking for a hand to hold, for a hand to guide them.

I went there and held out my hands and I said, 'Here, hold onto them. Hold onto the love.' They needed to know they weren't forgotten. I promised them I would never forget. I knew it could have been me drowning in those waters. I had to let them know somebody cared, that I cared deeply.

"I had been through so much in my own life, and I know that if I had never gone through any of it, I wouldn't have been able to reach out like I did. I would not have been able to write the words I wrote to inspire the hearts of others if I hadn't been through so many hardships of my own. I am grateful for every obstacle that I faced in my past, that I am facing at the present, and that I will face in the future. I have been made a better person for all I have been through, and for that I am truly thankful.

"I believe in my core that hard times are for a reason. We're in it to go through it, and to say, 'I came out. I survived.' That's the joy. And then to take opportunities and soar above the clouds—that's an even greater joy. When I visited New Orleans, I said, 'I am still here. You are still here. And for that we shall be grateful. Together we will rebuild. Together we will come out from under this.'

"I dwell on that which is good. I dwell on that which is true. And for me, that is the greatest joy of all."

Hurricane Katrina . . . a day remembered by so many, as if it were yesterday. Yet through George, I learned that we must always look ahead to what tomorrow will bring, never dwelling on what the past has brought.

And I also remember the day when I asked, "George, should we go on with this interview?"

George took a deep breath and then spoke softly, "Lise, we must always go on."

Meeting Life Head-On

Sabrina Sloan
Top 24, Season 6

Just before Hollywood Week, my sister asked me to do her a favor. Hey, it was my sister, so of course I'd drop her off at the Burbank Airport—at six o'clock in the morning. Dressed in pajamas and flip-flops, off I went. As she hopped out of the car, she thanked me for the ride, told me good luck, and said she'd be praying for me. Little did I know that her prayers would be needed for more than my making it beyond Hollywood Week, which was six days away.

I never saw it coming. Driving home, I was appreciating the beautiful colors of the horizon, smiling inside, and thinking about my golden ticket. Three blocks away from my destination, my life—in an instant—was turned upside-down. The driver on my left had stopped, so when the big truck ran a red light and turned right into me—hitting my little Nissan head-on—I never had a chance to react.

The air bags went off into my face. I heard the sound of breaking glass and crunching metal. In an instant, it was over.

I was in total shock. I smelled the putrid odor of gasoline and the sickening smell of burning rubber. My head was pounding, and as I turned to look at myself in the mirror, I could see blood pouring from my nose, and my eye was a cut-up mess. People began running toward me and reaching into the car to get me out. They were afraid of an explosion, but as I tried to get out I realized I couldn't move. I couldn't feel my legs, and looking down, I saw blood coming from my ankle.

Everybody started screaming, "Stay there! Don't move!" It was so frightening. I'd never been in an accident before, and I kept thinking, *Am I in shock? Do I not feel anything?*

I looked at my bloody face again in the mirror and immediately thought, *Hollywood Week! Is my nose broken? I only have six days!*

The accident happened on Tuesday, and Hollywood Week began the following Monday. I had already been preparing—picking songs, practicing. I thought, *What if my dream is over before it really began?* That was when the ambulance came, and one of the paramedics asked me for a relative's number. I told him my husband was home asleep and gave him the number.

I knew that Chip was going to freak out, but I didn't have the strength to shout to the paramedic for him to tell Chip that I was okay.

The other paramedics were able to get me out of the car and onto a stretcher. There were so many people there—firemen, policemen, and several ambulances. It felt like complete chaos. They put me into the ambulance. Right then, Chip pulled up. He saw the scene—the street, the pieces of the car all over the road, the glass and the blood—and I heard him scream, "Is Sabrina in there?! Where is she?!"

That's when I started to cry. I was shaking. I was just so happy to see him, and he was just so happy that I was alive. He got into the ambulance and took my hand. As I lay in the back of the ambulance, I probably should have been thinking about how lucky I was to be alive, but all I could think was, *Am I going to be able to walk in the next few days? Will I be able to sing?*

At the hospital, they whisked me in and took X rays. I had a fractured rib, a sprained ankle, a black eye, contusions, and puncture wounds. Thankfully, other than my rib, nothing else was broken or fractured, but they said they weren't sure how soon I would be able to walk again.

By Thursday, whiplash had set in, and I couldn't move my neck. I was able to stand up by Friday, but I couldn't open my jaw without excruciating pain. I kept thinking, *Only three days until I have to be at Hollywood Week! Am I going to be able to walk into the audition? Am I going to be able to breathe with the agonizing pain from my fractured rib?*

It was so hard, and I did have this one second of feeling, *Really, God . . . it had to be now?* But I told myself, *You walked away from it, didn't you?* And that had to be by the grace of God.

I just kept encouraging myself, saying, *I'm not going to let anything interfere with this. This is something I've been working toward my whole life, and I'm not giving in to any pity party. I still have my voice. I may need to take more shallow breaths and it may hurt a little bit, but there is nothing that is going to stop me from being there.*

On Monday, nobody could believe I was ready to go to the audition. I even put on my heels! In spite of all the pain, I had to just push it away and say to myself, *This is my shot. I've got to buck up and make it through this week!*

I made it through to the Top 24 and got voted off the night before the Final 12. People tell me that if I had been stronger, and the accident hadn't happened, there is no way that I wouldn't have been in the Top 12. But you know what? It doesn't matter. I did the best I could, and the experience helped me get some perspective.

Six days before, my car was in pieces, I was lying in an ambulance, and I couldn't move. God spared my life, so whatever was supposed to happen after that, I knew had to be in his hands. It was meant to be that I got the golden ticket, that I was put through to Hollywood Week. It was meant to be that I was able to make it into the Top 24. And it was meant to be that I learned the lesson to value life so much more.

Who knows how much longer any of us will be here? Another six months? Another year? None of us knows the answer. I just know that whatever I do, I'm going to give it everything I have, and appreciate everything that happens in my life—even Ryan Seacrest saying, "Sabrina, you're going home."

I realize now that there are worse places to go than home.

Lost and Found

Kimberly Caldwell
Top 10, Season 2

No question about it: I had fallen hard. I was in love—in love with music.

I had just sung my first song in the little town of Katy, Texas. The venue was a local beauty pageant, and I was five years old, yet I already knew performing would be my life. It was what I'd been put on this Earth to do.

So many opportunities came my way. I did hundreds of pageants and talent shows. I landed a spot singing at the legendary Grand Ole Opry for George and Barbara Bush's fiftieth wedding anniversary. I won Ed McMahon's *Star Search* five times in a row, and I am very proud to say that I still hold the record for most wins as junior vocalist on the original show.

Then, at the age of twelve, I auditioned for a big variety production called *Country Tonite* and was chosen to be the featured performer. I was so excited. I'd be singing in front of thousands of people in two shows almost every day. But there was one problem: to fulfill this dream, my mom and sister and I had to move to Branson, Missouri, hundreds of miles from our Texas home—and my dad. He stayed behind, looked after the house, and kept the business running. He visited us every other weekend to keep our family together.

The show was a huge success, and my original four-month contract evolved into three-and-a-half years.

My childhood consisted of home school, rehearsals, makeup, autograph signings, and photo shoots—not bikes, games, and school dances. Although I experienced excitement and was given opportunities many other kids dream of, I sacrificed the "normal" life I might have had.

Don't get me wrong—this was my decision, and I loved my life. Though my parents didn't push me, my mom did instill in me the confidence that allowed me to step in front of a huge crowd every day. But she always said that the moment I wanted to quit, she would completely support me.

The show migrated from Branson, Missouri, to Biloxi, Mississippi, for six months, and I followed. But I had just turned fifteen and was curious about life as a normal teenager. I reached a point where I felt fulfilled with what I had accomplished and was willing to let it go for a while in order to get my Brady Bunch–like family back in the same house.

But it wasn't to be. Not long after we were all home again in Texas, my parents separated. It was like a slap in the face. They had never fought in front of us and had seemed perfectly happy when we reunited on weekends. But my family was broken, and I knew I couldn't fix it. I now lacked the two things in my life that I felt made me who I was: my stable family and performing.

I felt lost.

I began searching for something to make me whole again. I acted out to get attention and to find release. I had no stage to sing on, no costumes to dress up in. I didn't know who I was or what I was living for. Sad, angry, and depressed, I went off the deep end and did many things I'm not proud of.

One day, I walked past the living room where my mom sat, totally enthralled with some new singing show called *American Idol*. I didn't bother to see what it was all about, but the next year she practically pushed my lazy backside off the couch and out the door to audition.

With no steady job, no college education, and no income, I had nothing to lose—but I didn't even have gas money to get to the auditions in Austin. That's when my grandma stepped in and saved the day. So I polished my song and got myself prepared. I knew I was in "the zone."

I not only earned the prized golden ticket to Hollywood, but I made it into the Top 12—on the biggest show in America! Ultimately, I didn't become the *American Idol*, but I got everything I dreamed of and more: I sang in front of millions of people every week. I went on a forty-five-city tour. I got a job as a host on the TV Guide Channel. I'm now recording a country/rock album, produced by one of my favorite artists, John Rich. I bought a house in Los Angeles with my sister. And I travel the country almost every weekend to sing live.

The icing on the cake? I have four new little sisters from my parents' current marriages.

I can't imagine my story any other way, and I have no regrets about the decisions I've made in my life. I've learned from my experiences—good and bad—and feel they've made me a stronger woman.

I will be forever grateful to *American Idol* and honored to have been a part of it—not only for the fun, excitement, and friendships I've made, but most importantly, because *American Idol* gave me back my life.

Fourth Time's the Charm

Gina Glocksen
Top 10, Season 6

My friend Nicole was curled up on the couch, her mouth swollen from just having had her wisdom teeth pulled out. The TV blared.

"*What* are you watching?" I asked.

"It's called *American Idol.* You mean you've never heard of it?" She seemed incredulous.

When I told her I hadn't, she said, "You should go try out."

"Yeah, right," I laughed. "I'd never be able to make it on something like that."

That was Season 1. Nicole's words stayed with me, and when Season 2 came around, I went to Detroit to audition. I didn't make it past the first round and decided it wasn't for me—but I continued to watch religiously and never missed an episode.

I didn't audition again for Seasons 3 or 4, but when Season 5 rolled around, I reconsidered and decided to audition again, this time in Chicago.

That year I made it all the way to Hollywood Week, and

trust me, Hollywood Week is stressful. Talk to anyone who's been there. Ask them, "If you could do Hollywood Week again, would you?" They'd probably say no. But despite all the pressure and anxiety, I had great auditions. Then, on the last audition, I flubbed my words a little and that was that.

Afterward, I was standing in the lobby, crying with two other rejected singers. Paula walked over to us and said, "You guys should really try out again." Then she looked directly at me. "Really. Don't give up. Come back again next year." She repeated, "Just come back next year."

I thought, *I wonder if she means that, or if she says the same thing to everyone.*

The next day, I went home to Chicago feeling awful. I just kept thinking, *I can't ever do that again. Really. I can't go through all that stress another time.*

But when *Idol* held auditions for Season 6, my boyfriend Joe stepped in. "Gina, it's your year. I know it's your year. I can feel it. You just have to go."

I didn't know if I could handle the rejection again. But it wasn't only Joe who was encouraging me this time. All my friends were saying that they could feel this was my year.

Okay, fine, I thought. *I'm a dental assistant. I didn't go to college . . . and I don't want to suction saliva from people's mouths for the rest of my life.* When I went to the Los Angeles auditions, I was hoping that everyone would remember me from the prior year. I liked to think that I had stood out a bit. I sang for the first judge.

"We're not putting you through," he said.

I was shocked. "You're kidding me, right?"

"You just brought back what you did last year," he said.

I guess he did remember me.

I bawled to Joe, "This is really, really it. I can't take this rejection anymore. I just feel so beaten up."

That feeling lasted all of about ten minutes, and then I

pulled myself together and was more determined than ever to try again. I wasn't going to let them tell me no and that I couldn't follow my dream!

Back home, my boss and coworkers at the dental office didn't want me to give up either. Not only did they encourage me, but my boss also offered me a week with pay to go to Memphis and audition again there. I couldn't say no. This seemed important to so many people—not just to me, but also to Joe, my family, his family, and everyone in my office. I thought to myself, *I know I feel beaten up, and I'm questioning whether or not it's worth it. But if I can't do it for myself, I have to do it for everyone else.*

When I realized how much I'd be letting other people down, not making it through wasn't even an option.

I know it's a cliché, but I really believe that whatever doesn't kill you makes you stronger—and I wasn't dead yet. So I went in stronger. This time I sang a different song in front of a different judge—and here I am today, a Top 10 finalist for Season 6. I'm grateful to everyone who believed in me and helped me to keep going.

Sometimes it takes a cause bigger than yourself to give you the strength to do something difficult.

And I'm proud of myself for not giving up. Some things in life come easily, and for some, you have to go the extra mile. But if you hang in there and don't give up, you might get lucky like me and find that the fourth time's the charm.

Measuring Success

Tanesha Ross
Top 24, Season 1

"It's your turn, Tanesha. Are you ready?" Ryan Seacrest looked at me with excitement in his eyes.

"Yes," I lied. I had made it to Hollywood and was now a part of the coveted Top 24, but I wasn't ready. My heart drummed so loudly in my ears, I almost didn't hear Ryan. The truth is, I didn't even want to be there anymore. I wanted to bolt for the door. Instead, I made my way to the stage, trying to keep my emotions in check.

I greeted the judges, and then boom, I was off. The piano player started with such intensity that I thought the notes would run me over. As the song went on, I struggled to keep myself composed, but my breath betrayed me note after note. The song ended, and a sea of tears flooded my face. I tried not to drown in them as I responded to the judges' comments.

"You didn't shine like a star," Simon stated flatly. He was right.

Back in the green room, I was greeted with sympathetic smiles. I had handled myself well, "with grace and class,"

American Idol host Brian Dunkleman had said. Yet during the post-performance interview, my tears continued to flow.

My voice—my ticket to success—had betrayed me. What was I going to do now? The worst part for me was the feeling that I was letting others down.

I'm the oldest of four children, the responsible one. I grew up in poverty. Often, I didn't know what or if I was going to eat that day or where I would end up sleeping. My job was to protect my brothers and sister from the horrible things that had stolen my childhood—and my innocence. As events progressively spiraled downward, protecting them seemed like an impossible task. But I had a spark of hope inside that I was determined wouldn't be snuffed out.

When I was younger, I found comfort—and escape—in school and music. I threw myself into every activity I could, especially if it involved singing. I was determined to give my family something they could believe in.

I was the only member of my immediate family to graduate from high school, let alone think about going to college. But the summer after my high-school graduation, I packed a U-Haul and left. I was consumed with guilt. *With me away at college, who would protect my family?* Yet I knew I had to go, even with guilt as my constant traveling companion.

During my college years, things at home escalated from worse to devastating. My sixteen-year-old sister begged me to get her out of there, so I brought her to live with me. I worked two jobs to support us and received my bachelor's degree in music. I made a career out of performing and experienced more success than most people my age.

Success. Everyone wants it, but too often people measure their worth by it, as though the amount of success they achieve defines them. I thought it would define me

and make my life worth something. I wanted it badly—
not just for me, but for my family.

When Ryan called my name that fateful night on
American Idol, I couldn't figure out why I was so nervous.
I've sung in front of people so many times before, I thought. *I'm
a professional! I've been singing for a living for the past five
years!*

As I began to sing, I had the fleeting thought that
maybe I should have shared more of my life story with
the producers of *American Idol*—or with America—but I
didn't want votes because of my sad story; I wanted votes
because of my talent.

As my performance concluded and my post-performance
interview began, I realized what the nerves and tears were
all about: I had believed I was going to save my family
with my success, and as I sang on *American Idol* that night,
for what I knew was going to be the last time, I realized my
success wouldn't have saved them any more than the
thousand and one other things I'd tried.

I didn't make it to the Top 12, but that night I received a
far greater gift. I realized that success and triumph have to
come from the inside out, not the outside in. I'd done my
best to help my family, but I realized that I couldn't do
everything.

As long as I am proud of who I am, as long as I strive to
be a good and loving person, as long as I can look in the
mirror and like who I see, that's enough.

And only I, and no one else—not the judges and not
America—can truly measure my success.

Taking a Chance

Melissa McGhee
Top 12, Season 5

"You are unique in this competition; no one has a voice like yours."

I was thrilled with Paula's comment after my performance of Reba McEntire's "Why Haven't I Heard from You." And when Simon added that he, too, loved my voice, I was on cloud nine! If I got voted through that night, I would only have one more performance before making it into the Top 12.

On *American Idol*, I was known for my low, raspy voice. People wondered how my voice came to have that sultry sound and frequently asked me if I ever smoked cigarettes. My answer was always the same, "I've never smoked. I've thought of my voice as a gift from God."

I had been singing since I was four years old, but I'd never worked my voice as hard as I did when I was on *American Idol*. I thought the pain and discomfort I was feeling was just a result of too much singing. But when it was time to perform each night, I would have to drink a shot of olive oil to soothe and lubricate my vocal cords. I'll bet there's not a singer out there who has tried *that* and liked it! It helped me through each night, but I began to worry. *Was there something really wrong?* I was losing my voice after singing only three songs.

Singing was like breathing to me. My dream since childhood was to be a successful singer, and now it was happening. When I made it into the Top 12, I knew that I was really on the path to my dream coming true. I also knew that I should go see a specialist, but I was afraid of what I might be told.

During the tests, which were relatively painless and simple, the doctor didn't give an indication that anything was seriously wrong. But when he walked in with my test results, the look on his face made my body go numb. He slowly sat down and told me the news—what gave my voice its uniqueness could also cause me to lose my ability to ever sing again. I had hard knots on my vocal cords called polyps, and papilloma, which is a benign form of cancer.

I was terrified. Nothing felt real. I started to shake, and then the doctor said the unthinkable.

"Melissa, unfortunately, this surgery will probably change your voice."

I sat speechless, as tears ran down my cheeks. I felt the panic grow inside me.

He continued, "If you don't have the surgery, you will probably never be able to sing more than a couple of songs back-to-back."

How could this be happening to me? I thought. *It just doesn't seem fair.*

But I knew what I needed to do. I scheduled the surgery.

The week before my operation, I was performing in concert with Ruben Studdard and other *Idols*. My frustration was enormous, as now I was only able to sing two songs before my voice began to fade. But like an angel from heaven, Anthony Fedorov, a Season 3, Top 10 finalist who was also performing with us, became my comfort. Anthony had undergone a tracheotomy as a toddler in Russia due to a birth defect in his windpipe.

"My doctors told my parents that I would most likely never be able to speak again, let alone sing," he told me. "Obviously, they were wrong." Anthony had come through his ordeal with an amazingly beautiful voice. He calmed me down and prepared me for the journey I was about to take.

The day for the surgery arrived. To compound the trauma of the operation, I had always been terrified of needles. Just to start my IV, the nurse had to give me medication to calm my nerves. She told me to start counting backwards. "10, 9, 8, 7, 6, 5 . . ." That was the last thing I remembered.

For the two weeks following the surgery, I was on 100 percent vocal rest. Notes, hand signals, and text messaging were my only forms of communication. At the end of the two weeks, I had a follow-up appointment with my doctor. He looked at my vocal cords to make sure everything was healing properly. When it all checked out, he announced, "Okay, Melissa, you can talk now!"

I should have been excited to try out my new, improved cords, but all I could do was nod my head. Every time I began to speak, I stopped myself. I kept thinking, *Why am I not letting myself speak? The doctor said my cords look great, and I can talk now.* And then I realized I was terrified of what my "new voice" might sound like—so terrified that I literally could not get myself to say a word.

Finally, my doctor insisted, "Melissa, you *really* have to talk. I need to hear what your voice sounds like." Here it was, my big moment, and I could only eke out four words: "I can talk now." I quickly covered my mouth with my hands.

I was devastated—I sounded like Mickey Mouse. As my eyes started to well up with tears, my doctor assured me that my voice would not sound that way for the rest of my life.

"Don't worry, Melissa. Your vocal cords just need to warm up and work out. They're still new and tight. I promise, everything will be fine."

I wanted to believe him, but every time I spoke, I wanted to cry.

Then he continued, "But no singing for three more months."

No singing for three more months! How can I live through three months? I wondered. *Ever since I was four, I've hardly gone three minutes without singing!* His words broke my heart—my passion had to wait. My voice had to heal. Three months of no singing, even though I could talk, was much harder for me than those two weeks of complete silence.

The next few months were difficult for me. The vocal lessons and speech therapy that followed were strenuous. And, while I was thrilled for my fellow contestants' successes, it was tough seeing them all making albums and moving on with their careers, while I was only able to wish them well and watch from the sidelines. If it weren't for the support and compassion of my friends and family, I don't know how I would have pulled through.

But I made it, and I am singing once again—with a voice that is better and stronger than ever. Although I lost a little rasp, I gained a unique falsetto.

I did what I needed to do, and at the end of the day, I learned a lot about myself. I can make tough decisions even when the outcome is uncertain. I have an amazing network of people to turn to who love and care about me. And, most of all, I've learned to appreciate the little gifts in life, like the feeling I get when I know that I can sing the whole night long.

God Had to Be Fair

Kim Estep
American Idol Fan

We always knew our daughter Kendall was going be a performer of some sort. She entertained people in our small town by putting on shows on our front porch when she was only three or four. Blonde-haired, blue-eyed, and beautiful, she sang like a little angel and mesmerized everyone.

When Kendall was five, we began to notice that she was blinking a lot and clearing her throat frequently. We had her tested for allergies, but the doctor said she wasn't allergic to anything at all. After the problem worsened, we took her to our local children's hospital where she was diagnosed with Tourette's Syndrome.

It was pretty devastating because other children constantly made fun of her, and sadly, even a teacher teased her. When the tics were especially bad, Kendall had to wear a neck brace. She only had one or two friends, but that was okay because they were—and continue to be—real, the kind who stick by her, no matter what. Through all this, Kendall continued to sing and entertain.

Remarkably, her tics disappeared when she sang.

We took our daughter from doctor to doctor, but all they did was give her medication that just made it worse, so we decided to go the natural route. Through chiropractic therapy, changes in her diet, and other natural treatments, the tics gradually lessened.

In 2005 when Kendall was sixteen, we thought she was pretty much out of the woods—or at least heading in that direction. However, as if Tourette's Syndrome wasn't enough for a beautiful young girl to deal with, a freak accident happened.

At a birthday party, Kendall hopped on a friend for a piggyback ride. He bent lower than she expected, and she jumped higher than he expected. Kendall flew over his back and landed on the cement floor—on her neck. An ambulance rushed her to the hospital where she spent the next week, paralyzed from the neck down. Ironically, her biggest concern wasn't whether she would walk again, but whether she would be able to audition for *American Idol*.

Doctors said Kendall had central cord syndrome. The pain was excruciating and required morphine to control it. Sometimes it was so unbearable she had to bite down on a toothbrush to take her mind off it. As the days dragged on, feeling returned to her left side, but she was still paralyzed on the right. We didn't know for sure how much of her movement would ever come back.

I believe Kendall wanted the *American Idol* audition so much that she *willed* herself to move again. One of her friends brought a microphone to the hospital and put it on her bed. Every day, Kendall tried hard to pick it up with her right hand. It was more important for her to pick up that mic than a spoon or fork.

Sometimes we all cried because of the pain we witnessed. But on the day Kendall walked into the stadium to audition for *American Idol*—a mere three months after her accident—we cried tears of joy. And our tears turned into shouts when she was given a golden ticket to Hollywood.

As a parent, you always think your child is the best ever—that's just what parents do. But after seeing Kendall perform, I *know* she's one of the best, even though she didn't make it into the Top 24.

Kendall is eighteen now, living every day to its fullest. She's recorded a CD with some of John Mellencamp's band members. She's also on CMT's *Music City Madness* for an original song and video, and is having some good success. I'm absolutely sure she's going to make it big some day. Kendall just puts it all in God's hands.

When she was a little girl trying hard to be strong, she looked up at me, her big eyes brimming with tears, and asked me why she had to have Tourette's Syndrome. My heart ached to make the world right for my child. But I looked right back at her and told her the truth as I see it.

"Kendall, God gave you a pure heart, an angelic voice, a strong mind, and a beautiful presence. With all of that, he had to make it fair for everyone else."

And the Top 10, Too

Mandisa
Top 10, Season 5

It was the evening of January 17, 2006, and I was on cloud nine. The premier of *American Idol*'s fifth season was about to air, featuring Chicago, my audition city. My friends, Chance and Jennifer, were hosting an *American Idol* premier party for me. They had made a fabulous feast and lit candles throughout the house, and more than twenty of my closest friends had gathered to celebrate and watch my debut. As I chattered excitedly with my friends, I felt like royalty. Chance had "crowned" me with a plastic tiara, while other friends had printed almost a hundred brown T-shirts that said, "Mandisa is my *American Idol*—All Hail the Diva," beneath a shining star.

The amazing thing was that none of them had even known whether I was still in the running. I already knew I'd been selected for the Top 44, but I hadn't been able to break my silence and share the news with my friends until tonight. When I did, the room erupted in cheers. I told them I wasn't sure if tonight's show would include my performance, but I had a strong positive feeling about it because I had seen commercials featuring my triumphant exit from the audition room.

After dinner we moved into the family room, crowding onto the couch and filling every chair. When the *American Idol* theme song began, I almost pinched myself to make sure I wasn't dreaming. Little Mandisa had finally found the courage to stand up, leave the house, and take a chance.

The minutes ticked by, and I kept wondering when my audition would come on. I barely noticed when the phone rang, but Chance pulled himself off the couch to answer it. A moment later I saw him signaling for my attention and felt a fleeting second of irritation. Whatever it was, couldn't it wait? Then I realized that something was up.

"That was Kevin on the phone," he said. "They're watching the show in real time. You just sang."

"So?"

"So, after you left the room, Simon said something rude about your weight."

I felt like I'd been slapped. Tears stung my eyes, and a sob stuck in my throat. My emotions, at a high pitch all day, now plummeted into despair. I thought about walking out the door and not coming back. Instead, I took a deep breath, thanked Chance for the warning, and rejoined the group. My friends barely noticed my return; they were so focused on the show. And then, there was my face filling the screen.

After just a few lines of my song, the judges stopped me. Paula, Randy, and Simon all said nice things and then announced they were sending me through to Hollywood. The camera zoomed in on my beaming face, and then showed me leaving the room in a joyous fit.

My friends exploded into cheers and applause as I tried to keep my chin from quivering. That day had been so good. Why had Simon gone and ruined it?

Only a few were still watching the screen when the

camera zoomed back in on Simon, but those who saw my face quickly turned their attention back to the television. Before a national television audience, Simon looked at Paula and asked, "Are we going to get a bigger stage this year?"

Paula slapped him good-naturedly and said I reminded her of Frenchie Davis, a contestant from a previous season. Simon grinned and retorted, "She's more like France."

I tried to smile when the friends who'd heard Simon turned to look at me. "It's okay," I said, my voice shaking. "I'm okay."

Dead silence overtook the room. I looked down, not knowing how to react. I'd gone from my life's highest moment to one of its lowest.

One friend broke the silence. "Simon's a jerk," he said, and immediately others came to embrace me. I accepted the sympathy, but I really just wanted to disappear. We watched the rest of the show, but the gathering now felt more like a funeral wake than a party. Those "All Hail the Diva" T-shirts, scattered throughout the room, seemed to mock me.

But little did I know that Simon's words would turn out to be a blessing in disguise. I now believe that if Simon had been uncharacteristically kind and never mentioned my obvious weight problem, I would never have been able to touch so many lives.

Make no mistake: Simon's words hurt me deeply. I cried myself to sleep that night. But as I wept, I realized what I had to do. The people on the receiving end of Simon's comments don't usually make it to Hollywood, so he never has to face them again. In my case, I made it to Hollywood, and once there, I knew that at the risk of not being put through to the Final 24, I had to be the voice of so many people who had been hurt by Simon and weren't able to tell him what his words had done to them. And I knew that I also had to be the voice for so many women who have been held back and told they weren't beautiful because of their weight.

I made it through every round during Hollywood Week, and when the day arrived that the Final 24 would be chosen, my childhood dream of becoming a world-class singer was within my grasp. But this was also my chance to share my truth with Simon. I knew the outcome could go either way, but I also knew that being true to myself was even more important to me than the possibility of becoming the next *American Idol*.

I heard my name called and, like a warrior marching to battle, I entered the elevator. And as the elevator doors opened, I started walking down the long stretch we called "The Green Mile" to the lone chair opposite the three judges. I sat down, looked Simon squarely in the eye, and began.

"Simon," I said, "a lot of people want me to say a lot of things to you right now, but this is what I want to say. I want you to know that you hurt me. I cried, and it was very emotional for me. But the good thing about forgiveness is that you don't need someone to apologize in order to forgive them. So, Simon, I want you to know that I have forgiven you, because if Jesus could forgive me for all the things I've done wrong, I can certainly extend that same grace to you."

As I delivered my message, Simon's grin disappeared. Although I didn't take my gaze off Simon, from the corner of my eye I could see Randy raise his brows and Paula break into a smile as bright as the lights overhead.

In the silence that followed, Simon uncrossed his arms and hung his head. "Well, I feel about this big," he said, holding two fingers about an inch apart. "Mandisa, I'm humbled. Come here and give me a kiss."

I can't tell you how many women have shared what it meant to them that I refused to swallow his comments

and just go on as if his words had never been spoken—
and then forgave him as well. I just felt that if I didn't
speak my truth, then his truth would have been the final
word—and once again another woman who struggles
with her weight would retreat with her head hanging and
her heart broken. But I've always been a fighter, and my
purpose in life is to shine through my integrity as well as
my voice. I knew that I had to stand up for all women who
struggle with their image, period.

I needed to say those words to Simon for me, but by
doing so, I also hoped to help change the image of true
beauty for all the young girls in our society. The possibility of realizing that goal made it worth the risk. And it continues to be worth it over and over again.

Last December, I was invited to tobyMac's Winter
Wonder Slam Concert in Nashville. I was sitting in the
audience when a mom and her two little girls came up to
me. The precious girls, who I guess were about ten, stared
at me with big brown eyes and nearly blinding smiles.
Moved by their awe, I gave them each big hugs and
signed the tickets they held in trembling, outstretched
hands. Then one of the girls got up the courage to speak.
She looked at me and proclaimed in a high-pitched voice,
"You are sooooo beautiful!"

As I looked deeply into that young girl's eyes, I knew
that I had changed her perception of beauty, and I hoped
I had made the rest of her life a little easier for it.

As they turned to go, the mom stopped and whispered
in my ear, "You have no idea what it means to me to have
a role model like you—a woman who is not only beautiful,
confident, and honest, but who also loves the Lord. Thank
you for giving my girls someone in this crazy world that
they can really look up to."

As they walked back to their seats, a huge smile took over
my face, and I thought to myself, *That, and the Top 10, too.*

4

YOU LIFT ME UP:
STORIES BY IDOLS TOUCHED
BY OTHERS

*Hold fast to your dreams, for if dreams
die, life is a broken winged bird that
cannot fly.*

Langston Hughes

Tau's Story

Carrie Underwood
American Idol, Season 4

I have always been grateful to *American Idol* for all the amazing things that have happened in my life over the last two years, but I've never been more grateful for anything than having been allowed to be a part of *Idol Gives Back*.

It was a hot, muggy day when we visited a South African clinic. Tau was four years old and enjoying his time playing with the toys on the floor of the clinic waiting room. His mother and grandmother were with him, watching him fit the letters onto a brightly colored foam puzzle. They seemed so proud of him and made a fuss every time he completed the alphabet. He seemed like a typical young child in his overalls and lime-green shirt, only perhaps a bit shy—and sad.

Though he was only four, I believe he knew that being there wasn't a good thing.

The situation in this South African clinic is one that far too many children and families have to experience.

I tried to talk with Tau. I asked him his name and how old he was, the typical conversation one has with a small child. I smiled as I spoke to him, and he smiled back, seeming only a little nervous.

The nurse walked in and called Tau's name. We all got up to follow her. We were led to a small white room with one window and diagrams on the walls. There was a table in the center that held alcohol, cotton swabs, small metal tools, and other doctors' instruments. Close to the edge of the table were two little packages lying side by side.

When we sat down, the doctor explained what she was about to do. Tau nodded when she told him that she was going to prick his finger. He seemed confident and calm, but the doctor was worried that he would cry and make the task difficult, so she asked the boy's mother to comfort him as she took the various objects out of their sterile packages.

Tau didn't move a muscle as the doctor pricked his tiny index finger. There were two small, square plastic test plates. The tests were very much like pregnancy tests, and the doctor was looking at lines. A certain number of lines would mean the test was negative, while another number would mean it was positive. The results, she said, would appear in about ten minutes.

Those ten minutes seemed like an eternity.

Again, I tried to talk to Tau. I told him what a good job he did and what a brave little boy he was. He smiled and shook his head no when I asked him if it hurt. He held the bandage over his finger. He seemed proud of himself for being so brave and enduring such a mighty pain.

When the ten minutes were up, the doctor looked at the tests, then back at all of us waiting patiently for the results. Without hesitation, she delivered the difficult news: this tiny, sweet, young boy was HIV-positive.

The doctor explained that he should start his medications right away and would need to come back for frequent follow-up visits. She explained that it was very possible for Tau to live a normal life. But I could feel my heart break.

I could only imagine what his family must have been feeling.

To think that this precious little boy did nothing wrong. He was kind, smart, and so adorable. Yet, he had this virus that could potentially cause him so much suffering and even end his life long before his time.

We left the clinic that day lost in our own thoughts. The boy and his family had to deal with this horrible news. And I began to think about my life and the great fortune I've had.

Like Tau, I have done nothing to deserve the things that I have stumbled upon in my life. The only difference is that I get the chance to *have* a full life.

Neither one of us did anything right or wrong. It's just the hands we each were dealt.

The purpose of our trip was for us to visit the poorest areas of South Africa and give back to these people. Hopefully, we changed many of their lives for the better.

Because of my time with Tau, his family, and all the beautiful people of South Africa, *my* life has been changed forever. I now appreciate each day I have on this Earth so much more.

I never imagined when I agreed to go and "give back" that I would receive infinitely more than I could ever have given.

My Earth Angel

Vonzell Solomon
Top 10, Season 4

It was down to the Final 10 in Season 4 of *American Idol*. I was sitting in the contestants' lounge, waiting to go downstairs and rehearse when the phone rang. It was my dad calling to tell me about a young girl in our hometown of Fort Myers, Florida, who was ill with cancer. Her name was Madison Merrifield, and she was only ten years old.

He had just seen Madison interviewed on the local news. She had expressed her passion for singing, and talked about how much she admired me and wanted to be an *American Idol* herself one day. There was only one problem—her cancerous tumors, called Ewing's sarcoma, had spread to her lungs, and she had been given less than a 5 percent chance of survival. The doctors had stopped all treatments because they said there was nothing else they could do. They gave her three to six months to live.

I obtained a CD Madison had made and was so overwhelmed, while listening, that I decided to give her a call. When she came to the phone, I thought there was no way I could be talking to the right person. This didn't sound like a child suffering from terminal cancer with a few months to live! She was like no one I had ever spoken to before—she was so full of joy, faith, and life.

We chatted about *American Idol*, and she said one of her dreams was to be in the audience at a live show some day. I told her I could arrange it, but she shared with me that there was no money for that. Her medical treatments had drained all of her family's resources. If I had had the money, I would have given it to her in a minute, but I didn't—and I was sad that maybe her dream would never come true.

When I told my dad about Madison's wish, he said that somehow, some way, he was going to get Madison out to the show, and he had an idea.

He went to the management of a local restaurant called Leapin' Lizard and asked if they would be willing to host a fundraiser to get Madison and her family to Los Angeles for the show. The management "leapt" at the chance, and the fund raiser was a huge success.

With the money raised, Madison and her family would be able to go to two live *Idol* shows in Los Angeles, plus there was enough left over to cover all the recording and production expenses for Madison's CD—aptly named "Miracles."

I was so thrilled that I was going to finally meet Madison.

In our phone conversations, she was a source of inspiration for me and often brought me to tears. She was so young, but she touched my heart deeply.

Finally, the night arrived when Madison and her family would be in the audience. When Ryan Seacrest called my name and I got into position to sing, instead of being nervous about forgetting the words or being "pitchy," I was excited because I knew I was going to look out in the audience and see them sitting in my "friends and family" section. The band started, the stage lights went on, and as I sang my first words, I immediately saw Madison.

I knew it was her. Her beautiful smile radiated and filled me with joy. The chemotherapy had left her with no hair, but she was so confident in herself that she didn't need to wear a wig. At first I was surprised, but then I thought how typical it was of Madison not to care about little things like having hair or not. She just dealt with every obstacle in her path with a self-assured smile on her face.

As I sang my last note and stood in front of the judges, I hardly heard what they had to say. All I could think about was jumping off the stage to give Madison a big hug. Of course, that wasn't allowed, so I had to wait until after the show.

At last, it was a wrap, and my little friend Madison and I were finally together. The crew was so kind to her, and she was invited to meet Randy, Paula, and Simon. They invited her to come into their dressing rooms, and Simon even told Madison and her family they could be his personal guests at the show anytime!

Then we left the studio and headed to my favorite restaurant. Normally, my immediate family and closest friends came to the show, and we went out for dinner together afterward. That night was no different since, through our correspondence and phone conversations, the Merrifields and I had become like family. It was as if we had known each other all our lives.

At dinner, we told stories and laughed and made plans to never lose touch.

But it was a bittersweet evening. I was so happy to be with Madison, but so afraid that, if the doctors were right, this would be the last time I'd ever see my beautiful friend again.

A few weeks later, it was Wednesday and, of course, elimination night. I was overwhelmed with nerves. All of the remaining contestants walked on stage and took their seats on the couch. My family and friends were in the audience, cheering as usual, but my dad was shouting something that I couldn't quite understand. I didn't want to be squinting with a puzzled look on my face when the camera was on me, so I waited until the show went to commercial break to find out what my dad was saying.

The news was amazing: Madison had gone in for tests, and the doctors had found no sign of cancer! It was truly a miracle. I was so elated that all of my nervousness disappeared. At that point, I was usually praying that I'd make it to the next round, but that night all I could do was try to keep from crying and just keep saying, *Thank you, Lord, Thank you, Lord,* over and over.

Today, Madison is thirteen years old and a three-time cancer survivor, having fought cancer at ages eight, ten, and twelve. She is not only my Earth angel, but she is an inspiration to everyone she meets with her beaming smile, her unwavering optimism, her simple but strong faith, and her beautiful singing voice.

We have kept our promise to never lose touch.

You Just Never Know

Clay Aiken
American Idol Runner-Up, Season 2

It was December 2003, and Christmas was just a few weeks away. I was in Atlanta as part of a radio tour around the country when I received a very special and unexpected holiday gift.

Six months had passed since that amazing night when Ruben and I stood on stage at the Kodak Theater for the *American Idol* Season 2 Finale. In those months, I had loved being on the *American Idols Live!* tour, making my first video and album, traveling from city to city, singing live at radio stations along the way, and meeting with thousands of fans to chat and sign autographs.

At the beginning, all the adulation had been difficult for me to accept, but I was finally starting to get used to people telling me how hearing my songs or watching my videos had changed their lives. Yet, it was still a challenge for me when a fan would tell me something dramatic like, "I was thinking of ending my life— and then when I put on your CD and heard your song, I realized that I actually wanted to live, and I cried tears of gratitude to you."

Could I really be having that kind of impact on people's lives?
I'd ask myself. *Because, if I am, I should be the one crying tears
of gratitude to have the fortune to be in this position.*

Since my fans mean everything to me, I would do my
best to be gracious when they'd tell me these things, even
if I was caught off-guard.

This particular December day, a very petite and pretty
girl came up to me as I was signing autographs and said,
"Your video, *Invisible,* made such an impact on my life."

I didn't want to argue with her, but I was sure she must
have gotten that video confused with some other video I'd
made. I thought, *It couldn't have been* Invisible. *That was just
a self-congratulatory video of me singing on a stage in the middle
of Hollywood Boulevard with a bunch of people cheering. There
was no story line. There was nothing inspirational about it. How
in the world could that video have impacted her?*

"Are you sure you don't mean some other video?" I
asked.

"No, I'm sure it was *Invisible.*"

I asked her to explain.

She paused before she said, "Well, I used to weigh about
200 pounds."

"Wow, you look great, but how does that have anything
to do with *Invisible*?"

"When I saw that girl on stage in the video, and you put
your arm around her, I could hardly believe it. I mean, she
was overweight, and you looked so happy to have her up
there with you. Because you accepted her, I was able to
accept myself. After that, my whole life changed."

I had to think back to that video for a minute before it
dawned on me what she was referring to. While we were
making the video, the music director had pulled someone
out of the audience and put her on stage with me. She
wasn't hugely overweight. She was just a healthy-looking
girl, but she didn't exactly fit the image of the kind of

women you usually see in music videos. She wasn't stick-thin or model-gorgeous—but I had never thought anything of it until that moment.

"Well, thank you so much for sharing that with me," I said. But a simple thank-you was hardly adequate for the gift that young lady had given me that day.

Without her even knowing it, her words had rocked my world.

I've always tried to remember that people are looking at what I say and do to find out what's valuable and important to me, and I've always tried to set the right example. But that day I realized that I can't know all the ways my actions may impact someone. I couldn't have imagined that video would have affected anyone in any kind of positive way—but, lo and behold, it had.

Based on that conversation, I decided that in my videos, I would always have normal, everyday, average-looking people. I had to fight with the producers from my record label about this, but I insisted. When we made *The Way*, I told them I didn't want any stick-thin girls or model-perfect guys in the video. If we were going to include beautiful people, I wanted the gorgeous girl to be with the overweight guy and the average-looking girl to be with the model guy. I want people to know that it doesn't matter what you look like. Everyone is good enough.

This is one of the reasons America loves *Idol* and the show has the impact that it does on so many people. You rarely see a contestant with a music-video look! It's about real people. Season 2 was so exciting because not only were the Top 3—Ruben, Kimberley, and me—all from the middle of nowhere, Podunk, USA, but we were also *extremely* normal, average-looking people. We would never have gotten record contracts if it hadn't been for *American Idol*. Ruben was such a big guy; Kimberley was gorgeous, but a plus-size woman; and me—I was, and am still, such a dork! And then, the next season there was Fantasia—a struggling single mom that so many people could relate to. We're just normal people from next door or down the street.

That momentous day in Atlanta, I also realized that it's not just people in the public eye who have an impact on others. You don't have to make a music video to make a difference in someone's life. You can be a bagger at a grocery store or a teller at a bank. You just never know when something you say or do is going to impact someone else's life, and maybe even change it forever. . . .

The gift I received from my fan in Atlanta is proof of that.

Making a Difference

Jasmine Trias
Top 10, Season 3

I wish I could say that from the time I was little I sang because I wanted to touch people's hearts. But to be honest, I sang because I enjoyed the praise, I craved the recognition, and most of all I loved being the center of attention. Whether it was a wedding, a birthday celebration, or a local Mililani talent show, no one ever had to coax me to get up and perform. Before the request was out of anyone's mouth, I was on stage with a mic in hand.

But although I loved to perform, my most cherished dream was to one day become a nurse, since I also felt so much happiness when I was helping others. I knew that I wanted to touch people's lives and make a difference—maybe even save a life—and nursing seemed like the perfect vehicle.

I sailed through high school, performing in all the plays, singing in the concerts, and even being chosen to represent my school in the biggest high school talent show on the Islands, called The Road to Fame. I would be singing in front of thousands of people from every corner of

Hawaii, and the winner of this show would be receiving a $3,000 college scholarship.

There were so many amazing singers at The Road to Fame. My heart was pounding when my name was announced as the winner, and I loved basking in the recognition. I was also thrilled that I was one step closer to becoming a nurse since I would be using the scholarship money to attend the Hawaii Pacific University Nursing Program to which I had already been accepted. As I was handed the envelope with the scholarship certificate, I thought, *My dream of touching people's lives and making a difference is going to come true.*

As I stepped down from the stage, envelope in hand, an elderly gentleman with penetrating brown eyes walked up to me and said, "You have a gift from God. He gave you a beautiful voice and you are destined to sing. You are supposed to touch people lives and make a difference with your voice—maybe even heal them. That's why you won today." I was speechless. No one had ever said anything like that to me about my singing before. When I turned around he was gone.

It was as if his words turned on a switch inside of me. Could singing and not nursing be the way I fulfill my dream? Shortly afterward I found out that the *American Idol* auditions were coming to Oahu.

As I waited in the crowded stadium and stood in front of the judges, I still had no idea how fate was going to hand me the fulfillment of my most cherished dreams.

When it was down to the final three on my season, Fantasia, Diana DeGarmo, and I all went back to our hometowns for our "Homecoming" celebrations. As I entered my high school auditorium and our school president Mr. Baker spoke, all I could do was cry tears of gratitude.

"Every Tuesday and Wednesday night the streets of

Hawaii are deserted between 7 and 8 PM," he said. "I am so proud of Jasmine. Nothing like this has ever happened here before. Jasmine has brought together not only families, our school, and our town but the entire state of Hawaii."

I thought, *It doesn't get much better than this.* And then it did.

One night, I was sitting backstage at *Idol* in the lounge where we wait for hair, makeup, and wardrobe when I got a call on my cell phone from my dad.

It seemed that my uncle had been watching television and there was a piece on the local news about an elderly woman in a hospital in Hawaii. My uncle told my dad that the news report said the woman had suffered a stroke and had since been in a coma. Her granddaughter was sitting at her bedside day and night holding her grandma's hand and praying for her recovery. The night before, while the girl sat with her grandma and watched *American Idol*, all of a sudden her grandmother spoke.

"Is that an angel singing to me?" she asked.

Her granddaughter's heart jumped and tears of joy rolled down her face as she explained to her grandma that no, she had had a stroke and had been in a coma and that was Jasmine Trias from *American Idol.*

When I hung up the phone with my dad, I knew that the prediction of the man with the penetrating eyes had come true and my dream of touching people's lives, not in a nurse's uniform, but with my voice, was my destiny.

The lady in the coma fully recovered and to this day she says her life was saved because she heard the voice of "her angel."

What I Set Out to Do

Lisa Tucker
Top 10, Season 5

My entire life, I always wanted to perform. Not so much for the praise or the glory, but to touch people's hearts and hopefully make their lives a little happier.

As soon as I appeared on *American Idol*, I began to receive fan mail. It was so humbling to read the letters and realize how much I meant to my fans. I hope they know how much they mean to me.

Although all my fans hold a place in my heart, there's one fan in particular who has touched my life in a special way.

At the beginning of the *American Idols Live!* tour, our group of Season 5 *Idols* soon became aware of fifteen or twenty girls who called themselves the "*Idol* Junkies." They said the name was given to them by Jennifer Hudson when they showed up at almost every city during the Season 3 tour.

These girls from all over the country had met on an *Idol* Forum and at random *Idol* events. Some worked two or three jobs to earn the money to go to the concerts. Sweet and sincere, they always came decked out in T-shirts and pants decorated with "*Idol* Junkies" and their favorite *Idol's* name on the front. When they presented us with *Idol* Junkie T-shirts, Kellie, Paris, Mandisa, and I wore them at that night's concert. The girls were thrilled.

I first met Marissa at a meet-and-greet. I was happy to have her as one of my "Junkies." I always knew when she was in the audience because she held up a big "Lisa" sign. I'd last seen her at a concert in Hartford. Now school was starting, so although the *Idol* tour continued, the Junkies' touring was over.

I continued to get letters and postings from Marissa, but one day I received a letter that stopped my world. Marissa had been in a horrible car crash. On her way to field hockey practice, a car sped through an intersection. Hit on the driver's side, her car did a 180. Frightened and hurt, Marissa was trapped inside.

While she waited for the ambulance to arrive, she was in intense pain and very scared. But she managed to reach over for her iPod, and when she turned it on my song from the Season 5 CD was playing. She told me she just closed her eyes and felt that my song pulled her through. Her face was burned and her body was bruised, but when the ambulance driver arrived, he told Marissa that she was going to be okay.

He said that the seat belt she was wearing had saved her life, but she told me she knew everything was going to be okay because she felt like I was with her.

When Marissa recovered, I sent her tickets to our next concert in New York. I knew she was there—there's no mistaking when Junkies are in the house! The concert was difficult for her because the loud music worsened the ever-present headache she'd had since the accident. But I planned a surprise that eased the throbbing.

For my solo, I sat at the piano to perform "Your Song" by Elton John.

"I'd like to dedicate this song to someone very special. She says I'm an inspiration to her, but she is a bigger inspiration to me than I can ever be to her. I dedicate this song to an amazing girl named Marissa."

Marissa told me it was the most incredible moment of her life. She was touched that someone she "*Idol*ized" cared so much about her and made her feel special that night.

After the concert was over and I was sitting alone in my bed on the bus, I was thinking that my whole life I just wanted to perform to make a difference in people's lives.

Somehow, I knew I'd made a difference in the life of one person that night. I realized what a gift God had given me and knew if I stopped performing that very day, although I'm only seventeen, I would have already accomplished what I set out to do.

Tylee

Nikki McKibbin
Top 10, Season 1

The 2002 *American Idols Live!* tour was coming to an end. One of our last cities was Seattle, and as always, we were backstage after the performance mingling with fans at what is called a meet-and-greet. I don't know why, but whenever there were little children at the meet-and-greets, they always gravitated toward me. Seattle was no different.

Tylee was the cutest little girl I'd ever seen, with her tan corduroy overalls and little bald head from her chemotherapy. Her big brother, Tre, and her mom were with her. She was only five years old and already a huge *Idol* fan.

From the minute she walked into the meet-and-greet room, she didn't leave my side. She hugged me and kissed me as we drew pictures together. Whatever her disease was it had to be serious, but despite it, she was such a perky and happy little girl.

Although I'm usually tired by the time the meet-and-greets are done, I was sad when this one ended because I had to say good-bye to Tylee.

With the tour over, I headed back to Dallas and looked forward to spending some time just chilling and being with my four-year-old son, Tristen. I'd hardly seen him over the last three months.

Just as I was starting to settle in and get some semblance of normalcy back into my life, the phone rang.

"Nikki McKibbin, please."

"That would be me."

"This is the Make-A-Wish Foundation®. There is a little girl you met on the *American Idols Live!* tour who was just given a chance to make a wish. She said that her wish was to spend a day with you. Her name is Tylee, and we don't know if you remember her, but we'd be very appreciative if you could make her wish come true."

"Of course, I remember her," I said. "How could I forget her? She was so adorable."

"If you want to fulfill her wish, you need to get on a plane to Seattle tomorrow. She's not expected to live through the weekend."

She's not expected to live through the weekend? I thought. *No, that can't be true!*

My mom and grandma pitched in to help me get ready. On the way to the airport that Saturday morning, I stopped and bought pants that matched Tylee's tan corduroy overalls.

The Make-A-Wish Foundation® set up our meeting in a hotel suite not far from Tylee's hospital. I don't know who was more exited when I walked in—her or me. Tylee's mom, dad, brother, stepmom, and grandmother were all there.

I almost didn't recognize Tylee when I saw her. Some of her hair had grown back, and she was all dressed up in the cutest little pink frilly dress. Pink must have been her favorite color since she also clutched a pink Beanie Baby teddy bear in her hand that she never put down.

"She carries it day and night," her parents told me.

We talked and laughed and took lots of pictures and videos. We even ate hot dogs together. She showed me a little book she had made called Nikki Notes that contained the photos we had taken together at the meet-and-greet. She had me write in it.

After a while, Tylee wasn't feeling well, so she took a nap, and her grandmother and I went shopping. I knew she loved Barbies and teddy bears, so I bought her a new Barbie comforter sleeping bag, Barbie pillow, and a teddy bear. I signed them all, "Tylee, I love you."

When we got back to the hotel, she was awake and feeling a little better, so she sat on my lap and we went through her Nikki Notes again. At one point I gave her a little tickle and she laughed, so I gave her another tickle, and she jumped off my lap and we ran around the room playing tickle tag.

Her parents and grandparents were overwhelmed with emotion. They said they hadn't seen Tylee have the strength to play like that for as long as they could remember. They said they felt like it was the best day of her life.

As we were saying our good-byes, Tylee went over to her mother and whispered something in her ear. Her mom blinked back her tears and said, "Oh course, honey, if that's what you want to do."

Tylee came over and gave me her pink teddy bear, the one she carried with her night and day.

The rain pounded the roof of my cab as I rode to catch my flight home.

Tylee lived a few more weeks.

5

YOU'LL NEVER WALK ALONE:
STORIES OF SUPPORT FROM THE BEHIND-THE-SCENES CREW

It is one of the most beautiful compensations of life that no man can sincerely try to help another without helping himself.

Ralph Waldo Emerson

Eyelashes

Mezhgan Hussainy
Makeup Artist

When the two men arrived at the door of our house in Afghanistan, even though I was only eight years old, I knew something had gone wrong. The anguish on my mother's face told the story. That was the day my family— my parents, three brothers, and six other relatives—were to begin our escape from the country that we called home. It was the early 1980s and the Soviet invasion had just begun.

"There is no way we can take the van. The Russians are watching the roads. Our only hope for escape is by foot," the men told my parents. These were professional smugglers who made their living getting people out of the country. We'd hoped to make it to Pakistan and then ultimately, one day, to the United States.

My mother had only enough food for the two days it was supposed to take to drive through the seldom-traveled back roads—a bag of hard-boiled eggs, some cookies, and a few bottles of water. There was no time to get more food for the twelve of us. The men made it clear that either we left at that moment or we would be caught.

After the start of the Russian invasion in Afghanistan, you couldn't leave just because you wanted to. You were always watched, and if there was any suspicion that you were planning to escape, you would be killed immediately.

For the next ten days, my entire family walked in the darkness through the nearly impassable mountains covered in fog so thick that if you took one wrong step, you would fall into the deep canyons. We hid in little villages during the daylight hours, hardly moving or speaking. At first I thought it was some sort of fun game, especially since it was special to be spending this time with my cousins, but after the second day when the hard-boiled eggs were long gone, with no food or water, the horror really began.

It was freezing cold at night and sweltering hot during the day. Everyone had blisters on the bottoms of their feet. I had developed sores all over my body—the most painful were the ones in my mouth. My little brother, who was only five, suffered from such severe dehydration that we had to stop my mother from slitting her wrists because she wanted him to have something—anything—to drink.

My most vivid memory was the night we came upon a little puddle of water. The top was covered with moss and scum, but my mother scooped the water from the bottom of the puddle for each of us to drink saying that we were going to die one way or another anyway.

By some miracle, we made it over the border into Pakistan. We paid the smugglers—and others too who later helped us reach America—with money my mom had put in bags and sewn underneath her dress along with my father's college diploma.

My dad had gone to school years before in the United States. He had a degree in computer programming and spoke fluent English, so that helped our transition.

Although the rest of us didn't speak one word of English, we adjusted well in our new country, eventually settling in Los Angeles.

The first thing that struck me about school in America was how much the kids talked about rock stars and movie stars. All the girls seemed to know everything about them, and pictures of their favorite stars were everywhere—on their notebooks, backpacks, T-shirts, and bedroom walls. It really intrigued me, and I soon became enamored with Hollywood, too.

However, working in Hollywood happened completely by chance. After high school, I went to school to become a dental hygienist because I love beautiful smiles. One of my friends from dental school happened to be working part-time for a makeup line and thought it would be fun if we did makeup together. I told her I had no experience with it, but the next thing I knew, I was working for the cosmetic company Lancôme.

That led to a job working with the stars I'd dreamed of in school. I became a makeup artist on some small TV shows, and I loved it. In fact, I actually rejected an offer from *American Idol* for Season 1 because I was working on other shows. I kicked myself when I saw what I'd turned down, but I got lucky when they gave me another chance to work with the show on Season 2. That time, I said, "Yes!" immediately, and I've been with *Idol* ever since.

I feel incredibly fulfilled working with the contestants. I get to take these kids—many of whom come from farms, the inner city, or small towns—and transform them right before their eyes. What I try to do with all of them is to bring out their inner beauty.

I remember the first time I met Jennifer Hudson. She had never worked with a makeup artist before. Everything about her was so genuine, coming from her heart. She had no ulterior motives.

The irony of Jennifer's story is amazing. She walked in, sat down in my chair, looked in the mirror, and asked, "Can you make me look like Beyoncé?" That's all she ever talked about, "Beyoncé, Beyoncé, Beyoncé."

I told her, "Sweetheart, Beyoncé is amazing, but you are Jennifer Hudson, and you can be as big as Beyoncé. You just have to believe in that."

I never want to make these kids someone they're not. When one of them says, "Make me look like Beyoncé or Pink or Christina Aguilera," I tell them, "No, I'm going to make you look like you. When you're true to yourself, that's when you'll really be happy, and when you're truly happy, that's the only time you can step on that stage and make others happy."

In this business it's so easy for them to lose themselves, but if they stay true to who they are, they'll do much greater things.

One of the most rewarding parts of my job is watching a contestant when they look in the mirror for the first time, and they love the way they look. To see their reaction and catch them sneaking an extra peek at themselves makes me smile. I have to tell them not to cry—or we'll need to start all over again! Then, when their moms and dads see them, they tear up, too, and thank me for what I've done. We have to keep a lot of tissues handy!

After the contestants are made-up in a way that makes them feel beautiful—inside and out—they go onstage and perform with a new level of confidence. It's an honor for me to work with these contestants who were beautiful long before they ever sat in my chair.

It's still amazing to me that I get to do what I love the most and make a good living, too—one of the many perks of living in America!

I'll always be grateful to my parents for the courage they had to give their children a life of freedom in this country. The remarkable irony of my life story is that if my family had stayed in Afghanistan after the Russian invasion and the Taliban taking control, not only would I never have been able to wear makeup, but I would have been living my life under a burka, with my entire face covered. Women in my country can be killed if they walk out of their front door with their faces showing.

And here I am, making up the faces that are seen on television by more people than any other faces in the world.

Perhaps my mother had an intuition about what my destiny would be—Mezhgan, the name I was given at birth, means eyelashes.

I Have Connections

Debra Byrd
Vocal Coach and Arranger

I remember when I first met Ruben Studdard.

"Boid," he said (everyone calls me by my last name), "back home in Alabama, a woman prophesied about you. She told me I would meet a singing teacher in Los Angeles, it would be in a contest, and the teacher would be the greatest help and the one that would get me through."

"Really," I said.

"Yeah. So I'm very glad to be with you, Boid."

I've been a performer all my life. I've done backup, made records, been in movies, and starred in five Broadway shows. Basically, my career has been 97 percent performing and only 3 percent coaching. So when I moved to Los Angeles from New York and got this gig as vocal coach for *American Idol,* people said, "How did she get that job? I've been in L.A. for years, for decades, looking for that type of job!"

Then they watched me work with these kids.

"Oh, now I get it," they said. "It had to be you."

Every day before I come into the studio, I thank God for

helping me to meet every singer's need. Each of these kids needs something different—there are no stock answers. When I'm stumped, I close my eyes and ask for guidance. Like neon across my forehead, an answer comes, instantly. *Thank you*, I say. "Now, this is how we fix this. . . ."

I know this is my ministry. A lot of people put their spirituality only into Sunday morning, but I believe in ministering to the world every day. *American Idol* is bigger than I am. I'm just a vessel and have to "get myself out of the way" so that I can be used.

If the contestants are caught up in their anxiety, and I've given them all the techniques and information I possibly can, then I just say, "Okay, you have to let go and let God. When you stand on that stage, just let the God energy flow through you."

It always works, and the audience feels it.

During Season 2, I heard a contestant named Charles Grigsby, and his singing hit me right in my heart.

"Charlie," I said to him, "when you sang that song, I could tell you were letting grace flow through you. People are going to love you, and they won't even know why."

He gave me a beautiful smile that said, *Do you think so?*

At that very moment, a woman from the office was walking by. She stopped and said to Charlie, "I just want to say that—I don't know why—but I just love you."

Charlie and I looked at each other and grinned from ear to ear.

I tell contestants, "You are not here to sing for yourself. It's about touching people's hearts. Your voice can heal, inspire, and elevate. The fact that you're here is bigger than you think. There is someone out there who needs to hear what you have to sing." I know this from my own experience. Once, when I was performing at the Universal Amphitheater in Los Angeles with Barry Manilow, I felt bad after the show because I hadn't sung my featured songs well that night.

"I didn't do this right," I had whined. "I forgot to do that . . . waah, waah, waah."

I was completely caught up in my own frustration when a man walked up to me and said, "Thank you for singing that song tonight. You have no idea how you healed my broken heart."

I never complained again.

People say to me all the time, "You should be doing this! Why aren't you doing that? When are you gonna. . . ."

And I say, "It's not my time."

I just wait for God. Most people don't know how to wait on God because it's very hard to do. I'm one of those people who likes to be led through life by the Spirit. I don't like to butt my head up against walls. I've been told I have the patience of a saint, but really I just believe in divine timing.

Coaching at *American Idol* is a huge responsibility. I don't take it for granted—I'm incredibly grateful for it.

When I was a teenager, my mother used to say, "You have to 'walk on your knees,' give thanks, and be grateful all the time." I do. And I am.

I'm grateful for the smallest things. I remember during Season 1, Executive Producer Nigel Lythgoe said, "Byrd, I love you to your bones." That meant so much to me. I'm still grateful for it.

And when I leave the studio at the end of a day, I always say to God, "Thank you for speaking to me, and that I hear your voice. Thank you for being with me." Then I get into my car and all the songs in my CD player are songs about gratitude. I call them my thank-you songs.

Most of all I'm grateful that I'm aligned with what I'm destined to do. Whenever people ask me how I got this amazing job, I just tell them, "I have connections—God gave it to me!"

It's About the Music

Dorian Holley
Vocal Coach

It was my first day working as a vocal coach at *American Idol*. All the other coaches and Rickey Minor, the musical director, were having a meeting with the executive producers, Ken Warwick and Nigel Lythgoe. Ken and Nigel were standing authoritatively with their arms folded, and because I'm used to being the captain of the ship and not necessarily a foot soldier, I was a little apprehensive about what I was getting myself into. I had an idea that they both had some form of musical background, but when they started talking, I was blown away.

It was '70s week and we were discussing the songs that were being considered. Someone would suggest a song and Ken would start singing it. Then Nigel would join in, or vice versa, and they would sing the song all the way through. They could sing any song that anyone suggested. It was incredible to me. Then I found out that they both were also dancers and choreographers. They weren't just great producers, they were music lovers, too!

Although we couldn't tell the contestants what to sing, in that meeting we were all trying to come up with ideas for songs that would be the best fit for each of them. Whenever Ken and Nigel had an idea for a contestant, it was always right on. They were amazing.

That first day, I thought, *I'm going to love this job.*

I've had a great passion for music my whole life. I've been singing since I was twelve, when I got my first voice training at church. I attended a school where we studied four hours of academics and four hours of music every day. Although it was a private school, it was free. We earned the right to be there by the singing jobs we did. We performed at concerts, masses, bar mitzvahs—even at the *Carol Burnett Show.* Later, I got backup work touring with Michael Jackson, Queen Latifah, and Rod Stewart—I even sang in the movie *Happy Feet.*

Before working at *Idol,* I also taught singing. I firmly believe that everyone can sing, even people who think they're tone deaf. One day I was working with a girl from Germany who was as close to tone deaf as anyone could be. I worked with her for three sessions. During that short time, she went from not being able to sing a melody to delivering a song so movingly and perfectly in tune that it brought me to tears. But the tears were mostly because I saw her great effort and hard work and how badly she wanted it. I love witnessing the satisfaction someone feels when they go beyond what they think they're capable of doing.

A lot of the kids who've made it to *Idol* had, before the show, gotten by on talent alone. Back home, these kids were used to always being the best. They were the ones who got all the solos and the leads in the school and community shows. They were up against people who weren't nearly as good, so they got by just on their instincts and raw talent.

Then, when they get to Hollywood, they realize that they're suddenly surrounded by hundreds of outstanding singers. So once they're in the Top 12, they really have to get to work; they have to learn and hone their craft—or else they'll be voted off. Some of the contestants are willing to work hard to learn what we're trying to teach them, and some aren't.

When people hear someone like Aretha Franklin sing, they think, *What a gift she's been given.* Yes, it's a gift, but it's also hard work. Aretha will tell you that.

I tell the kids, "You can't worry about what the next guy is doing or how well or poorly the person before you sang. Everyone here is unique. Everyone is here for a reason. All you've got to do is work hard and then go out onstage, be yourself, and let America see your passion for the music."

When I look back at each season, I believe America chooses authentic musical talent. It's the media that focuses on how cute people are, or how much they weigh and how well they dress. With *American Idol,* the public ultimately overlooks those things in favor of ability. If America judged people according to their weight or style, we would never have had the Clay and Ruben phenomenon.

People with little talent can be marketed—the ninety-pound girl who jumps around in her underwear but can't sing at all, or the good-looking guy who lip-synchs his performances—but in the end, America really cares most about the singing.

And that's what this show is all about—the passion for and love of music. As I predicted on my very first day of work at *Idol,* I love this job. I get to share my passion for music with everyone from the executive producers to the wonderfully talented contestants each season—and with millions of people across America.

Family Ties

Debra Williams
Stage Manager

When contestants come to *American Idol*, many have never been in a city as big and overwhelming as Los Angeles before. You can tell how scared they are. They are fragile, like little flowers that are opening. They're so eager to absorb all of the excitement and attention.

I tell them, "If you soak it all up, you'll have a very rich experience. Go out onstage and enjoy every minute of it. No matter how tired and worn-out you feel, remember— you may never get another moment like this."

As stage manager, I feel as though I'm the mom, and this is my house. When people come to my house, I want them to feel comfortable and like part of the family. Although I run a tight ship, I try to create a fun atmosphere that can help them relax and enjoy themselves.

When the kids are nervous, and they usually are, I know what they're going through. My parents were gold medal ice-skaters in the 1940s who then went on to create a family act on ice. I was literally born on the road and started performing when I was two years old. We moved every week until I was fifteen. That's when we tried to be a normal family—I went to school and hung out with other children. But performing was in my blood, so I soon became a dancer on *The Donny & Marie Show* and then moved on to other television shows.

That's why I understand how difficult performing can be for these kids. They have so much to learn in so little time. It's tough. It's exhausting. It's emotional. Some are in tears every week during rehearsal. But they know they can come to me whenever they're nervous or upset—after all, performing in front of 30 million people twice a week can be intimidating! I want them to feel comfortable and safe, like they would feel with family.

And just like with any family, we have all types. We have our whiners. We have our divas.

So we nurture, but we also try to teach contestants to respect the people around them. We tell them, "The people out there are your fans. They are the ones who can make it or break it for you. If you go home tonight, leave the stage like a professional. Everyone will want a little piece of you—an autograph, a handshake, a picture. Be kind, be gracious, be respectful, be grateful." Some of them handle it very well. Some don't.

All of us are touched by how far these kids have come, but we worry about instant fame. That's why we do our best to try to keep them humble in the face of grandeur. After all, tomorrow they can be yesterday's news.

One thing we all love is the spontaneity of the show and the element of surprise. We have no idea in advance who is going to be voted off. And we definitely don't know who'll end up soaring to stardom. Nobody even noticed Kelly Clarkson for the first five shows of Season 1. Then she got bigger and bigger until, at the Kodak Theater Finale, fans were in a frenzy over her.

Knowing what I know now, it seems unbelievable that

I almost turned down the job of stage manager for *American Idol* when it was first offered to me. My son was graduating from high school the week the show was supposed to start, and I sure wasn't going to miss his graduation, so I told the producers, "I'm sorry, but I can't do it." Fortunately, they came back to me and said, "We'll have someone else start the first week if you'll come the next."

I had no idea how big this show really was, even after I worked on it, for the entire first season. It didn't sink in until I saw 10,000 fans show up at the MGM Grand Hotel for the special we aired live from Las Vegas after the end of Season 1. The fans had signs saying, "We Love Justin," and "Tamyra is My *Idol*," and they were dressed up like Kelly Clarkson. I remember turning to Ryan and saying, "I guess people know about us."

I tell the kids that it's a gift and a privilege to be part of this show and to treat it like that. I know that's the way I feel. For me, being part of the *American Idol* family has been one of the greatest gifts I've ever received, and I try to give back in the best way I can—by being there for each one of these kids from the moment they walk into my house.

It Doesn't Get Better Than This

Michael Orland
Vocal Coach and Pianist

I remember going to see *Mary Poppins* as a kid. I sat through it three times in a row and then went home and taught myself to play the piano by ear. From that moment on I became so attached to playing that you would have to tear me away from the piano to get me to do anything else.

I started as a pianist at *Idol* at the end of Season 1—though I nearly passed up the opportunity. I knew Debra Byrd and Kevin Bassinson, the *Idol* Season 1 musical team, from when I was a rehearsal pianist for Barry Manilow. Kevin had been the conductor and Debra had been singing backup for Barry at the time. One day, the phone rang and it was Debra calling to say that they needed an extra pianist on *American Idol,* beginning the next day, and she and Kevin had thought of me.

I told her, "I'm really sorry, but I can't do it. I promised to do a favor for a friend. This is someone who has never asked me for anything before, so I'm not going to let her down."

What a dummy—I said no to *Idol!* But at the time, I had no idea what I was passing up.

Three weeks later, out of the blue, I called Debra and left a message, "It's Michael Orland. If you ever need anything, give me a call."

And they did! They called right back and asked me to come to the Kodak Theater the next day to be part of the Season 1 Finale.

I know it was all meant to be, because I never call people to follow up and leave messages like that—but I did for some reason, and the position was still available. I started my job with *Idol* the night of the Finale. I thought I had died and gone to piano player heaven.

Before that, I was working mostly in piano bars. I worked in great places and enjoyed a lot of success, but I was playing and conducting primarily for people over the age of fifty, which was fine, but at *Idol,* all the people I work with are under thirty, and the energy and excitement are like nothing I've seen anywhere else.

This show introduces kids to music that their parents know and love, and vice versa. A few seasons ago when we had the rocker boys, Constantine and Bo, they introduced me to songs I had never heard of, and I loved it.

This is by far the most rewarding and creative job I have ever had in my life. Some people complain about having to go to their job for twelve hours a day. I sit at a piano twelve hours a day working with these great kids, Rickey Minor and his amazing band, and guest mentors like Tony Bennett, Elton John, and Stevie Wonder. I mean, where else does that happen? Of course, I'm a wreck around those stars, but I act as though I'm not.

The relationship between singers and their coaches is one of the closest you'll ever find. Besides being a pianist and musical mentor, I'm a parent, a friend, and a therapist, all in one. I develop unbelievably close bonds with the contestants. I watch them grow, and I give them not only musical mentoring but emotional support. I dry lots of tears and give lots of hugs.

What's really rewarding is that after they leave *Idol* and become huge stars, we still stay in touch, and we get to look back on the day they first walked into the studio.

When Jennifer Hudson got the part in *Dreamgirls*, she called me, saying over and over, "I can't believe it. I can't believe it." Then she invited me to go to the premier. It was so exciting. I sat there and cried through the entire movie because I was so proud of her. I had to go back again so I could actually watch it.

Another thing I love about this show is that you don't have to win to have a successful career—Jennifer, Chris Daughtry, and Clay Aiken are the greatest examples of that. This show has been the catalyst for so many kids to go out and realize their dreams.

I hope *American Idol* lasts forever. And it might. Every year it gets bigger and bigger and keeps bringing in bigger and bigger stars. *Everyone* watches it.

The other day I was talking to a huge Hollywood star, and I'm talking *huge,* and he told me that he had voted that night. I was like, "*YOU* voted?" And he said, "I vote every week."

If this job has a downside, I would say it's how emotional it can get being part of this show. I am the chief crybaby. These contestants become like my kids—I love every one of them, and I'm always so proud of them. The nature of the show is that everyone has to leave, but sometimes I feel they don't leave in the right order. On results night, I am the biggest gusher of all. People walk by and say, "Michael, are you crying again?"

My goal in life has always been to be a hit songwriter. I've written a lot of songs and had some successes. It's still what I ultimately want to do, but you know that question that people ask, "If you won the lottery, would you give up your day job?" I would never give up this job. For me, this job is *better* than winning the lottery. I couldn't be happier—and it also makes my mom the most popular woman at her beauty shop.

Holding Steady

Bruce Gowers
Director

I love the power of the camera. And I particularly love the steady cam—it can be a wonderful ally to an *American Idol* contestant. It's a handheld camera we use to float smoothly 360 degrees around the performer. It's perfectly stable, and enables a performer to make great eye contact with the lens because he or she is only a few feet away.

I always tell the kids, "The steady cam will come onstage, and as it moves around you, I'd love you to play to it. Just burn that camera with your eyes. Make love to the lens."

Constantine Maroulis took me seriously. I'd have to laugh when I'd see the stories they'd write in the magazines after the show about how he had smoldering eyes. I'd think to myself, *My god, what have I done?*

The other person who was like a pro from the start was the little country girl named Carrie Underwood, who's now a major star. When she was a guest at the Season 6 Finale, it was like things hadn't changed. The steady cam came around, and she played to it exactly as I had taught her to a few years earlier.

But some of the contestants are totally unpredictable. We can't be sure what they'll do. Sometimes they're very specific during rehearsal—"I'm going to come to this side of the stage, and then I'm going to cross to the judges, and then move to that side"—and then, when we tape the show live, they do it completely backward! You have to be really nifty with the camera to follow these kids. Since it's live, whatever happens happens. It's like fielding the ball in softball: practice all you want, but you never really know what the play is going to be.

I thoroughly enjoy working on *Idol*. And it's been the culmination of quite a journey. Born and raised in England, I started in the industry in the '70s, doing some directing. At that time no one had really made a music video. Some artists had made short clips to go along with their singles, but if it weren't for a British group called Queen and the music video we made to their song "Bohemian Rhapsody," I probably wouldn't be in this country, let alone directing *American Idol* today.

The video we created for Queen was rather avant-garde for 1975. People hadn't seen this type of thing before—a video in which we filmed the group performing their entire song and added unique visuals. After its release, it became regular practice for record companies to produce videos for their artists' singles. Some give the video of "Bohemian Rhapsody" credit for launching the MTV age. I never thought that producing that one music video would change my entire life.

When the video came out, I started getting numerous calls from the United States to come and work over here. So, for three or four years I was constantly going back and forth, working both in London and in L.A.

One day, I had just gotten on a flight to go back to London. I'd buckled my seat belt and sat back, when I suddenly had the thought, *Why am I doing this? Why am I going back to London? I love L.A. My future is here. I'm staying.* So I unbuckled my seat belt, apologized to the air hostess for the inconvenience, got up, left the flight, and moved my life to Los Angeles.

I directed a few more music videos and then began to do in the United States what I had loved doing in London—directing network TV shows. My first gig was directing the *Tony Tennille Show*—with the Captain providing a little help every now and then. After that, I went on to direct a bunch of specials for HBO, like Eddie Murphy's *Delirious* and Billy Crystal's *A Comic's Life.*

Today my staple is directing the awards shows. I've done the *Billboard Music Awards, People's Choice Awards, Kid's Choice Awards, Teen's Choice Awards,* and *Miss America.* This year I'll be directing the *Emmys,* too. Half of the year I do awards shows, and the other half I do *American Idol.*

When I first started on *American Idol,* I thought the show might not make it. Because I was in my own little world doing the show every week, it wasn't until the third season that I realized the effect it was having on people and how big it really was.

I went home one night and turned on the news, and it was all about *Idol.* So I switched the channel to *Entertainment Tonight,* and they too were doing a piece on *Idol.* On the next channel was a show called *Extra,* and they said to stay tuned for an "*Extra* Exclusive," which sounded rather exciting, and sure enough, it was on *Idol.*

I thought, *I didn't know we were that popular.* I mean, I knew people watched the show, especially the year with Clay and Ruben, but it hadn't rung a bell yet that the following was now almost cultlike.

I've gotten a lot of awards in my day, Emmys and the like, but the nicest thing happened to me at the Roosevelt Hotel after we did last year's Finale. This little man, who I didn't know from Adam, came up to me and said, "You are really, really blessed." I asked, "What do you mean?" And he replied, "You bring so much pleasure to so many millions of people."

I thought, *That is the nicest thing anybody could say.* It was nicer than getting an Emmy. And that's why I love *Idol*, and I will be here as long as they want to employ me.

I Have a Feeling
We're Not in Iowa Anymore

Dean Banowetz
Hairstylist

I was born and raised on a farm in Iowa, the thirteenth of fifteen children—eight boys and seven girls. I have thirty-seven nieces and nephews, with another one or maybe two on the way. With such a big family, I can never keep track.

Going from Iowa to Los Angeles was a dramatic change. At age seventeen, the age Sanjaya is now, I was still milking cows on the farm. When I started cutting hair in Iowa, maybe thirty people would see the work I did—maybe sixty-five if they went out to the local tavern. On *Idol*, almost 60 million people see my work every week.

My journey to L.A. began when I somehow got a photo shoot in Morocco for Matrix hair products. A headhunter in Santa Monica then saw my work and gave my name to some production companies. I interviewed for the television show *Extra* and beat out 170 hairdressers. They hired me two days later, and two weeks after that I packed up and left the farm for California.

Maybe they hired me because of my strong work ethic or because, with so many siblings, I could get along with anyone. I'm careful not to say hurtful things, even if I'm in a bad mood, because the words can never be taken back.

I've been on *American Idol* since day one, so I've worked with every contestant. I've found that those of us who work here go through changes, just like the contestants. We have sudden "aha!" moments. Just last week, I was walking backstage and saw Diana Ross in this *unbelievable* red dress. I just stopped in awe, and after I pinched myself, I thought, *This just does not happen in Iowa!*

These days, I'm living in a different world. I'm at the gym on the treadmill and David Boreanaz from *Buffy the Vampire Slayer* is next to me. The next day it's Stockard Channing. The next day, Lauren Graham. *I am definitely not in Iowa anymore!*

During my years at *Idol,* there've been a number of defining moments.

In Season 2, Kimberley Locke, one of my favorite contestants, said, "I never thought I had a weight problem until I moved to Los Angeles."

I don't think Kimberley's overweight, by any means— she's an absolute knockout, but sometimes people have a distorted self-image. When I straightened her hair, she looked in the mirror and tears welled up in her eyes. "Oh my god! I look gorgeous!"

It gave me goose bumps. "You've always been gorgeous," I said. "You just have to look at yourself in a different light."

One of the keys to success on *American Idol* and in the industry in general is to make changes frequently. The quickest way to get press is to change your look. Look at Madonna, Cher, or any iconic woman. Every time they produce a new album, they have a completely new look. In the eyes of the viewer and the consumer, if you've changed your look, your music has also changed. You've got a new sound, a hip new vibe. I don't want *Idol* contestants to stay the same visually throughout the entire competition, because change is important to capture the viewer's attention.

Another turning point for me came during Season 1, when we were down to the last five or six contestants. There was one contestant I really wanted to stay on the show. He was a good kid and a great singer. And then he got booted. I was devastated. I drove home crying, when suddenly I thought, *What the hell am I crying for? It's a television show. It's not like he's dead, right? It's not as if there are no more opportunities.*

I realized that caring for people doesn't stop when they get booted. I'm still in touch with a lot of past contestants, and I'm excited to watch them continue to progress. There is life after *Idol!*

I've also learned to be aware and considerate of the thoughts, feelings, and reactions of contestants. Everyone handles stress in a different way. Some talk, and the more stressed they get, the more they talk. Others obsess over one aspect of themselves.

I've found that if someone obsesses about their hair, it's really not about the hair. I coddle them about their hair, but I also know when to change the subject. I'll talk about their singing or whatever else I need to in order to get their mind into a different, peaceful place. When a contestant obsesses over one thing—anything—it starts to consume them, and they lose their perspective on everything else.

I try to help them enjoy the moment they're in. This show is a big deal for them. It's a big deal for us, too, so we all need to enjoy it for what it is. It's not going to last forever.

Some people get so worked up about their hair. Not me. My motto, especially in this city, is: *It's just hair.* It's fine if you want to keep the same hairstyle you've had since you were five, but if you're ready for a change, I'm happy to do something different, something fun. When friends say, "Oh, my god, you can't look at my hair," I say, "I'm not." And I'm not. It's just hair.

Am I bothered when someone criticizes a contestant's hair? No. I can't please everybody. Take Sanjaya, for example. He's crazy with his hair, and he loves to do fun, funky things. He's so gutsy. That's why America loves him and hates him. I think he looks good in whatever he does. But as long as Sanjaya's happy, that's all I care about. And that's true for all the contestants. They're the reason I'm here.

Don't tell my boss, but at the end of the day, I think, *I don't even care if I get paid, because I'm so enjoying the experience.*

I like to create a safe and peaceful place for people to be while I'm doing their hair. People call my house the Zen house. As she leaned back in the shampoo bowl yesterday, Gina Glocksen said, "Wow, can I get my hair done by you every day and just come and hang out?" And people tell me everything. You can't imagine the things I know!

My whole thing is about changing lives, one head at a time, because *American Idol* is not only about singing, but also about a person's confidence level. Contestants can take things to the next level not only with their performance but with their style as well. The contestants need to feel good about their presence without coming off as too cocky or too sure of themselves. Everyone is always walking a fine line here.

But, truthfully, when they look good, they radiate more self-confidence and the audience feels it. They're attracted to the contestant, and they start dialing 866-IDOL–whatever. So hair can make a huge difference, but, at the end of the day, *it's just hair.*

No Traffic on the Extra Mile

Rickey Minor
Music Director

I've got nothing to complain about, living at the heart of the music scene in Los Angeles, working with *American Idol*. It's quite the life. And it's been an amazing journey getting here.

When I was a young boy in Louisiana, my grandmother went out to California to visit her sister. She saw the promise and the hope in Los Angeles and decided to stay. Working as a domestic, she had to take three buses to work every day. When she sent for the rest of the family, my mother sold everything we couldn't carry and took the bus from Louisiana with my brothers and sisters and me.

So I grew up in the projects in South Central L.A. Much of the time I stayed with my grandmother, and by the time I was twelve, she had taught me how to pay the bills, balance a checkbook, do grocery shopping, mow the lawn, and take care of the household. She was all about going the extra mile to do things right, and I picked that habit up from her early on.

My grandmother was an early riser, so I never got to sleep in on weekends. She would say, "You never know when company may drop by." So I would always have to get up early and make sure I had made the bed and was ready for anything. Because of my grandmother I have never had to use an alarm clock, and I've gotten a whole lot more done in a day.

When I was fourteen, I started a little singing group in the projects. We all wanted to be like the Jackson 5. After winning a couple of talent shows, we decided we should be a real band with instruments. I played bass because I'd been singing the Jermaine Jackson part. I figured that if Jermaine could play and sing, I probably could too. We won more talent shows and started working professionally while I was still in high school.

After I graduated from high school, I got a scholarship to UCLA in math. I expected to follow in my uncle's footsteps and work for a corporation like Rockwell or IBM. But I had such a love for music—I just hear music all the time—that I couldn't take the corporate route.

When I was nineteen, I was doing a gig with a big band, when the trumpet player, Nolan Smith, came up to me afterward and asked, "Were you reading all that music?!?" It turned out that he was the music director for Marvin Gaye. He took a chance on me as a young bass player, and from that I got a call to tour Europe with Gladys Knight and the Pips. I had never been on a plane before, let alone across the ocean. I signed up just for three months, but at the end of that time, I decided to leave school and stay on with the Pips. The rest, as they say, is history—and I know I made the right choice.

While I was with Gladys, I met a guy named John Simons, who was working with Stephanie Mills. He said to me, "Rickey, I got this girl who sings in my church and is trying to get a record deal. Will you put together a band for her in L.A.?" I was twenty-two at the time. So I put together a little band and we did a showcase for the girl. All the record companies passed, but the girl and I became friends. That girl was Whitney Houston, and our friendship has lasted over twenty years. During these years, we've produced records, made TV specials, and performed at the Super Bowl. I only stopped traveling with Whitney in 1999 because I wanted to pursue more work in television and film. I'd been on the road since I was nineteen and it was time for a change.

People ask me about the secret to my success. I tell them it's spirit, perseverance, humility—and another thing I learned from my grandmother. She used to always tell me, "Rickey, you can catch more bees with honey than vinegar. Treat people the way you want to be treated, and if you're sincere, they will know it. They can tell if you are being phony. Use positive energy."

I have no use for anything negative. You can complain about other people or circumstances, or you can suit up and get in the game. It's easy to sit in the stands and say, "How did Kobe miss that last shot? We could have won that game." Instead, get out there on the court and get in the game yourself—stop complaining about the way other people are doing things.

People also ask me why I'm so happy. Happiness is not having what you want; it's wanting what you have. That's what will bring you joy. That's the energy I use.

I think everyone I've worked with—Stevie, Elton, Gladys, Ray Charles, Natalie Cole, and so many others—recognize this. And they know that I will go the extra mile. There are a lot of great arrangers and musicians in the world, but one thing I've noticed—there is no traffic on the extra mile. That's why I never have to worry. People ask, "Who's your competition?" I say, "I have none. All I'm concerned with is being better than I was last year."

At *Idol*, we live in the flow of life. It's organized chaos, a madhouse. How this show gets on the air sometimes, I will never know. But it's simple, really, when you think about it. I say to the people in the orchestra, "Guys, stay in your lane. There can be fatalities if you don't stay in your lane. We all have a space here at *Idol*; just don't cross over into someone else's territory."

Every week we have a different orchestra, and it looks like we represent the whole world. We have people in the orchestra from the Islands, from India, from Mexico; there are women, men, and every race. In the orchestra this week, there's a woman from the Czech Republic, an Asian trumpeter, and another trumpeter who's Spanish. But I never say, "I want to hire an Asian trumpet player." I just want to hire the best musicians, with the right spirit. And I like to spread the work around because there's not a lot of work out there right now for musicians. So we change most of the band every week so that hundreds of musicians get a chance to experience being a part of *American Idol*. I wish that every musician could have the opportunity to experience what we do here at *Idol* on a daily basis. It's such a gift.

When I work with the kids, the first thing I say is, "I'm not here to make anyone win. I am here to make you a better singer, a better performer, and a better person. But the key is simple. There will come a time when your ego will pass your talent. You are the only one who can keep that in check. This show is the top of the game. The rise is quick, but the fall is quicker, and harder. You will hit a solid concrete pavement, and it will hurt. You'll think, *Where did all the people go? The fans were screaming my name. I was on* Entertainment Tonight *and the* Today Show. *Where's everybody now?* You have to remember to use this moment fully and enjoy it. Don't let it pass you by."

As for me, the possibilities are endless. Complication is internal. It's not from the outside. On the outside it is what it is. I just like to enjoy the moment. It's a sweet ride. These kids are the *American Idols*, but I'm living the American dream.

I'm Stylin' Now

Miles Siggins
Stylist

I moved to the States because I believed in the American dream. I owned a big clothing company in England, but I wanted something different. I thought America—specifically Los Angeles—was the place to find it. My friends disagreed. "You will fail," they said. "L.A. is so horrible. You'll be back in six months."

But I had already sold my company and had put away some money, so I came to Los Angeles and had the luxury of being able to sit by the pool for a year. I basked in the sun thinking, *Wow, this is great. I love America.* Then I went to the bank one day, thinking I had ten grand left, and discovered I was down to a hundred bucks.

I had to do something—fast.

My roommate was an accomplished stylist, coordinating clothes and accessories for Janet Jackson and a lot of other well-known names. When she saw the bind I was in, she gave me a job assisting her. I loved the work, and from there, I moved on to working with stylist Kate Harrington and photographer Herb Ritts. Then, one of my neighbors who happened to be a producer on *American Idol,* Season 1, told me they were looking for a stylist for Season 2 and got me an interview with Ken and Nigel.

When we met, Ken said, "Oh, you're English. Where are you from?"

"Liverpool," I told him.

With a big smile he said, "So am I."

"Well," I admitted, "I'm not quite from Liverpool, I'm actually from the Wirral" (a peninsula across the Mersey from Liverpool). As it turned out, Ken and Nigel and I were all born within five miles of each other.

I think that's the real reason I got the job. But I had no idea what I was getting into. Absolutely none. I had never even seen the show.

"Don't do TV," counseled my friends when I told them about the job I was going to take. "The people are horrible—you'll hate it." So, once again, I braced myself for the horribleness. But the minute I started with *American Idol,* I thought everyone was absolutely fantastic. The people are in a flow of inspired energy. Everyone is expressing their creativity, and it's an amazing scene. There's an aliveness and juice that you just don't find anywhere else.

And I think I have the best job of all. I get to go shopping with the contestants and help them play dress-up. You can't beat that.

The only difficult part for me is that while most stylists work with a client once every few months, I get to see these kids every day for weeks and weeks so we become close, and when someone leaves, it's very emotional. I've gotten used to it somewhat, but I miss so many of them, even now. Some stay in touch; some we never hear from again.

Two of my favorites, Clay and Ruben, were contestants during my first season with the show. They were quite the pair! During the season finale, they both had very quick wardrobe changes, with five different outfits each. Clay was really quick to dress, so as soon as he was ready, he would help me dress Ruben. In the process, we all laughed so hard we practically cried. Those were bonding moments—and Clay and Ruben always made it onstage in time. They were great friends and have always supported each other.

I've loved all the kids. Since every week I only have two hours with each person to find outfits for both Tuesday and Wednesday, we have to be quick. The contestants get recognized wherever they go, so we bring security staff along. Everyone wants an autograph and a picture, and the kids try to be gracious to their fans, but their shopping time is short, and we have a lot to accomplish.

The right clothes give contestants confidence and a different attitude. When the kids walk onstage, before they even open their mouths, people form opinions based on how they look. They need to make a powerful visual impact. Although it's a singing competition, in reality, they're also judged on the outfit, the hair—the whole package.

The *Idols* must be comfortable when they walk onstage and not be too worried about their outfits, but sometimes we do get them to stretch a bit. Melinda Doolittle hadn't worn a dress in years, but when she put one on, she looked absolutely smashing and confident. Wearing something stylish can make a real difference in how they perform.

When I took Carrie Underwood shopping for one of the last shows, we found a fabulous tank top, but she refused to buy it because it cost $80. She also loved a pair of Jimmy Choo shoes.

"This is outrageous!" she said. "They're $350!"

I made a bet with her that she'd own at least four pairs of Jimmy Choos by the next time I saw her.

"Absolutely no way," she insisted.

The next time I saw her, she had five pairs.

All my peers watch the show now and say, "You are the biggest stylist on the planet! You have the biggest audience of anybody in the world."

But it just makes me nervous to think that way. If I make a mistake, I think, *Oh, great, the whole planet just watched me mess up.* And I certainly don't ever want to feel that I contributed to someone getting voted off.

Although I guide them and give them my honest opinions, in the end, the contestants make the final choice about what they want to wear. But, if they *really* don't look good, I say, "You know, Simon will slaughter you." It's my secret weapon. I know what you can't wear unless you want to be slaughtered. Cowboy hats are at the top of the list—and he hates red.

Truly, I just want the kids to look their best, and if it takes playing the "wrath of Simon" card, I'll play it. It's only because I care about these kids. I really do.

6

THE WIND BENEATH MY WINGS:
STORIES OF FANS TOUCHED BY IDOLS

If you ask me what is life's most urgent question, it would certainly be, "What are you doing for others?"

Martin Luther King, Jr.

The Turn of a Page

Lexie Matthews
American Idol Fan

My four-year-old son cuddled closer to me. It was after-noon nap time, and he had asked me to lie with him as he fell asleep. He always wanted me to be close while he slept. I was tired, too. My husband's random tirade the night before had made sleeping in the house impossible once again.

I had learned long ago that the only way to survive was to become invisible. I had learned to hide my real self away so that my husband's angry words and actions no longer hurt me. After a while, I became invisible even to myself.

My son drifted off quickly. He hadn't gotten enough sleep the night before either. As his soft breath became even and I knew he was deep in the cherished peace of slumber, I saw a rare opportunity to temporarily bring myself out of the shadows.

I retrieved Clay Aiken's autobiography from the bottom of a drawer where I had carefully hidden it. My husband had told me that I wasn't allowed to read Clay's book. He hadn't given me a reason, but the less of a reason he had, the louder he yelled, and I knew not to argue.

As I opened the book, a wave of relief washed over me. I wasn't completely invisible just yet. There was still a spark that gave me the confidence to defy orders—if only for a few precious moments. I sighed in silence and opened the book to a random page.

As I read Clay's words that told of the abuse he and his mother suffered at the hands of his biological father, I nearly stopped breathing. I began to tremble as he shared the account of the strength his mother had to find in order to leave the man who had oppressed her and her son for so long—and how that act of strength helped Clay to become the man that he grew into, that wonderful young man who has inspired millions with his own strong and gentle spirit.

I shut the book quietly so as not to wake my son, sleeping so innocently beside me. As he lay in the refuge of his dreams, I looked into his beautiful face. In that face, I saw two futures laid out before him, one dramatically different than the other. And in that moment, before his nap had ended, I had made up my mind. Like Clay's mother, I would find the strength to make a better life for the two of us.

The next morning, while my husband still slept, I quietly and triumphantly packed a few of our belongings into my car. I buckled my son into his seat, took a deep breath, and started the journey toward our chosen future.

Several months after our escape, my son and I celebrated our newfound freedom by attending a Clay Aiken concert. Tears streamed down my face as I held my son's hand and we watched Clay perform. But these were no longer tears of fear or sadness or hopelessness, but rather tears of gratitude—gratitude for this man who will never know how the turn of a page changed our lives forever.

Of Feathers and Rainbows

Jennifer Crain
American Idol Fan

I grew up with Paula Abdul.

My first encounter with her was in 1988. I was eight years old. When I snuck into my older brother's room, I noticed a large poster, thumb-tacked to his closet door, of this really pretty girl. Although at the time I didn't know who she was, I decided to like her because my brother did. I asked my mom to buy Paula Abdul's cassette for me. It was the first cassette I ever owned, and I played it until the tape unraveled out of its plastic case.

After that, I asked for her music as birthday and Christmas presents, and I always saved every penny I earned to buy "Paula stuff." I used to cry and beg my parents to take me to meet her, just so I could tell her how much she meant to me. My mom lovingly explained that meeting someone so famous was almost impossible. As I got older, I began to understand that my mom was probably right—meeting Paula in person would always be an unattainable dream.

Still, I was a dedicated fan. I admired her from afar—

not only her performance skills, but the way she cared about her fans and others around her. In 2002, I started watching *American Idol* simply because Paula Abdul was a judge. I immediately took a liking to this newly popular show in which normal, everyday people like me sang their way to stardom.

Then, in 2005, a dark and destructive storm devastated my area of Louisiana. Everything that I had taken for granted my entire life vanished before my eyes. My family and I fought to stay alive without food, water, or even gasoline to drive away from the devastation. I lived through the worst time in my life, and it seemed that it would take a miracle to put a smile on my face again. When it was time for *American Idol* Season 5 to air in 2006, we finally had electricity and our lives were slowly returning to normal. Yet I still longed for a miracle to pull me out of the despair in which Katrina had left me.

Around March of that year, Paula announced her own jewelry line. Fans everywhere were excited at the opportunity to own and wear something their *American Idol* judge had designed. I learned that QVC was inviting a studio audience to the taping of Paula's first live jewelry show in Philadelphia. This could be the opportunity to fulfill my dream of meeting Paula!

It was the first time I had ever traveled more than an hour from my hometown alone, but knowing where I was going, I was up for the adventure.

Just the other side of this plane ride, I repeated nervously to myself, *I'll meet my Idol.*

When I arrived at the studio, I was more nervous and excited than I'd ever been in my life. Before the show began, a QVC representative asked audience members who had traveled the longest distance to get there. Having come all the way from Louisiana, I won, hands down!

A few minutes later, we all stared at the hallway in amazement as Paula appeared in the midst of theatrical smoke. I could hardly believe she was real. I had seen her for so many years in magazines and on TV, but I never thought that this moment would really happen to me.

Before the show went live, Paula spoke briefly with the audience about her jewelry line. "I'm excited!" she said.

"I'm nervous!" I blurted, without thinking.

Paula looked at me, smiled, and said, "Don't be nervous, but I do want a picture with you after the show."

With me? It seemed that since I had traveled the farthest, I got the picture!

Watching the show being filmed fascinated me, but the thought of meeting Paula and having a picture taken with her kept me on pins and needles. And then it got even better. Halfway through the program, Paula walked into the audience to pick someone to model her jewelry. I held my breath as she got closer and closer.

"Come here," she said, motioning for someone to come forward. When I looked to see who the lucky one was, I realized she was smiling and pointing at me. My eyes got as big as baseballs.

"Me?" I asked in amazement.

"Yes, you!" she exclaimed.

I swallowed hard and managed to stand without passing out. I engulfed her in a big hug even as I fought hard to hold back my tears.

She took a bangle bracelet set from her own arm and put it on me. I also modeled a butterfly necklace and a feather necklace. Through my daze, I heard her talk about the feather's symbolism. "Fly without strings. Spread your wings and fly." At that very moment, I felt like I was flying!

Paula hugged my trembling shoulders and whispered, "You can keep the jewelry."

After the show, I thanked her for the jewelry and the

opportunity she had given me. I posed for a picture with her as the other fans gathered around asking for autographs.

Ironically, during Season 6, *American Idol* traveled to New Orleans to do a benefit for Hurricane Katrina victims. I watched *Idol Gives Back* with a smile on my face and a tear in my eye. I was still wounded from that terrible storm and the impact it had had on my life, but my heart was still soaring from the time when Paula Abdul made my eighteen-year-long dream come true. She was the miracle I needed to put the storm in my past forever.

My mother always says, "If you want the rainbow, you've got to be willing to put up with the rain."

Paula Abdul was my rainbow after the storm.

Thank You, Katharine

Nicole Merchut
American Idol Fan

Four years ago, I was sitting in class listening to a lecture about eating disorders. The teacher spoke to us about bulimia and why people binge and purge. She explained that bulimics desperately want to be in control of some part of their lives, and that they usually suffer from feelings of guilt or low self-esteem.

I knew just how those people felt. She was talking about me.

I never thought I was good enough and constantly put pressure on myself to be someone I wasn't. I'd put myself down and only saw my flaws, never the likable parts of myself. This self-hatred—plus the eating disorder that was my only comfort—had gone on for a long time.

But I never thought I could be killing myself. I was horrified when the teacher said that a significant percentage of people with bulimia die from it. Still, even knowing the danger I was putting myself in, I was so gripped by my illness that I felt hopeless. I honestly believed I would never be able to beat it.

But it's funny how lifelines can show up in the most unexpected places. . . .

One night I opened up a *People* magazine and read an article in which Katharine McPhee spoke about her own battle with bulimia and how, with her family's help, she was able to overcome it.

It couldn't be true! Katharine McPhee battling bulimia! How could she possibly have low self-esteem? She's not only incredibly beautiful and kindhearted, she has one of the most amazing voices any of us has ever heard—a voice that can bring a smile to your face and joy to your heart.

As a teenager, you want more than anything to be accepted by others. You want to be liked for who you are. But if you try to be someone you're not, just to be liked, you're not being true to yourself. You're letting others down by not letting them know the real you.

Katharine could have hidden her bulimia, which is what most people do because it's not an attractive disease. But she didn't. Risking the possibility of complete rejection, she was brave enough to let the whole world know about her struggle. Why? Because it was part of her, and she chose to be real. By doing that, she let thousands of other young women like me do it, too.

Reading her story gave me the courage to tell my family—before it was too late.

All of the *Idols* have struggled in their own way to get where they are. They all inspire us to reach higher and to not give up on our goals, showing us that anything is possible. But Katharine McPhee is an especially powerful role model for young women everywhere. Whenever I hear her voice or see her picture in a magazine, I know what she's gone through to get there.

Her incredible strength gave strength to the rest of us.

So I thank you, Kat, not only for the joy that your voice brings to me and millions of others each day—I thank you, Kat, for my life.

One Simple Word

Amy Johnson
American Idol Fan

Mackenzie was diagnosed with leukemia when she was just a year old. She began treatment right away, but when she was two and a half our world was crushed again when the doctors said, "This news is not good. Mack has relapsed."

As intensive chemotherapy began, so did Season 5 of *American Idol.* Chemo was extremely difficult for Mack's little body to tolerate, but no matter how bad she was feeling, she always wanted to join our faithful gathering around the television every Tuesday night. This reality TV show gave us a brief escape from *our* reality!

In the beginning, Mack came just to enjoy being in the inner circle of the couch with her four older sisters. Then, one night, a contestant named Ace Young came out and sang a song called "Father Figure." Mack was lying there, limp as a dishrag as usual, when Ace sang a song that contained a part about being naked, we all heard the word "naked," and there was a brief moment of silence as Lindsay, Taylor, Kali, and Lexie sat in embarrassment, their cheeks turning pink. Then Mack sat up and began laughing hysterically, "Ace say 'naked'!" she blurted out through her laughter, and all five girls burst out giggling.

Mack was transformed—laughing, happy, and full of life. This one simple word was the start of her adoration for Ace Young. She watched that performance over and over again, until she had every word memorized. And sisters, being sisters, began fueling the fire. "Do you love Ace?" "Is Ace your boyfriend?" As conversations about Ace became more frequent in our home, we could see that twinkle return to Mack's eyes. We loved seeing her experience pure joy in the midst of her suffering. As her mom, I felt it was the greatest gift anyone could have given us.

The week Ace was voted off, we were at Cincinnati Children's Hospital for Mack's cranial radiation. I had a feeling Ace might be going home that night, and I tried to prepare her for the disappointment. But when Ryan said, "Leaving us tonight is . . . Ace Young," Mack jumped up and down on her bed, clapping her hands proudly, saying, "See, I told you!" With a sinking heart, I realized she thought Ace had won. When we broke the news to her, she instantly collapsed into uncontrollable tears. We tried everything to console her, but nothing could stop those tears from rolling down her swollen cheeks. Out of desperation, I pulled out the trump card.

"Mack, you'll see Ace again. We'll go to the *Idols* concert!" As if I had just flipped a switch, the tears ceased and her smile returned. That was all she needed. She looked forward to that concert and counted the days until she would finally see her *Idol*.

I could only get tickets for the nosebleed section and was concerned that Mack wouldn't be able to see Ace. So I called a local foundation called Bare Necessities that grants wishes for sick children. They called Ace and asked him if he could meet Mack, and he graciously said, "Yes."

Then they called the local papers who, in turn, interviewed Ace about his upcoming meeting with Mack. As
word got out, it spread to the blogs run by some of Ace's
fans, who called themselves the Highrollers with Heart,
and they spread the word further.

The big day finally arrived to Mack's cries of "Mommy,
it's here, it's here!" At the stadium, Mack bolted over to
the souvenir counter. "Mommy, it's Ace in the picture!" I
couldn't pay the vendor fast enough. She hugged the picture, kissed it, and waved it in the air throughout the
show. And when Ace came out on the stage, Mackenzie
could hardly contain herself. She jumped to her feet
screaming, "Dare's my boyfwend!" The binoculars were
glued to her eyes and she was in her glory, totally mesmerized by this man.

After the show we made our way backstage, as Ace had
sent word that we should come back to see him after the
concert. The room was full of people, but Mack left us all
behind, weaving in and out of the many legs that towered
over her, making her way right to Ace. Then she stood,
staring up at him with adoration shining in her big brown
eyes, as if he would know exactly who she was.

Ace knelt down to her, and Mack wrapped her arms
around his shoulders. Ace held her tightly and whispered
into her ear, "Hello, Mack. Can I give you a big hug, too?"
Mack put her head to Ace's heart and just melted, tears of
happiness streaking her radiant face.

Watching Ace, I could see that he genuinely cared. It
was as if they were the only two in the room. For a little
girl at the tender age of three, who has endured more than
most of us will in a lifetime, it was magical. I realized that
Ace truly has a great heart, and it was his tenderness and
compassion that drew our little girl in.

In the months to follow, Ace's fans rallied around our
family, pouring out their hearts in support of Mackenzie

and giving selflessly to help carry some of our burdens. They had even formed an organization, Highrollers with Heart, to help other sick children as well. It was amazing to be on the receiving end of so much love from people we had never met.

Then, when Mackenzie was four, our lives were turned upside down once again with that haunting word *relapse.* We headed back to Cincinnati Children's Hospital for a prolonged stay, as a bone marrow transplant was Mack's only chance for life. This time we had an army of Highrollers going with us into battle. In a matter of days, the mail began rolling in and Mack's walls filled with pictures of Ace and letters from his incredible fans. The hospital staff was amazed as, every day, I rolled in big canvas post office bins full of mail and packages for Mack.

But the greatest surprise of Mackenzie's life came when she heard a knock at her hospital door. She sat up and saw a curly-haired figure peek into her room. Her eyes grew round. "Ace? Is that you? *Ace!*" she screamed. Mack jumped out of bed and ran into his arms. Then, wasting no time, she quickly pulled him into her world.

"Jump on the trampoline with me, Ace! It's easy . . . I'll show you!" Ace climbed up without hesitation and together they held hands and jumped. Mack rode her bicycle up and down the hospital halls for him, and she brought him into the playroom where they sat on the floor singing together with other children.

Ace's visit meant the world to Mack and clearly made a difference in her health. She went into isolation for the transplant after his visit, and she did very well. When her leukemia went into remission, after 136 days in the hospital, the doctors said, "It's a miracle."

Mack still has a long road ahead, but Ace Young continues to inspire and motivate her, every step of the way. He has been a bright light during a very dark time in her life, and our whole family is deeply grateful to him.

As Mack and I sat together on her hospital bed one morning I said, "Mackie, what would you wish for if you could only have one wish?" My daughter looked at me, lit up, and said, "I want to mawee Ace."

But although Ace Young is probably not the groom in Mack's future, thanks to him, Mack's brilliant doctors, and the love and support from the Highrollers with Heart, we are hopeful that we can now look forward to her wedding to someone, someday.

Clay Aiken, My *American Idol*

Melissa Shown
American Idol Fan

On January 28, 2003, my life changed forever.

I had finally convinced my parents we should start watching *American Idol* like the rest of the world, so at 8:00 PM we turned on the TV and settled in. Halfway through the show, in walked a skinny, redheaded kid with glasses. I thought he was someone the producers put on just for laughs. But when this kid opened his mouth to sing, I knew it wasn't a joke.

That moment began the four happiest years of my life.

The skinny redhead was, of course, Clay Aiken. Once he made it past the Wildcard and into the Top 12, I decided nothing was going to stop me from making sure that Clayton Holmes Aiken was the next *American Idol*. Week after week, song after song, vote after vote, I became more excited and more convinced that "my guy" was going to win.

After weeks of staying up until 1:00 AM to vote and skipping play practice so that I wouldn't miss *American Idol*, I sat in front of the TV that fateful night in May that was going to make it all worthwhile. I was on pins and needles through the two hours of pre-results buildup. Finally, the moment arrived when Ryan Seacrest announced, "And the winner of *American Idol 2003* is . . . Ruben Studdard."

I was devastated. *How could this be happening?* I went upstairs to my room and cried myself to sleep. I was afraid that I would never get to see or hear Clay again. Boy, was I ever wrong.

You see, I have cerebral palsy and am confined to a wheelchair, unable to walk or do most things other kids my age do. I loved Clay because I identified with him. He was different like me, and he taught me not to care what other people thought about me. When Clay lost *Idol*, I felt as though I had lost my best friend and the person who gave me something to look forward to each week.

In February 2004, Clay began The Independent Tour with Kelly Clarkson. In March, I went to my first ever live concert. Even though there were thousands of people there, being in the same room with Clay was the most surreal experience of my life, and I knew I had to do it again. When he came back to Baltimore in July for his solo tour, I was in the audience, and that concert was even better than the first one.

And in September 2006 when Clay came out with his second CD, *A Thousand Different Ways*, I listened to it every day and went to my third Clay concert—where something happened that made my world stop spinning.

As I waited for the concert to begin, happy to be in row 22, an usher approached me and invited me to move my wheelchair to be part of the group sitting *on the stage*. Yes, I was no more than *ten feet* from Clay Aiken!

As the concert began, I yelled, "I love you, Clay!"

Clay turned, looked me directly in the eyes, and smiled. "Thank you very much," he said.

To some this wouldn't seem like a big deal, but for me, in that instant, knowing that Clay knew that I existed, I felt connected to him and a part of something much bigger than my everyday life.

People always ask, "Why do you love Clay so much?"

My answer is always the same: "Because he makes me happier than I have ever been."

Clay's music takes me away from the limitations of my life into a world where anything can happen, and dreams do come true. I like to think he's speaking just to me, and believing in me and encouraging me to be all that I can be.

They say when you love someone you can't explain why. Although Clay Aiken lost *American Idol*, he won my heart forever.

The Youngest *Idol* Fan

Michelle Rossi
American Idol Fan

Maybe because he was surrounded by music since before he was born, Marcello has always known the music he prefers. And we're not being doting parents; we're being absolutely objective.

My husband is a singer and songwriter. He has played trumpet for thirty years and keyboard for twenty, and taught music classes for scores of students. That's why from the time of Marcello's conception, he was exposed to every kind of music, from classic to pop to the sweet baby songs his dad and I composed just for him. But even before he was born, Marcello's favorite piece of music was the *American Idol* theme song. He always started kicking like crazy whenever it came on.

Marcello was born during Season 3 and just starting to walk at the beginning of Season 4. Some people associate their children's milestone "firsts" with world events like, "I remember little Johnny took his first step the day the Berlin Wall came down." We associate Marcello's firsts with who got voted off that week.

Now, Marcello is no ordinary *American Idol* fan. He knows how to pick the winners. During Season 4, he cooed and laughed when a good singer performed at the initial auditions. He wailed, cried, and raced on his newly discovered legs into our arms for comfort, frightened when an awful singer belted out painfully unpleasant notes.

His favorite was Carrie Underwood. The first night she appeared on the screen, Marcello was sitting contentedly on the kitchen floor, playing his Fisher-Price Baby Grand Piano. The second he heard her voice, Marcello stopped what he was doing, ran into the living room as fast as his little legs would carry him, and stood directly in front of the TV. He stared, absolutely transfixed, until she disappeared from view. Of course, at that time we had no idea she would be that season's *American Idol*.

But Marcello did.

From that night on, with no prompting whatsoever, whether he was in his bedroom with cousins, in the den with his aunt, or in the middle of his dinner, whenever he heard Carrie's first note, he would come racing into the living room and not take his eyes off of her until she was finished and had left the stage.

I know all moms think their kid is destined for greatness. But, I must say, if Randy, Simon, or Paula ever decide to retire, I know a great replacement.

We'll just have to wait until he's potty trained.

An *American Idol* Love Affair

Nicky Pratt
American Idol Fan

It's funny to think that there used to be a day when I couldn't get my husband to watch *American Idol* with me.

"Please just watch it once," I begged. "I know you'll love it."

But my husband always had something else to do. So I sat alone and cried when Kelly Clarkson was tearfully crowned the first *American Idol*. I was so happy for her, and I wanted to share that feeling with my husband.

Along came Season 2, and I asked if he would please just *try* watching it. Again, he always had something he had to do.

Then one night while Ruben Studdard was singing "Music of My Heart," I caught my husband peeking around the corner. I pretended I didn't see him, crossing my fingers that he liked what he was hearing.

When the next week came along and he asked me when *American Idol* started, I nonchalantly told him and again caught him peeking around the corner! Imagine my delight the following night when he started asking me questions.

"So, who's this Ruben guy?" "Who do you think is going to win?" "Don't you think that Carmen girl is cute?"

All I could do was smile.

At this point in our marriage, we didn't have any TV shows in common. That might not sound like a big deal, but when I was a child I remember my parents laughing together while watching *M*A*S*H* or *All in the Family*, and how later in the evening they would start talking about it and laugh all over again. I wanted what my parents had. After that night in the kitchen, I had it. My husband was hooked.

Week after week, we sat together and watched *American Idol*. We expressed our awe as contestants got better. We yelled at the TV when our favorites got voted off. We jumped up and down in glee when our favorites won. And by the end of the season, we were officially having an *American Idol* love affair.

We couldn't wait each year for *Idol* season to begin. We even did a countdown. My husband's friends teased him for watching.

"Laugh all you want," he replied, "but it's our thing. It's our 'us' time and I love it."

I finally had what my parents had—and then some.

But when Season 5 rolled around, sadly my husband and I had split up. It's not that we didn't love each other, but our pressures and responsibilities had caved in around us. We had separated to reevaluate our life together.

Fortunately, *American Idol* creates miracles for more than just the Top 10; it creates miracles for us ordinary folk as well. As Season 5 progressed and we watched in our separate apartments across town, we knew we couldn't make it through the season without each other. It just wasn't the same. So before it even got down to the fateful night when our favorite, Kellie Pickler, was voted off, we decided to give our marriage another try with renewed promises of love, honesty, trust, and *American Idol* forever.

With Season 6 under way, we sit on the couch together again—in awe as everyone gets better, yelling at the TV when our favorites get voted off, jumping up and down when our favorites win, and very happy to, once again, be having our *American Idol* love affair.

The *American Idol* Roller Coaster

Lise Hintze
American Idol Fan

American Idol has been an addiction from beginning to end—an addiction of which I never thought I was capable.

During Season 2, I heard so much talk about the show—especially about Clay and Ruben—but I passed it off as, "That's nice," while thinking to myself, *I don't watch shows like that.*

Then came Season 3, and my two girls, ages nine and seven, asked if they could please watch—after all, "everyone else" was. Following some brief deliberation, we sat down, turned on the TV, and watched as young people from all over America, who believed in their hearts that they could actually sing, gathered—hoping to become the next *American Idol.* The three of us looked at each other with horror. *Was this really what people were talking about? This was it?* We went to bed in complete disbelief.

The next week was soon upon us and *American Idol* was back with more sinful singing. That week we were initiated into Simon Cowell, who, with his cryptic tongue, proceeded to systematically destroy some of the contestants and make them cry. He soon had my two girls crying as well.

"That man is so horrible, Mommy."

"Yes, he is, girls. Let's go to bed."

It was now week three and we were back on the couch. As we continued to endure the torture of pipes gone wrong, my girls' skins were getting tougher. They were no longer horror-struck by the Brit with the lashing tongue. My seven-year-old was warming up to Simon and was actually agreeing with his suggestion that some of these kids should give it all up and go home.

"Simon's right, Mommy. That guy stinks."

The girls were starting to recognize those with talent and forming bonds. And so was I. I fell for the soulful man from the South whose smile, graciousness, kindness, and light swept me off my feet—Mr. George Huff.

Thus, our official obsession with *American Idol* began. Tuesday and Wednesday nights were completely written off.

"A party invitation? Sorry, can't make it. *Idol* night."

"An interview? Can't do. *Idol's* on." It was bad and I knew it.

I voted for George Huff every week and went through a few rough nights when some of George's songs weren't as strong as they could have been. Of course, it's not easy for a man with a Teddy Pendergrass voice to handle a Barry Manilow tune. True?

And there was one night when I knew that the Huffinator was in trouble, but we had a rule in our house—one vote per person. So we each dialed our "01's" or "02's" and off to bed we went. I tucked the girls in, we said good night, and then . . . I did the unthinkable. I snuck downstairs. I had to help my *Idol*!

I tiptoed into the living room, gently picked up the receiver, went into the bathroom, slowly closed the door, and began to dial at rocket speed. Faster! "Thank you for voting for contestant #2." *Faster,* I thought! I had to dial as many times as I could. *American Idol can't lose its best contestant ever. I must dial, dial, dial!* And then . . . I heard them!

"DADDY! MOMMY'S CHEATING!"

As they stormed down the stairs, I quickly dialed again. *Good. I got in one more vote. That will do it. That will save George.*

Then, like a little SWAT team, my girls swooped into the bathroom, ripped the phone out of my hand, and screamed at me, "Mommy, you have to get in trouble for this!"

And my lovely husband, who now believed I had completely lost my mind, said to my seven-year-old, "You can pick Mommy's punishment, Sophie."

With that I was handed my sentence: "Okay, Mommy, next week you can't vote at all."

"WHAT?! NO, SOPHIE, PLEASE! DON'T DO THIS TO ME! I HAVE TO VOTE NEXT WEEK!"

And up the stairs the three of them went, laughing and singing, "Mommy can't vote next week. Mommy can't vote next week."

There I sat, alone in the bathroom, stripped of my right to dial "0-whatever" and put in my call for my man George. I went to bed discouraged, but ready to put Plan B into action—buttering up my seven-year-old so she would change my punishment—and I had one week to do it.

Sophie got extra dessert all that week, along with, "Sure, Soph, you can have an ice pop before dinner, honey. Anything you want." My plan worked. It was now Tuesday and I was back on top as "Best Mommy in the Whole Wide World" and George got my vote yet again. I was going to get that man into the Top 5 if my life depended on it.

At that point I could safely say I was a committed (or a should-be-committed) full-fledged, *American Idol* junkie. I was so over-the-top, I was sporting a Huff Daddy baseball cap, which I had proudly had made by a local merchant. I wore it running. I wore it to the beach. I wore it to bed.

The ride of Season 3 ended for me when George was eliminated on a dark Wednesday night. It was like someone ripped my heart out of my chest. His name was read and I burst into tears. My girls had tissues ready and their words of condolence were kind. My phone started to ring: "We're so sorry, Lise."

A few weeks later, Season 3 ended with Fantasia winning fair and square.

But the ride wasn't over yet! There was the *American Idols Live!* tour. Once again I found myself, phone in hand, dialing at mach speed and managing to get the best seats available for the show. And just before we were about to leave for the concert that warm summer evening, the phone rang. It was Uncle Gary, a concert promoter in Detroit.

"Hey girls, do you want to meet the *Idols*?" I don't know who jumped higher—them or me.

When we arrived at the venue, we were guided to the meet-and-greet room. Of course, I proudly wore my Huff Daddy hat. My girls whispered, "There he is, Mommy. There's George!"

I walked up to him and just extended my arms. He stood up so graciously, and with that big smile on his face, he put his arms around me and hugged me as tightly as he could. I hugged him tightly back and silently I said, *George, you were so great. I voted for you every week. Your spirit and light were so bright and your determination and good sportsmanship were wonderful for young people to see and learn from.*

And I think he heard what my heart was saying because he held my two hands and said, "Thank you so very much."

As the season retired, so did my Huff Daddy hat. Now signed, it resides on my office desk. No one is allowed to touch it.

So thank you, *Idols*, for the fun and the ride. A ride I never ever thought I would get on—the *American Idol* roller coaster.

Angels Brought Us Here

Jane Marquit
American Idol Fan

Single moms like me search for a little bit of comfort wherever we can find it. As the winter winds whistle outside my window, I often curl up with a bowl of chicken noodle soup and a bologna and mayonnaise sandwich—the foods I loved as a child. These serve as temporary Band-Aids, but inevitably the tidal wave of work and bills floods over me yet again.

My ultimate goal in life is to raise a happy daughter. As the new year of 2005 rolled in, Megan was going through a terrible period of transition and teenage angst. She was overwhelmed with school, and I with work. We were both just trying to keep our heads above water. Moments of peace and tranquility were like butterflies dancing just out of our reach.

When we discovered the magic of *American Idol* Season 4, everything began to change. Megan and I grew closer, inspired by our mutual love and admiration for the sweet country girl, Carrie Underwood, and the humble yet gifted Anthony Federov. Carrie's talent, beauty, and authenticity left us breathless. Anthony's soothing, lyrical voice both delighted and amazed us, especially when we learned that as a child he had had a tracheotomy, and the doctors had told his parents that it was unlikely that he would ever speak again, let alone sing like a nightingale.

I loved to watch my daughter take endless delight in spending two hours every Tuesday night voting back and forth, once for Carrie and once for Anthony. The inspiration she got from these two unique individuals was a godsend. I saw joy coming back into her life—and hope into mine.

When we found out that the *Idols* would be going on tour, we decided to indulge ourselves and attend the *American Idols Live!* concert later that year, even though we were just treading water financially. So one sunny September afternoon, Megan and I set off on our *Idol* adventure. As we drove across the bridge from our home on Cape Cod to the concert venue in Providence, Rhode Island, we joyfully sang songs from the *Idols'* CD as our hearts beat faster in anticipation of seeing Anthony and Carrie live.

The concert was beyond anything we could have imagined. Megan had spent hours making a sign, and when she held it up and Anthony pointed at it and smiled, she nearly jumped out of her skin with happiness. When Carrie sang "Inside Your Heaven," it brought tears to my eyes. Not surprisingly, given their similar natures, Carrie and Anthony had become friends and their interaction on stage was especially sweet to watch.

After the concert, Megan and I, both bubbling over with excitement, strode along with the crowd to the *Idols'* tour bus. Moments later, Anthony appeared and patiently posed for pictures and gave autographs to his many fans. He signed Megan's ticket and we took a picture of her beside him. As she ran on the wings of bliss to our car under the starlit sky, my heart overflowed with joy and gratitude to these *Idols* for giving her the happiest night of her young life. I remembered a song that Carrie had performed during the *American Idol* competition called "Angels Brought Me Here." At that moment, I felt as if angels had swooped down from heaven and brought us there, bringing happiness and fun back into our lives.

But we still had our struggles, and that winter they were compounded when a severe windstorm devastated Cape Cod. One afternoon it violently swept across our area, felling hundreds of trees and taking out almost all electricity on the Cape. My daughter was stranded on a school bus surrounded by fallen wires for hours. I had no idea where she was—a parent's worst nightmare. The process of locating her was impeded by the power outage, and the next five hours were the longest of my life. Finally, we were reunited, and then lived with no power or heat for several more days. That glorious night in Providence was the happy memory that kept us warm and sustained us through those trying days and nights. We vowed that once it was over, we would do everything we could to attend one more live concert.

The following summer we once again crossed the bridge, this time heading to Connecticut. Carrie, now a superstar, put on a concert to remember. Every note in every song was pitch-perfect. We sang and swayed and soaked in every single minute of it.

After the concert, we got in line at the merchandise booth and a few minutes later, to our surprise and delight, Carrie appeared. I was struck by how tiny she was as she shined her warm, genuine smile on her dazzled fans. She signed an autograph for my speechless daughter as I snapped a picture. I then mumbled something mundane like, "It's so nice to meet you, Carrie," to which she politely and humbly replied, "Why, thank you," with a huge grin and a slight drawl. As we floated to our car, Megan kept screaming, "I met her! I met her! This is the best night of my life!"

A few months later, as Carrie accepted her CMA Award for female vocalist of the year, with Anthony Fedorov watching proudly from the audience, she said it was the best night of her life. The joy she so generously bestowed on my daughter and all of her other fans had deservedly returned to her.

I will always be grateful to *American Idol* for bringing hope and enjoyment back into our lives at a time when we were on the edge of despair. Sometimes in the darkest night, a light will shine from the most unexpected place. For my daughter and me, that light came from our television set the January night we discovered *American Idol*— and it's only gotten brighter. Since then, despite the persistent glare of the spotlight of fame, Carrie and Anthony have continued to shine, each with their own simple, humble, unpretentious inner light—light that appeared in our lives when we needed it most.

The Rocker and the Writer

Cynthis Borris
American Idol Fan

I admit it. I'm an *American Idol* addict. With the high cost of gas, the desire for entertainment with a competitive edge lures me to my television week after week.

Live from Los Angeles, the familiar theme welcomes me like an old friend. I crank the volume to high, determined to hear every note. Pitch-perfect or "oh my," I'm in for the season.

Song after song, my house rocks with my party of one. Windows rattle and the cats hide. My toes tap to the music. I'm alive and in the moment. I settle into my chair, glass of wine in one hand and phone in the other. A seasoned *Idol*er, I feverishly jot down the 866 (not 800!) number and mark my night's favorites: 5701, 5703, 5706 . . .

An equal-opportunity viewer, I cast a fair vote: a vote for a job well done, a vote for a valid try, yet another vote for a winning attitude. I marvel at how the contestants either step up to the plate and deliver or turtle back to the dugout in defeat.

I check my scoreboard for a recap. Tears, attitude, or apologies land a strike across their four-digit number and the phone lines stay vacant. I take note. One number is circled, underlined, and highlighted with an asterisk. In a season filled with awesome talent, discovering the one performer who draws me into the music and out of my chair to dance is phenomenal.

Chris Daughtry was the one during Season 5.

Rarely does a contestant capture my attention and, more importantly, my heart. Chris was not just gifted with a voice; under the lights he showed that the mark of a man's success is measured in more than octaves.

Me and heavy metal? Me and a rocker? I glance at my CDs and thumb through the titles: Chris Botti, Josh Groban, Harry Connick, Jr. Under a film of dust, some country and blues, even a little Cajun. But rock? Not exactly the rhythm of my soul. Then, with his soft, seductive "I Walk the Line," I looked beyond the music.

With a constant strength of spirit, Chris gave his best, listened to the critiques, accepted the challenge, and delivered with excellence.

Captivated, I coached from the sidelines.

"You got it."

"Great job!"

"Not so loud. You'll strain your vocal cords."

I reached for a throat lozenge and let the eucalyptus cool my frayed voice, as I edged closer to the television and inhaled on the upbeat. Chris proved to be a team player, and I was on his team. Whew! The song over, I exhaled and waited alongside my player for the judges' critique.

What, no wow factor? I tossed popcorn at Randy and scowled.

Say what? You put my man in the dog pound. What's up, Dawg?

Some nights they offered, "Fantastic." Some nights, "Not my thing." Some delivered their reviews with a bite.

Still, Chris walked the line. No moans, no groans, no attitude. Manilow, Elvis, and Bocelli, the rocker stayed the course and humbled himself to explore other avenues of song. I stayed the course, too, and learned to appreciate his chosen path.

He captured my heart and I decided to step up. Just as Chris could embrace Manilow's lyrics, I could stretch and train my ears to heavy metal. After all, fair is fair. Can I ask anything less than I'm willing to give?

So I listened.

And one night, one performance, he knocked me out of my seat with his rendition of "Have You Ever Really Loved a Woman." I knew then I was part of something special. The goose bumps ignited and the magical spark that connects souls entered the room, a palpable entity.

Shouts of "Yeah!" cascaded across America.

No question. My vote sealed, I grabbed the phone and entered the number, push after push. A blister bubbled on my finger and I hustled to the bathroom for a Band-Aid. Armed with survival gear, my mantra was: "Redial, redial, redial."

More Tuesdays came and went, and then we were down to four contestants and anyone's win. The singers inched off third base and rallied for the final run. Heightened performances filled the hour and expectations escalated.

Then came the vote. Somehow, Chris's team was caught off base and the other *Idols'* fans cast votes beyond our count.

Smiles turned upside down across America. Disenchanted viewers bombarded the website, demanded an explanation, cried for a recount. I traded my Chardonnay for Scotch on the rocks. A double.

Shocked and bruised, the Daughtry fan-base shook with controversies, rumors, and tears. Tabloids broadcast the outrage and how-could-this-happen headlines. Over and over, talk shows replayed the elimination moment that stunned viewers.

In the turmoil, Chris strode to the front and quieted the fans with thanks and empathy for their disappointment. In an act so public and humble, he reached out and comforted his supporters. Me. He comforted me. Funny, I thought it was the other way around. *Shouldn't I be sending Chris a cyber-hug?*

For Chris, the contest ended there. But the mark of a man, of this man, was branded forever on our memories.

Now, Daughtry's CD plays, and I listen to the music. Still learning to rock, I struggle to decipher the words; I flip open the booklet that was included with the CD and read the lines.

Old ears, old eyes, young heart, I hold my reading glasses inches above the lyrics and speak them softly. I hear the rhythm, feel the meaning, and grasp the stroke of the artist's touch. I understand, and the words awaken the music of my heart.

What's this? A thank-you note?

"'Now a very, very, very special thanks to my amazing, die-hard, crazy, hard-core fans.' Chris Daughtry."

That's me! A fan. The crazy one.

At the top of my CD pile, Daughtry smiles. I smile, too.

It's All Clay Aiken's Fault

Mary Baust
American Idol Fan

If you had told me four years ago that my life was going to be changed forever because of a TV reality show, I would have told you that you were crazy. But here I am, fifty-eight years old and telling you exactly that.

It was Season 2 of *Idol*. I hadn't watched the first season and had no plans to watch the second, but my father-in-law was a fan and had convinced my husband to take a look. So one evening I was upstairs peacefully working on a scrapbook when out of nowhere I hear my husband laughing hysterically downstairs. I continued working, trying to ignore my husband's ever-more-boisterous appreciation for whatever he was watching until finally I couldn't stand it anymore. I went to see what all this was about, and as I sat down and proceeded to watch the parade of talentless singers march across the screen, I, too, began to laugh out loud. As fate would have it, that night as I was sitting and watching *American Idol* for the very first time, a geeky-looking young man from North Carolina stepped up in front of Randy and Simon (Paula was ill that day). I shook my head, made a wisecrack to my husband, and braced myself. Then he began to sing. When he was done, I turned to my husband and said, "That's him. He's the winner. They don't need to audition anyone else." That young man was Clay Aiken.

I was hooked. I followed the audition process each week, and was in shock when Clay was sent home, but my dismay turned to delight when he was called back for Wildcard Night, and was eventually chosen as one of the twelve finalists. Each week I would watch the show with eager anticipation of what he was going to sing, how he was going to look, and what he was going to say. I wept during "Bridge Over Troubled Water," and loved him even more when he messed up the words to "Vincent." I was so absolutely certain that he was going to be the winner that I didn't even start voting until the last few weeks. On the night of the finale, I voted nonstop for hours—undeterred by the frustrating busy signal—trying to get in as many votes as possible, but, as we all know, there weren't enough to declare him the winner. I was devastated. *How could this have happened?*

During the weeks that followed, I found myself in a state of withdrawal. I hadn't realized how listening to this young man sing for a few minutes each week was the "fix" that kept me smiling for the other 158 hours.

When summer arrived and the *American Idols Live!* tour was on the road, although there was a show only fifty miles away, I didn't go because I was afraid to make the trip alone and couldn't find anyone to go with me. Still being in my state of "withdrawal," I decided to "Google" Clay. I was amazed at the number of sites devoted to him and started checking them out. It was on a fan's site on the Internet that I first saw Clay's performance during the *American Idols Live!* tour. Once again I was amazed by him—he wasn't just a singer, he was a performer, and one who held the audience in the palm of his hand. Right then and there, I made the decision that if the opportunity to see him live were ever presented to me again, I would overcome my fear of traveling alone and would be there no matter what.

One day I was searching the Web and I saw a site that frankly scared me a little. It was called the "Lecherous Broads for Clay Aiken" or LBFCA for short. Nonetheless, I checked it out and that's how the purple pages of "the Broads" became my Internet home. The pages were written with intelligence and wit by women who loved Clay Aiken. They loved Clay Aiken the singer. They loved Clay Aiken the man. They loved Clay Aiken the hottie!

It was such a relief for me to realize that I was not the only fifty-something out there who had feelings that had snuck up on me about this young man. We took pride in his accomplishments just as we would if he were one of our own kids. But when he was performing, the feelings that we had were far from motherly. I would become a fifty-eight-year-old teenager—yelling and screaming like a fifteen-year-old! Except now, I had credit cards, a house, and no curfew!

But the most wonderful part of this whole experience for me has been the relationships that I have formed with the other Broads. I remember the first concert I went to. It was in Philadelphia for the Independent Tour, when Clay was co-headlining with Kelly Clarkson. A group of Broads was meeting for dinner before the concert. I sat at the table reserved for the group, and as each one arrived, there would be screams, smiles, and hugs, as if we were greeting long-lost friends. A few days later, I attended another concert in D.C. and took my mother-in-law. Once again, it was dinner and hugs and laughter and even presents. Afterward she told me that although she enjoyed the concert, she was overwhelmed seeing the sisterhood she had witnessed among all of us Broads.

The friendships that have formed in this group are real, true, lifetime friendships. These are women who not only chat online but call each other on the phone, send cards on birthdays and holidays, and share pictures and stories of their families. Some of these women are as young as my daughters and some older than myself. They are from every corner of the United States. They are rich and poor. Some are overcoming hardships and some are dealing with life-threatening illnesses. But they are all kind, caring women who have one thing in common: we love Clay Aiken. What other performer has had this amazing effect on his fans? Clay said very early during the *American Idol* experience that what he wanted most from life was to make a difference. I think he got what he wished for.

So if you're ever at a Clay Aiken concert, and you see a group of wild women, wearing purple, and probably even a feather boa and some outrageous beads and hats, and looking like they are having the time of their lives, it's a pretty safe bet that you're seeing a group of Lecherous Broads. If you ask them why they're having such a good time, they'll tell you, "It's all Clay Aiken's fault." It's his fault that we met, his fault that we travel all around the country (often alone!), his fault that maybe we spend a wee bit too much time on the computer, but most of all, it's his fault that we are having the most wonderful time of our lives.

My Favoritest *Idol* Ever

Emily Weaver
American Idol Fan

Garrett rushed into the family room and plopped himself down on the couch.

"Hurry," he yelled to us in the kitchen. "It's almost time!"

We brought in warm popcorn drizzled with melted butter for our Tuesday night ritual. My husband handed our four-year-old his own little bowl, a napkin, and glass of root beer, which Garrett carefully arranged on the coffee table.

"Sit down, Mommy!" he insisted. "You're going to miss *American Idol!*" Garrett's eyes gleamed as the familiar theme music blasted from the television.

We can't remember exactly when our preschooler became so enthralled with this reality show. We'd watched *American Idol* since Season 1, but it wasn't until sometime early in Season 4 that Garrett started to show interest.

At first, he enjoyed the music but didn't pay much attention to anything else. As the weeks progressed, however, it was evident that little Garrett was, in fact, a miniature Simon Cowell. No *Idol* evening was complete without his critique of each contestant.

"Aww, c'mon Carrie, what's with the hair?"

"Do you think Bo was a little pitchy, Mommy?"

"Was Mikalah singing or screaming?"

No contestant was safe from our little guy's "expert" opinion. No one, that is, except Scott Savol.

There was no question that Garrett was captivated by the teddy-bearish, soft-eyed, twenty-eight-year-old from Cleveland.

"He is my favoritest!" Garrett proclaimed after each of Scott's performances. "Simon better not say anything mean to him!"

Scott's performance of Phil Collins's "Against All Odds" was, without a doubt, the highlight of the season for Garrett. He just couldn't get enough of it. We had recorded the show, and he listened to his *Idol* singing the song over and over again.

On elimination night each week, Garrett literally held his breath in a dramatic show of support for Scott. And when Scott went safely to the next round, Garrett heaved a huge sigh of relief before running around the house in glee.

"Scott's safe! Scott's safe!" he yelled.

So, on the night of May 4, 2005, when Scott Savol was sent home, Garrett's world came crashing down.

"What just happened, Daddy?" he asked. "Did Scott get voted off?"

"Yes. I'm sorry, Garrett," his father said. "Scott has to go home now."

"Does that mean he's not going to sing next week?"

"That's what it means, son."

Garrett stood up and ran to his bedroom. He sat on the edge of the bed, covered his face with his hands, and cried.

"I'm going to miss him so much, Mommy!" Garrett

sobbed. "He was my favoritest *American Idol* of all!"

Startled at his emotional reaction, I tried to offer some comfort.

"I know he was your favorite, honey. But only one person can win."

"But it was supposed to be Scott," Garrett cried.

"Things don't always turn out the way we want them to," I told him. "We have to be thankful for all the times we were able to hear Scott sing."

"Did Simon make him go home, Mommy? I think it was Simon's fault."

"It wasn't Simon's fault, sweetheart," I said. "It's no one's fault. Scott did his very, very best, and we have to be proud of him for that."

Garrett wiped the tears from his little cheeks and drew in a deep breath. He tried his hardest to accept my words, be proud of Scott, and not cry anymore.

As the weeks passed, it seemed Garrett had forgotten the painful elimination of his favorite contestant. He still asked how many days it was until Tuesday. He still watched *Idol* every week. He still critiqued the remaining singers.

When the season ended and Carrie Underwood was crowned, Garrett begrudgingly praised the young singer. He didn't admit he'd grown to like the sweet and charming girl from Oklahoma, though the smile on his face lingered long after her last notes of "Inside Your Heaven" faded away.

Later that night, after we had tucked Garrett safely in bed, we thought we heard music coming from the family room. As we quietly crept to the edge of the door, we recognized the familiar strains of the Phil Collins tune. And there in the darkened room was Garrett, standing in front of the TV, watching in awe as his favorite *Idol* sang those familiar words.

"You were my favoritest *Idol* ever," he said to the TV. "I wish you would have been that one person who could win, but you tried your best."

Now it was our turn to cry as our son crept right up to the screen and cupped his hand next to his mouth as if to whisper a secret.

"Just so you know," he said softly, "I still think it was Simon's fault."

7

I GOTTA BE ME:
STORIES OF STAYING TRUE TO YOURSELF

Do not go where the path may lead, go
instead where there is no path and leave
a trail.

Ralph Waldo Emerson

The Body Shop

Bucky Covington
Top 10, Season 5

If you asked me what my favorite subject was in high school, I'd have to be honest and tell you flat out—it was lunch. I wasn't into the books very much. In fact, I wasn't into them at all. I didn't need to have my head buried in books and world maps because the map of my own life was already planned out for me. Carved in stone the day I was born, actually.

When I got out of high school, I'd head up Mill Road to the body shop where my grandpa and dad worked the 9-to-5 and did very well for themselves in our small town of Rockingham, North Carolina. My twin brother, Rocky, and I carried on the respected tradition of the Covington men. I couldn't break the tradition that had been in our family for over fifty years. They were counting on me to keep the shop growing, and the way I was raised in the South, you do what is expected of you and never disappoint the people you love—you just don't.

And so, I didn't.

Ten years passed, and one morning my faithful alarm

clock rang, as it did every morning. I woke to the silence of our small town. Not too much stirs at 7:30 here, other than the sound of an old dog barking or my mom's kettle whistling on the stove. My routine was the same as it had been for the past decade, and with each passing morning, I wrestled more and more with the thought of doing it again and again . . . *and again.*

I could practically do it with my eyes closed, and that feat of mastery bothered me every waking minute of every day. I took no pride in the simplicity of my life. Something was empty. Something was missing—for me, anyway.

This morning was no different in some respects. My thoughts were elsewhere as usual, and not on Mr. Thompson's '87 pickup that needed sanding in an hour.

But today, I was charged with excitement as I rolled out of bed and into the bathroom. I stood in front of the mirror, focused on one thing. *How do I tell my father that I have just learned the* American Idol *auditions have been moved from Memphis to our home state of North Carolina?* I had thought long and hard about going to Memphis, but the trip would've been too expensive, and there was no way I could leave my father shorthanded at the shop for over a week. But then yesterday my sister-in-law called . . .

"Bucky!" she said. "The auditions have been moved to Greensboro! You can go now!"

I knew at that very moment that everything in my life could change. Greensboro was just an hour away and I knew this was fate calling me. I took it as a sign. I'm not sure if it was an angel or the Big Man himself, but deep down, I knew what I had to do. It burned inside of me. My hands were willing to go sand that old truck, but my heart told me something very different. It told me to sing.

Back in the bedroom, my old shirt and shorts were lying in a heap on the floor. I threw them on and punched my fist into my dirty baseball cap. I went into the kitchen, packed myself a lunch, and headed out the back door, letting the old wooden screen slam behind me. I jumped into my beat-up Chevy truck, started it up with a pair of vice grips, and headed out onto the one road where I had spent my life—Mill Road. My entire family did everything on this road. Covingtons lived on it, worked on it, and raised families on it. As I pulled my truck onto the trusted blacktop, I could think of only one thing—to get as far away from Mill Road as I possibly could. Sure I loved it, but I knew in my heart there were bigger roads for me to travel, and I was praying my music would guide me to them.

I drove to Bojangles drive-thru and ordered my usual—a sausage biscuit with jelly and a large sweet tea. I sat in the parking lot listening to the morning DJ while I waited for Rocky to meet me. His truck pulled in, and together we headed to the dusty garage that housed four bays.

I sanded three cars that day, and all I could hear was the voice in my head, *I am done! Man, I got to get out of here!* It's funny because I loved the body shop. I loved working with my brother, father, and cousin. And yet, all the while, I'd just hear that voice, *Bucky, you gotta get out of here and go do music!*

I was counting on my father to understand my story because he had gone through it himself. He had been an amazing athlete and a great football punter back in high school. There was only one guy that could outpunt him in the state, and he ended up playing for the Washington Redskins. I only hoped my dad would understand as we sat down together.

It was the end of the day before we had a chance to talk. When I saw my dad putting away his tools after finishing up the last job, I took a deep breath and walked over to him.

"Dad, do you ever think back on your life when you played ball? Do you ever think that maybe you should've taken that chance and gone pro?"

My father didn't utter a word. He just looked me in the eye and listened.

"Do you ever look back and think maybe you should've tried, Dad? Maybe you should've taken that one chance?"

His eyes filled with tears. "My life is good, Bucky. I'm okay with it. I have three great kids. I'm very happy with what I've chosen."

"Dad, I just don't want to wake up one day when I'm forty years old and say, *What if? What if I had taken that chance and dared to leave the body shop?* I don't want that feeling haunting me for the rest of my life."

I remember the silence in the shop as I continued.

"Dad, I need a yes or no answer. Do you think I should go? Honestly, what do you really think my chances are if I go to Greensboro?"

He just looked at me. Then, wiping his dirty hands with a ripped-up old rag, my dad spoke slowly and from his heart.

"Bucky, not only do I think that you have as good of a shot as anybody, I think you've got to go. You can't stay here and wonder your whole life, son. You gotta listen to that voice inside of you and go. I'll be fine here at the shop. We'll manage. Walk out that door and go sing, Bucky. Just go!"

So I went. First I went home and packed a bag, then I loaded my truck, and, with my father's blessing, I drove slowly out of town on ol' Mill Road. I knew every crack in the pavement. I thought about all the balls I had caught on it, and all the bike racing I'd done on it. I headed down that trusted road and prayed my fate would be at the other end. Not knowing where the road would take me, I pulled my strength from my father's parting words:

"And Bucky, you're gonna be great."

Signed, Sealed, and Delivered

Sanjaya Malakar
Top 10, Season 6

Singing is everything to me and my sister. It's in our blood and in our souls.

The first time I remember performing was during an assembly when I was four. I sang, "I'm a Little Teapot." But my mom told me that I really preferred doing Fred Astaire dance moves and singing songs like, "Steppin' Out with My Baby." I guess I have an old soul. When you're hardly out of diapers, you usually prefer songs from *Barney*. I preferred songs from *Singin' in the Rain*. My mom said she thought maybe I was the incarnation of Fred Astaire.

I was never like everyone else in school either. I wasn't much of a student; I preferred to entertain. My second-grade teacher moved my desk outside the classroom because I would spontaneously burst into song and distract the other kids. She thought that if she put me where I could still hear her, but I didn't have an audience, I might be able to learn something. I don't think it worked, because school is still not my thing. If my sister gets a B, she feels like she's failed; if I get a C, I think, *Wow, cool. I passed.*

When I was eight we moved to Kauai, and my mom put us into Children's Theater. My first show was *Oliver!* and my second was *Bugsy Malone.* I played Fizzy the janitor. I had a solo, and every night when I would hit the high note, I would receive a standing ovation. You've gotta love that more than social studies.

At first, my mom didn't want me to audition for *Idol.* She thought I wasn't ready and that I should wait a year. I couldn't understand why; she'd always been so supportive of me, but I realize now that she somehow knew that once I stepped into the world of *American Idol,* I would never be able to just walk through a shopping mall or go to a concert or do any of those normal things ever again.

Before our first audition, while we were in the big arena, two ladies on the *American Idol* staff asked Shyamali and me if we were brother and sister. We told them we were, but we didn't audition together or make a big we're-brother-and-sister deal. We even had someone in line between us.

I didn't make it through the first round but my sister did. I love Shyamali so much and was so happy for her. I believe that there's a master plan, and I thought that my making it through just wasn't part of it.

Then the strangest thing happened.

Shyamali went in for her second audition with the executive producer, Nigel Lythgoe. When he put her through, he said, "So it looks like you're going to be in competition with your brother."

"No," she said. "Sanjaya got cut."

Nigel looked confused for a moment and then called over his assistant. After asking her some questions, he said, "What? Well, find him!"

Apparently, those ladies who had seen us in the arena had told him, "When you audition the Indian girl, she comes with a brother."

So I went in and sang for Nigel.

"You have to work on your stage presence," he said, "but I'm going to let you through."

I stood there in shock for a second and then ran out to tell my sister. We were ecstatic.

When I sang in front of Paula, Simon, and Randy, they asked who I thought was a better singer.

"Shyamali," I answered honestly. They said they thought she was the better performer, but I was the better singer. I still disagree. I have a more powerful voice, but my sister has this smooth, sultry jazz voice. She sings perfectly.

It was hard in Hollywood when I got through and my sister didn't, but I know that she'll be a star. She'll just get there in a different way—and I'll do everything in my power to help make that happen.

Throughout my journey on *Idol*, there have been a lot of ups and downs, triumphs and disappointments. But the hardest part has been the judges' comments. Nobody likes to hear, "You're horrible," or, "You look like a bush baby." Getting that kind of criticism night after night, week after week, could wear anybody down.

I decided that I wasn't going to let it get to me. Instead of taking their words to heart, I took the constructive criticism and left the rest. I just wouldn't put the negative things in my head. At a certain point I decided, *I'm going to do this for myself and the audience. I'm not even going to try to get the judges' votes. I'm just going to be myself and hope America likes me.*

I think America does. And that's good for a lot of reasons.

My mom says it's good because I don't represent the black community or the white community—but rather the brown community—which includes pretty much the majority of the people in the world. I think it's good for people to see someone like me. It's good for people in more isolated communities to feel like they know, and like, someone who is different from anyone they've ever met in their real lives.

And then there's my name. Sanjaya is Sanskrit, and the vibrational quality is supposed to bring to the person who speaks it the love and protection of the universe. So even when people say, "Sanjaya stinks; he should go home," they're drawing a good and positive vibration to themselves.

Who knows, I might even be making a difference for people on some higher level. I like that thought.

And one other thing . . . Stevie Wonder is my role model. He never let his apparent "disability" get in the way of his success, and he has always stayed true to himself in his life and his music. I wish I could have sung Stevie Wonder on the show, but the judges said it was too big for me. I think if I sang "Signed, Sealed, Delivered" they would have liked it—but it's cool. I have a long career ahead of me, and I know that someday, somewhere, I'll get to sing some Stevie. I think maybe I'll wear my pony hawk when I do.

The Real Kisha

LaKisha Jones
Top 10, Season 6

I started singing when I was five. Whenever our church needed someone to sing, my grandmother would pipe up, "Kisha will do it." When I'd refuse and start to cry, my grandma would tell me, "Just go up there and open your mouth." The more I did it, the more I liked it, and over time, singing became my passion.

As I got older, my grandma continued pushing me to sing, while my mom was saying I needed something to fall back on. So after high school, I went to the University of Michigan in Flint to major in vocal music. But the theory and technical stuff overwhelmed me, so I switched my major to theater. Midstream, I moved to Houston, where I changed majors again, this time to communications.

My life was busy between singing, studying, and working—and then, at age twenty-three, I found out I was pregnant. I got engaged to my baby's father—we'd been together for four years—but the relationship didn't work and I became a single mom. I realized that now I really had to finish college and acquire a skill to support myself and my daughter.

I switched majors yet again—this time to business. The classes were tough, and I began a long grind of working all day and going to school at night. Leaving at 6:00 in the morning and not getting home until 11:00 at night, I never saw my baby except when she was asleep. It broke my heart; it just wasn't right. So, I left college again.

In 2003, when my daughter was five months old, I tried out for *American Idol* in Houston and didn't make it past Nigel and Ken. They said I had a wonderful voice but told me that I wasn't what they were looking for.

What are they looking for? I wondered. *Everyone tells me that I have it, so what am I missing?*

Deeply discouraged, I vowed I'd never audition again. I figured I would just sing for church and weddings and that would be that. But a move to Baltimore and a teller job at a bank ended up sending me right back to *American Idol*.

After only a few days at my new bank job, I discovered that my assistant manager, Patrick, sang in a band. I went to hear him, and he was totally rocking out. He had heard that I sang, too, and began asking me to sing.

"I want you to sing for me, LaKisha," he begged. "Just let me hear you."

I said, "No. Not a chance."

But he wouldn't let up, so finally I sang Whitney Houston's "I Will Always Love You" for him. Patrick freaked out, and after I shared a DVD of my performance in a local contest, he and my other coworkers insisted, "You are going to audition for *American Idol!*"

"No, no, and no," I kept saying. None of them knew I'd already auditioned once before. *American Idol* had already told me that I wasn't what they were looking for, and I wasn't interested in giving them another opportunity to reject me.

I don't know the exact moment when I changed my mind, but I knew that my coworkers were not going to give up; so with the New York audition only a four-hour drive away, I said I'd do it. Patrick arranged time off for me—pretty nice of him, considering I'd only been at the job for a month! And since I didn't even have enough money for gas, Patrick gave me $100 and sent me on my way.

I arrived in New York late Friday night with my baby, and stood in line for eight hours. After that long wait, I was finally able to register on Saturday morning, but my audition time wasn't until Monday. So I drove back to Baltimore to work my five-hour shift on Sunday, got a little sleep, and left again after midnight to drive back to New York. Then I stood in line for eight more hours on Monday to get to audition.

When I got in, I sang "And I'm Telling You." The producer asked for something a little softer, so I sang "I Will Always Love You." Next, he asked me to sing something a little up-tempo. Then he said the magic words: "You're going through to the next round."

Since the second round was the next day and I couldn't sleep outside with my baby, a cousin arranged for us to sleep in the guest barracks of a military friend. The next morning, I traveled by subway and cab back to the audition and stood in line all day again—and made it through that round.

Amazingly, Ken and Nigel attended every second-round audition in every city—except the day I auditioned. That day, it was two other producers who put me through, telling me I'd need to come back two weeks later to face Randy, Paula, and Simon.

Going back to New York again to audition in front of the judges turned out to be a family affair—my mom, my aunt, my daughter, and my ninety-year-old grandma (who fell for Ryan Seacrest—and he for her!) all accompanied me.

"This is your time!" my family said with confidence.

And it was. After I sang, all three judges said, "Yes!" and after a tearful scene caught on camera with special hugs from my baby as I came out of the audition room, I was off to Hollywood!

I know what it's like to be a single, working parent, living with eviction notices and no electricity. Making it to Hollywood and then on to the Top 10, I now know that I can overcome anything. My making it here is a testimony to the power of faith, hope, and never giving up.

My grandmother is my role model. She taught me to be the best I could be and not to compromise myself. She would say, "Just always be the real LaKisha." That's why I don't turn it on and off on the show. I can't flash that big smile on cue or be perky when I'm down. That's just not me. What you see is who I am.

When I sang, "Diamonds Are Forever," people asked what it was like to have $650,000 of diamonds on my neck and another $300,000 in my hair.

I told them, "I felt like Kisha with jewelry on."

It's nice to have good things, but material things don't do it for me. I feel thankful for whatever I have, because I know that no matter how bad things get, there is always someone who has less. So I'm thankful for every little thing.

Of course, I'm thankful for *Idol*. Now I know I'll never again walk into a dark and cold apartment because the lights and heat have been shut off.

And I'm excited about going on the *American Idols Live!* tour. But at the end of the day, I just want to come back to my baby and have her jump all over me. That's what's really forever. That's the real Kisha.

Not a Bad First Step

Kevin Covais
Top 12, Season 5

People say I'm a really fun guy. It's not that I try to be; it's just who I am.

When I was twelve, I counted the months until I was old enough to audition for *American Idol*. The fall after my sixteenth birthday, I couldn't believe it when *American Idol* announced auditions in Boston, only a four-hour drive from Long Island where I lived.

I went to Boston with no expectations, accepting the reality that I was not a candidate for sexiest man alive. At 5'4" and a kind of pale juvenile diabetic, I knew I was no Bo Bice or Constantine Maroulis. Gosh, I wasn't even a Clay Aiken—which is pretty scary. But when you aren't going thinking you're a shoo-in, if you don't make it, the sky doesn't fall on you.

Before I auditioned in front of the judges, I got a haircut. I asked for a trim, but the guy mowed my head. I looked like I just got back from the Marines. As soon as I walked into the room, Simon had this "you've-got-to-be-kidding" look on his face.

After I sang, Paula and Randy said they loved me. Simon said, "I think only people over the age of eighty will love him."

Wow, that's so cool, I thought. *I can go home and get my grandma to rally the troops.*

It wasn't a clean sweep but I got through—not a bad first step for the kid who is now known throughout the country for his uncanny resemblance to Chicken Little.

When I got through to Hollywood, the first song I chose to sing was, "If I Ever Fall in Love." I was petrified—much more than at my auditions back in Boston. I remember thinking, *I'll just go up and grip the mic really hard and plant my feet.* I never moved. I just bopped my body up and down.

When I was done, Randy said, "I loved what you did with the mic, dawg. And your body, man, that was a great game plan."

I was smart enough to smile and say thanks instead of admitting I had no game plan. I wasn't moving because I was numb.

As I progressed through each audition during Holly-wood Week, I never thought I was the best, but I felt as though it was one of those destiny things. My two most distinct memories are of being hungry and thinking, *This growing boy needs some chicken noodle soup,* and of sitting in the back of the room by myself thinking, *Everyone else looks like they're at a big party I wasn't invited to.* That is, until the day Ace Young came over to me for no other reason than that he's a great guy and invited me to be part of the party. He took me around and introduced me to everyone. It was like being best friends with the prom king.

A recurring pattern with *American Idol* and me was that I was always last. It was no different the day I had to walk The Green Mile to find out if I had made it into the Final 24.

The judges said no to the first ten people. All of 'em.

Every time someone came out of the elevator, the rest of us would say, "Wow. That's really too bad, man. Terrible."

But, of course, in my mind, I'm thinking, *Score! One more spot left for the kid.* Finally, when it was time for me to go in, it was down to three of us, and only one was going through.

When I walked into the room, Simon just laughed—a laugh that said, "This is so funny that you're still here."

Then he said, "Well, this was a really, really, really, really, really, really, really tough decision. But the answer to whether you're in the Top 24 . . . is . . . yes."

And, with that, my life as a sex symbol began.

The most fun part of this whole thing has been getting my cheeks pinched. And I haven't minded the Chicken Little thing one bit. People ask if I was okay with the split screen showing me on one half and Chicken Little on the other during the show. The producers were great guys; they asked if I felt it would be disrespectful or hurt my feelings.

I said, "If you can't have fun, then what's the point?"

It's kind of ironic that after every performance I thought I was going home, except for the night I was actually voted off. That time I thought I had done my best. Although I didn't make it into the Top 10, to be with this class of singers has been a great honor.

It's amazing how my life has changed. One day people don't know you and then the next day almost 60 million people tune in, watch you, and develop feelings about you. They love you, they don't love you—but either way, they're talking about you. It's really like nothing else to be a part of this *American Idol* experience and go from being a regular kid in high school to being "Kevin Covais."

Everywhere I go now, I get recognized—it's something I've had to accept as part of my life. I have to wear hats and shades sometimes to be incognito, although I'm barely riding the D list.

One day I went to Jones Beach with my friends to catch some rays—although I just go from white to burn, then back to white. We spread out our towels and I said, like, one word to my friends, and from twenty feet away, this dude looks up and shouts, "Is that Kevin Covais?" Next thing I know, I have this little autograph session going that lasted pretty much all afternoon.

Another time I was waiting for a plane, with my disguise in place, when some guy from the other side of the room yelled, "Yo, Chicken!" I mean, if he's going to yell from the other side of the room, he could've at least used my full title.

And now I'm costarring in a movie. A movie star, a sex symbol, *and* Chicken Little, too. Now *this* is really getting to be fun.

The Best Birthday Gift of All

Anwar Robinson
Top 10, Season 4

But my birthday is tomorrow. That's all that played in my
mind the night I was eliminated from Season 4 of *American
Idol*—not necessarily because birthdays are a big deal to
me, but because that was the first and only night my
mother and baby sister were in the audience throughout
my entire time on *Idol*. They chose that night to come to
Los Angeles all the way from New Jersey, because the next
day was my birthday. They came to celebrate.

All I could think to do when Ryan Seacrest announced
that I would be going home was to look my sister in the
eye and tell her not to cry. Her tears were ready to roll,
and I didn't want the cameras to capitalize on her pain. I
knew why she was crying; the angst that she, my mom,
my brother, and other family members were feeling was
because they assumed I was devastated by Ryan's words,
especially since the next day was my special day.

After the show, I was the guest of honor at the good-bye
dinner, but my mind was focused on returning to my
room to gather all the things I had brought to Hollywood

with me. Midnight and my twenty-sixth year arrived faster than I liked.

In my room, I packed my huge bags and said good-bye to my roommates. I knew I wouldn't sleep much, and I had to wake up again in just a few hours.

I also knew what was in store for me at 5:00 AM.

After a contestant is voted off *American Idol*, the following morning is spent being interviewed by almost fifty news stations. I would be sharing my thoughts on why the music teacher, said to be "technically the best singer," had just been eliminated.

Instead of giving in to my lack of sleep, I retained my composure throughout the interviews. "Once you get down to the Top 12," I explained, "the voters have picked out their favorite or favorites—and everyone is a strong contender at that point."

I mentioned my birthday in an attempt to ward off the interviewers trying their hardest to get me to speak negatively about my cohorts or the show. I refused to take the bait. Finally, after sitting in front of the cameras for about four hours, it was time to eat.

That's when the reality hit me like a steel wrecking ball.

I couldn't eat—which is very unusual for me, since I've been known to have a voracious appetite—because something just didn't feel right inside.

The burden of holding back my feelings throughout the whole elimination ordeal weighed heavily on my spirit. I tried my best to retain my composure. I managed to hold it together until I got back to the hotel room, and there I allowed myself to accept the reality that this part of my journey was really over.

The tears rolled down my cheeks as the faces of my loved ones ran through my mind. Most difficult was the thought of all the people in my life reeling in disappointment that day, especially my students back home. It was hard for me to handle the sadness and disappointment I knew they were experiencing.

Sometimes you can feel when a major shift is about to take place in your life, and about three weeks prior to my elimination, I had sensed something was changing for me. Many people saw my smile in images across the media, and I knew my life's journey included being on *Idol*. However, I started going through an internal examination to determine *what* role *Idol* played in my life. Why was I *really* there?

That morning it finally became clear—and I received what turned out to be the best birthday gift of all.

On my twenty-sixth birthday, I realized how much it meant to me to inspire young people, my students, my community, and friends and family, and how much I wanted them all to feel like they were a part of something big, something exciting. In spite of my heavy heart, I saw that I didn't need to be "the" *American Idol* to achieve this.

I didn't have to go any further or stay any longer. I had already gotten what I came for. It was time to move on.

Where Have You Been?

LaToya London
Top 10, Season 3

I'm a different me now than when I was on *American Idol*.
That was the prim and proper LaToya—the one who was
brought up to be poised and articulate. The one who actually went to finishing school.

I'm happy America liked my singing enough to put me
through each week, since I'm not at all sure they liked my
conservative personality. In fact, I'm not sure I liked my
conservative personality!

I was going through a time in my life where I was trying to figure out who LaToya truly was, and I kept to
myself during *Idol*—not wanting to say or do the wrong
thing. I lay low most of the time and never got that buddy-
buddy with anyone—although now I'm closer than ever
with Fantasia, Jennifer, George, and Jasmine. Back then,
we all looked at it as a competition.

I sometimes wonder if being the demure, sophisticated
LaToya may have hurt me a bit—not that I'm complaining
about making it all the way to Number 4! But I don't think
people could relate to me like they could to a lot of the other

contestants who showed more personality and feeling.

That might even be why I didn't get a lot of "airtime" during the preliminary rounds. I remember when I performed for the first time in front of the judges as one of the Top 32, all three of them were like, "Where have you been?"

If I were on the show now it would be a whole different story. I'd unleash the real LaToya and not be afraid to do or say the wrong things. I've learned that we're all human, and it's okay to be vulnerable. And as I've gotten older, I've become more comfortable with who I am. I'm not afraid anymore to be open and let people see the real me, and as a result, my life is so much richer. People meet me today and say, "You're so different from the person we thought you were on *American Idol*." And they're right.

That's why stepping into the role of Nettie in the Broadway musical *The Color Purple* has been the most natural thing in the world—I can feel Nettie and relate to her. She's a lot like who I am now. She's alive, vibrant, and hopeful—she's just a whippersnapper. She speaks her mind, she doesn't stand for nonsense, and if you need telling, she'll tell you where to go and how to get there!

On *American Idol*, I played the role of LaToya London, the poised and elegant. Now I'm playing the role of Nettie, the feisty and optimistic. What do they say about art imitating life?

So time goes on, with many lessons learned. And as I continue to grow and change as a person and entertainer, I know I'll look back in a few years on what I'm doing now and think, *I wouldn't want to change a thing.* I'm me and loving it!

I'm sure there's a lot more to discover about who I am. One thing I've learned that they don't teach you in finishing school—you're never really finished. There's always room to grow. But whatever comes my way in the future, I just want to be true to me. There's no one else I'd rather be.

Now I Know

Blake Lewis
American Idol Runner-up Season 6

Okay, I've got a big confession to make: I knew practically nothing about *American Idol* before I auditioned. I didn't know millions tuned in each week. I didn't know they had theme nights and celebrity mentors and guest judges. I didn't even know who had won when or who won what.

I just didn't know.

I didn't know about the night the three divas—Jennifer, Fantasia, and LaToya—were in the Bottom 3, or about Constantine's rebellious rock. I didn't know Carrie Underwood grew up on a farm. I would have totally come in last place in an *Idol* trivia game.

Honestly, I had never even seen a full episode before I auditioned.

Oh, I'd caught a performance or two as I walked by the TV at a friend's house. I remember watching Elliott Yamin. He had that neo-soul sound I love. He knew who he was as a vocalist. I liked him a lot.

Other than that, I didn't have a perception about

American Idol one way or the other. Well, maybe I did—I thought it was a bit cheesy. But, hey, I didn't know.

My friend Josh called me the night before the auditions hit Seattle. "Hey! The *American Idol* auditions are tomorrow. You have to come!"

I thought it over a bit and asked myself, *Why not?* After all, I had the same chance as anybody else. I had nothing to lose. I had just quit my job doing construction to focus on music full-time and was living with my family again. I told myself, *If you make it, you make it. If you don't, you don't.*

There was only one problem—I missed the registration. I was a bit disappointed, but later that night I was playing a show at the Triple Door in Seattle, and Josh called me again.

"Hey, I just went to Key Arena and registered for *American Idol*. You can go there right now. There's no one in line," he said. "It will take you two seconds and then tomorrow morning I'll pick you up at five, we'll make some sandwiches, and we'll go audition."

I didn't realize it was a conversation that would change my life forever.

The next few months were pretty much a blur. They were so full, so exciting, so packed that the details get all mashed together in my mind. I did some beat-boxing—that I know—and I did a lot of singing. I met some of my biggest inspirations, which was awesome.

It was cool to sing with Rudy Cardenas again. We'd been in two different Seattle-based a cappella groups—Kickshaw was mine and M-Pact was his. Rudy was the friend I could trust, the friend I confided in. My low point hit when he got cut from the Top 24.

I had a great time writing a song with Chris Sligh and playing guitar with my man Chris Richardson. But even when it was down to the Top 10, I still didn't really understand what the *American Idol* experience meant, outside of the little bubble we lived in as contestants day and night.

Then I made it into the Top 3, and flew back to Seattle to film the homecoming piece for the show. When I landed at Boeing Field, I started to get it. That's when I finally began to understand. To *know*.

Everywhere I went, there were hordes of people. Westlake Center was packed; people filled the plaza. Seeing all of those faces, those fans, those friends—all those who came to see me, to appreciate my art—that was really tight. And my mom and dad were there, of course.

I was getting it.

I met Pat Monahan of Train. I beat-boxed with Sir Mix-A-Lot. We hit all the FOX affiliates for TV interviews and went to four different radio stations. I had a house party with seventy friends. It was all incredible and overwhelming.

On the return flight, I sat and thought about it all. You see, I put myself and my goals out there to the universe all the time. I believe that things happen for a reason, and if you project yourself in a positive way and just be true to yourself, then good things will come back to you.

Just hold on and stay true, even through times of struggle. Never stop imagining, wishing, and planning. Someday those wishes will start to take shape. It's amazing. It works. For me, *American Idol* was absolute proof, validating that it can happen to anyone.

Trust me; I know.

Now I really, really know.

Pens, Anyone?

Jon Peter Lewis
Top 10, Season 3

I grew up assuming I'd be in the music business.

My dad was in a '60s group called the Marketts. "Outer Limits" was their one big hit that made it all the way to number three on the pop charts. Eventually, he left the group and got out of the business. The remaining guys went on to become Paul Revere and the Raiders.

My dad still loved music and always made sure there was music in our house. When he came home from work, he'd sit at the piano while we seven kids ran around singing at the top of our lungs. Music was always the most fun thing in the world for me.

In 2003, I was living in Montana, working for a theater company. I was twenty-four, living with friends, and getting paid to do something fun. You'd think it would have been a great time in my life. In reality, I was at a pretty low point. I was a bit lost and trying to figure out what I wanted for myself.

One night I came home from working at the theater, and I just wanted to sit down, relax, and watch a movie.

When I flipped on the VCR, it didn't work. For some reason, I just snapped. All the frustration I'd been feeling culminated in a little drama—I held the VCR high over my head and bashed it to pieces in front of me. Needless to say, it definitely didn't work then.

The next day, I went out and got a new VCR. I brought it home, set it up, and was so excited to test out my new pride and joy that I just grabbed every random tape within arm's reach.

While I didn't live in total isolation, I had been living in Spain for the two previous years and hadn't been back home for very long. So when I put in the first tape, I had no idea what I was watching. At first it seemed like some kind of star-studded variety show, except I didn't recognize any of the stars. For some reason, I couldn't stop watching it. I was absolutely mesmerized by this skinny, spiky-red-haired guy and this big smiley guy they called the "Velvet Teddy Bear." Both had amazing voices and were decked out in awesome threads. I figured out it was some kind of contest and all the other people on the stage had been in the contest also, but now it was down to these two guys. The big guy won.

That tape of the Season 2 Finale was my introduction to *American Idol*.

I can do that, I thought.

I immediately went on the Internet, looking to see how one gets to audition for this show. I figured this would be the one time I would give the music business a shot. But when I saw the dates, my heart sank. All were during the summer, the height of the theater season, and I had commitments for the next two months that I couldn't break. But I knew I had to find a way!

I went downstairs and watched the tape again, and then went back to my computer to recheck the dates. Strangely, I noticed something I'd missed before. Several months later, in the fall, there were going to be auditions in Hawaii.

Now, Montana to Hawaii is a trek, and I didn't have any money, but I was so determined that I took out a school loan (which I did pay back). I flew off without telling my family where I was going or why. In Hawaii, I stayed with some relatives and didn't even tell them why I was there. Because I thought auditions lasted one day, I had packed only three sets of clothes; one for the audition, one for church, and one for the beach.

Dressed for the audition, I made my way to Aloha Stadium where, along with thousands and thousands of others singers, I waited a day and a half for my chance to sing in front of the first producer. Happy doesn't come close to how I felt when he put me through to the next round. But when he told me to come back the next day, he added, "Dress to impress." *Great. Should I wear my church clothes, my beach clothes, or the ones I've been wearing now for almost two days?*

I had no money to buy anything new, so I had no choice but to wear my white shirt, navy dress pants, and tie. Little did I know those clothes would define me for the rest of my *American Idol* career.

When I sang for the executive producers, they commented on my shirt and tie but put me through in spite of the church look. Next, I had to face Simon, Randy, and Paula.

At that point, I was so nervous I was numb. Walking into the audition room, I braced myself, knowing that I looked a little different than the people around me. The first thing Simon said was that I looked like a pen salesman. That moment was replayed throughout the entire season, and to this day people say to me, "Hey, aren't you that pen salesman from Season 3?"

Call me what you will, when I was done singing, Randy said, "Absolutely yes."

Paula compared me to Aaron Neville and said, "Yes."

Simon shrugged his shoulders and said, "I guess I bought the pen."

Some say that I was the first *American Idol* contestant to be successful doing a performance-driven number when I sang "A Little Less Conversation" by Elvis. Until that point, it was mostly pure voice that carried people through, and I didn't want to be a balladeer. So, one day while I was rocking out to Elvis during a rehearsal, I thought, *Wouldn't it be fun to do something like this on the show?*

Debra Byrd, our vocal coach, would never tell us what we should or shouldn't sing. But if you were attentive, you could read between the lines and hear what she was thinking. So, when I sang the Elvis song during rehearsal, she said that she loved my dancing around. Since she didn't comment on any of my other songs that day, I knew, *That's the one.*

If Byrd likes it, I thought, *I bet America will, too.*

America voted and, sure enough, they loved it. That was the week they picked me as the Wild Card choice.

After that, jumping around and being a goofball became my thing. It may not sound that great, but I'm really proud of it. It was something different, and people liked it.

The night before I was eliminated, although I thought I'd given a great performance and had never been in the Bottom 3, I woke in the middle of the night from a dream. In my dream, Patrick Lynn, one of the producers, was sitting at the foot of my bed with his laptop. He looked up at me and said, "You're leaving."

The next night, Diana DeGarmo, John Stevens, and I were in the Bottom 3. Because she'd been in the Bottom 3 four weeks in a row, I was certain Diana was the one going home. But when she was sent back to the couch and we went to commercial break, Deb Williams, our stage manager, came over to John and me and said, "Whoever goes home, when you sing your last song, just go out and have a good time."

At that moment, I knew it was me.

John had sung a soft and slow Barry Manilow song that didn't exactly lend itself to a good time. So I thought to myself, *All right, I will have a good time!* So when Ryan said, "JPL, you're going home," I had the time of my life!

With all the pressure gone, I really cut loose.

All through *Idol*, I'd had the urge to jump off the stage and run around the audience—that was the year before they put the platform out—so I jumped down and I probably flipped out the camera crews, but I just made my way rocking through the aisles. I saw my dad, pulled him out of his seat, and danced with him. As I headed back, I fulfilled another fantasy. I'd always dreamed of rolling onto the stage. I don't know what zone I was in, but I went for it. I dove onto the stage, rolled over, ended on my feet . . . and said good-bye to America.

And that was that.

Nowadays, I'm still, as Randy might say, "doing my thing." I have a great band, a CD I'm proud of, and many more on the horizon. I also hear that my roll-up moment gets lots of hits on YouTube.

And fortunately, I haven't had to start selling pens . . . yet.

8

WITH A LITTLE HELP FROM MY FRIENDS:
STORIES OF THOSE WHO HELP US THROUGH

*K*eep away from people who try to belittle
your ambitions. Small people always do that,
but the really great make you feel that you,
too, can become great.

Mark Twain

'Til Death Do Us Part

Sherman Pore
Auditioner

My lady and I never liked the Denny's in L.A. We'd drive all the way out to the one in Canyon Country because the atmosphere there is much better. On one of our drives I think she had a premonition. She didn't know yet that she had cancer, but she was looking out the window and said to me kind of quietly that she felt like she hadn't accomplished anything in her life. I told her, neither had I. We drove the rest of the way in silence, each of us kind of reflecting on our own.

I met Melissa twenty years ago when we were doing *South Pacific* in community theater. It was the only play I'd ever been in. She was one of the singing nurses and I was Captain Bracket. Mine wasn't a singing part, which was too bad because I love to sing. I sing everywhere I go. I sing when I drive. I sing in line at the bank. That's just what I do.

When Melissa was in the hospital, everyone knew when I'd arrived because I'd be singing when I came down the hallway. I knew it made her smile even before I got to her room. It would make the other patients happy, too—and the doctors and nurses. I felt like it was the only thing I could do to ease my lady's pain. I had to do something for her. I felt so helpless. The hospital became my home. They set up a cot for me in her room. I'd go to work during the day and come back home to her at night.

It was her idea for me to audition for *American Idol,* even though she thought I was too good for it. I told her that I was singing in line at the market when someone said to me, "You are amazing! You should try out for *American Idol.*" When I told him I was too old—the age limit was twenty-eight, and I was sixty-four—everyone in line started saying, "That's not fair!" Back at the hospital I told Melissa what happened, and she also thought that it wasn't fair. So, as sick as she was, the day before they moved her from the hospital to the care home, she started working on a petition asking *American Idol* to make an exception to the rule.

She organized everyone in the hospital to sign my petition, which they did because they all loved my singing, and they loved her. Then she pushed me out the door and said I had to go and get more signatures. I went across the street to a pizza parlor and told the manager that I had a petition I'd like her to sign so I could get on *American Idol.* I said that I didn't want her to sign it just because of my age, but only if she liked my singing. So she had me sing for her customers right then and there, and everyone in the whole restaurant signed my petition. Then she went next door to another restaurant to get signatures and came back and said, "They won't sign unless you go and sing for them." So I went and sang there, and everyone in that whole restaurant signed it too. I was up to almost 100 signatures.

A few days later I went to the Rose Bowl where they were holding the *American Idol* auditions. The line outside must have been 40 people wide and 500 people long.

When I got in line, everyone assumed I was there to support another contestant. So I made an announcement that I was there to be a contestant and was looking to get my petition signed. People started yelling, "You have to sing first!" so I did, and then they all wanted to sign. When we got inside the Bowl, people were shouting to me from five aisles away that they wanted to sign my petition. It was so exciting, and I would have given anything for Melissa to have been there to experience it all.

I didn't get in to sing the first day, so I overnighted my letter and petition to the *American Idol* office. They would have received it on Thursday, and that was the day that Melissa started having serious trouble breathing. They transferred her from the care home back to the hospital, and I slept that night on my cot next to her bed. My hand was on hers, and as she fell asleep I sang to her "(I'll Be Loving You) Eternally." In the morning, Melissa died. A few hours later, I got the call that they wanted me back at the Rose Bowl on Sunday.

I wasn't feeling much like going, even though this was Melissa's dream, and she had gotten so many signatures at the hospital and the care home. I knew she really wanted this for me, but I didn't feel much like getting off the couch. So I asked Melissa to show me a sign.

Next thing I knew, I walked over to the bookcase and found a pile of greeting cards I had saved that we had sent each other over the years.

One card fell out of the pile.

It had a picture on the front of two little country kids. It said, "Take my hand," and when you opened it up, it said, "Tomorrow is waiting for us." Underneath I had written to her, "You light up my life," and put musical notes around it. I remembered the card, but in my mind the two kids were walking side by side. This time when I looked at it, I saw that the little boy was looking down, and the little girl was a few steps ahead of him and turned around with her hand held out, as if to say, "I'll help you."

That was all I needed. I guess everyone knows what ended up happening—on Sunday, I stood there in front of Paula, Randy, and Simon, and I sang a song dedicated to my lady. They liked it so much they put my audition on TV.

What most people don't know is that two gentlemen who heard me sing on the show called me up and offered me a record contract. The reason they thought I could be really popular was that one of them was sitting in the hospital with his wife who just had twins, and when she heard me singing on the TV, she just started crying, and then his mom called the hospital because she had heard me, and she was crying, too! It was the same hospital that Melissa had just been in.

And when I went to the office building to meet these gentlemen and sign my contract, it turned out to be the same building where Melissa had worked. I recognized it because I used to pick her up there. She did calendaring for a law firm, and had tried so darn hard to work even after she got sick. She never wanted to let anyone down.

Well, one person she never let down was me. I know her last few days on earth were happier because she saw me pursuing this dream. She knew I never would have thought to do the petition or gotten all those signatures without her encouraging me.

And I know she's still helping me and guiding me every day from wherever she is now. In fact, in some ways I feel closer to her than ever. People ask me why Melissa and I never got married, and I have always given the same answer: "It's not that we didn't love each other more than anything; we just never wanted to have to say, 'Til death do us part.'"

Everyone's Girl

Paris Bennett
Top 10, Season 5

Of all of the roles I played in high-school musicals, my favorite was Dorothy in *The Wiz*. Just like Dorothy, I wished I could go to a sparkling city and have a wizard make my dream come true.

Oh, my dream wasn't to find my way home. I had a wonderful home with a loving mom and grandparents, and even my great-grandparents were always there for me. But I wanted the Wiz to make me a "Daddy's Girl."

"That's a cool shirt," I said to my friend when she showed up at school wearing a brown T-shirt with "Daddy's Girl" spelled in bright pink. I wondered whether her dad had picked it out, or if she'd bought it for herself. I wondered if he knew her favorite color was pink.

It was a cool shirt, and so were all the "Daddy's Girl" things my friends had: mirrors and notebooks and picture frames that held photos of them hugging their dads.

When we all started going to school dances during my freshman and sophomore years, I could just see the pride in the dads' eyes when they looked at their daughters all dressed up and looking so fine. As their baby girls walked off hand in hand with their dates, I could just tell that those girls didn't have to figure out the boyfriend thing on their own.

In high school, I tried to be in all the plays and talent shows—partly because I loved to sing, but also because after the shows were over, everyone would tell me, "Paris, you were so good!" Some of the dads would even say, "I am really proud of you, Paris," and I'd feel like a Daddy's Girl for a brief moment. Then I'd watch everyone climb into cars with their dads and head off to some restaurant or ice-cream shop to celebrate.

And so I continued down the yellow brick road of life, hoping one day I'd find the Wiz who could make me a Daddy's Girl.

On *Idol*, I was grateful to be voted through week after week, but still, I had an empty place in my heart, especially when I'd look into the audience and see Lisa and Katharine's dads all choked up over their girls.

Then, one day, I landed in Oz.

The day that was a turning point for me started out like any other *American Idol* day; lots of rehearsing, working on wardrobe, being tutored, eating, and waiting. Then I went to a session we were having with Miss Byrd, the vocal coach for all of the *Idol* contestants. I felt so close to her and loved her talks. As always, she was so positive. She talked about the impact that we as contestants have on people's lives, and how that impact goes beyond our singing. She said this *Idol* experience is bigger than we can even imagine.

I have so much to be thankful for, I thought. *Why do I even let myself dwell on the fact that I'm not a Daddy's Girl?*

Then something in me simply clicked—just like Dorothy's ruby slippers. I remembered the moment Dorothy discovered she didn't need the Wiz or anyone else to help her. She'd *always* had the power to go home. And in that moment I realized that I, too, had always had everything I wanted all along—and more!

I could have had a T-shirt that said "Ace, Taylor, and Elliot's Girl" and worn it any day of the week. They would have been *proud* for me to wear it.

Rickey Minor and the band members—all of them— were my musical family. If I was having a bad day, I couldn't wait until I'd get to rehearsal; they'd have me laughing in no time. I knew I was Rickey's Girl!

And it even went beyond that. Mandisa was the auntie I had never had. Kellie and Katharine always had a joke for me. And Lisa and I were so close. Even though we're opposites—she's book-smart, I'm street-smart—I knew we would always be best friends.

As I sang my song onstage that night, I looked out into the audience, and there was Lisa's dad and there was Katharine's dad, and they were crying—for me!

I had been wearing the ruby slippers all along, but that day I finally clicked them together. My heart was so full when I realized that, even better than being a Daddy's Girl, I was Everyone's Girl!

The Judges of Judson High

Allison Pittman
American Idol Fan

I loved those Wednesday mornings. . . .

Thirty minutes before the first bell rang, and the high-school hallways were still empty. No sign of the slamming lockers and shouted conversations. No exuberant teenagers on their way to their first-period class.

With a fresh cup of questionable coffee in my hand, I would make my way down the hall from the teacher's lounge. No one in sight—except for Jennifer.

Tall, blonde, and beautiful, she stood by her classroom door, hands waving, shouting to me, "Did you watch?"

Did I watch? Of course I watched.

Immediately we were immersed in a deep, meaningful conversation. I heard another voice from around the corner.

"Oh . . . my . . . gawd. Do you believe last night?!"

It was Yoli, of course. Petite and pretty, with a sharp tongue and an impeccable manicure, Yoli launched herself into the debate as though we were all discussing the demise of the world as we knew it.

"Wait a minute, girls. Don't start talking without me!"

Carol, the conscience of the group, arrived to make our little circle complete. And now the conversation flew:

"What was she thinking, wearing that dress?"

"If he gets voted off, I'm never watching again."

"I didn't think the human voice could produce that sound!"

"Wasn't Simon crueler than usual?"

"What does 'cabaret' mean?"

To look at us, you could well imagine a cartoon scene: puffs of dust, hairpins flying, thousands of words converging into near-hysteric babble. Pity the poor innocent who walked past our little group. While most of our fellow faculty learned to simply shake their heads and keep on walking, every now and then the occasional neophyte would be compelled to stop.

And listen.

And ask.

"What are you people talking about?"

At which point, we would answer in a perfect harmony rarely achieved by contestants even during the Finale ensemble performance.

"*American Idol!*"

With a sigh, the poor victim would shuffle away, having the nerve to pity us.

Throughout our years as the unofficial *American Idol* faculty commentators of Judson High, the four of us developed a deep bond. When we absolutely couldn't stand to wait for our morning chitchat, we sent e-mails with a preview of coming attractions for the next morning's rant. For five solid months I signed myself off as Mrs. Taylor Hicks.

Then our little *Idol* universe changed forever.

In the spring of 2006, Yoli moved to a different campus. Jennifer moved to a different city. I moved back home to pursue writing full-time.

When January rolled around, I had to watch the early rounds without my comrades to confer with the next morning. I resorted to following my husband and sons through the house, making them talk to me about which contestant was bad and which was horrible.

After I watched the Hollywood round with no one but myself to talk to, I began bribing my children with ice cream to sit and watch with me. After the first night of the Top 24, I could take it no longer; I went to my computer, and like a voice crying out in the wilderness wrote:

"TO: Jennifer, Yoli, Carol

SUBJECT: *Idol*, anyone?

Hey—are y'all watching? You wanna talk? How much do you love Melinda?"

And, oh, the replies! RE: after RE: after RE: after RE: And I didn't have to look beyond the subject line to know who penned each message. Jennifer still held the authority as the only true musician among us. Yoli still cut through with her sharp tongue. Carol still loved everybody and made us all feel bad for being mean.

Me? I kept every message, even as they got longer and longer, creating an e-mail trail that spanned twenty pages.

Now, instead of hanging around a deserted high-school hallway to listen for footsteps and hollered greetings, I get up Wednesday mornings, make a bowl of cereal, turn on my computer, and drink it all in—the jokes, the nicknames, and the outrage. The voices of my friends echo on my screen as I see their faces—smiling, laughing, and tearful—illuminated in the monitor's light.

Ready to Rock

Haley Scarnato
Top 10, Season 6

I was always happiest when I was singing. Music came from deep inside and was just a natural expression of my heart and soul. Singing was where I felt best about myself.

I guess that's why the most difficult thing for me on *American Idol* was always the judges' comments. Often, they wouldn't be just about my singing, but about me personally. It's tough being judged for who you are. I felt like, *I'm delivering me and you're not accepting me,* and that was hard.

I wanted to stay true to myself, but I also wanted the judges to like me, and I began to take it personally when they didn't. I know they never tried to hurt me intentionally, but their words did hurt. And as the weeks went by, it got emotionally exhausting.

I know the judges didn't like it the night I cried. But when they finally said something good about me, I just lost it.

Singing has always been an emotional experience for me. I fell in love with it when I was ten. I was a gymnast at the time, and I remember I loved to sing while I tumbled.

Not entire songs, just notes and runs, just for the fun of it.

One of my teammates kept telling me I should take singing lessons from her aunt, so eventually I did. I loved the lessons, and that was that. I was hooked!

In high school, I performed in community theater and sang in the choir. When I graduated, I had no interest in going to college; I just wanted to sing. So I went to New York, auditioned for *RENT*, got a few callbacks, tried to get a record deal, and had a few bites from record companies . . . but nothing panned out. I sang with a band. I sang and danced at Six Flags in various shows including the Monster Mash Bash Halloween Show. In 2003, I auditioned for *Idol* and didn't even make it in to see the producers.

I enjoyed most of the gigs I played, but one of my most unusual gigs was at Sea World. *Shamu Rocks* was a wonderfully fun and magical show starring the world's most famous whale. Other than the trainers, I was one of the first entertainers to ever stand on the stage—so close I could practically reach out and touch the whales. I sang a rock ballad, and every night when I'd hit the high note, Shamu would breach out of the water and come crashing back down with a huge splash right on cue! The audience went wild every time he did it.

I loved those summer nights. The experience was just so sweet and innocent. I wasn't trying to get anyone's vote—and Shamu didn't care about what I wore. He didn't even care if I was pitchy or old-fashioned. He never thought I was forgettable—he breached every time, right on cue. He simply loved my high note, and everyone else loved us both.

I know this sounds corny, but I swear Shamu would smile at me when he came out of the water and slid onstage—or maybe he was just hungry. The show may have been called *Shamu Rocks*, but I think we rocked it together!

It's All Perfect

Charles Boyd
Supervising Producer

After having been a producer on *Pop Idol* in England, I was invited to come to the States for a six-week stint to work on the brand new U.S. version, *American Idol.* They hired me to work on the scripts and to coach the hosts, Ryan Seacrest and Brian Dunkleman.

The show was not yet a known quantity, so it was still a big question mark as to whether or not it would be a hit. Then the six weeks turned into a whole season, which turned into Season 2, which turned into Season 3, and then into Season 4 . . .

Meanwhile, I had a house in London, and a lady waiting there to whom I was engaged and had been with for seven years. Long-distance relationships are difficult, especially when you're almost on the other side of the globe. As a result, during the Christmas vacation before Season 4, I went back to England and we decided to part ways.

I remember the day when Michelle, the production coordinator, told me that she had someone she wanted to introduce me to. I said, "No. No. Absolutely not. I just finished a seven-year relationship and I . . ." And then I saw Dana out in the hallway. I fell head-over-heels on the spot but, silly me, I still resisted. She resisted, too. She was in fund management, and the last thing she wanted was to be with someone in the entertainment industry. I just "wasn't the kind of person she wanted to get involved with."

Now we've been married for two years. But that's all background. The story I really want to tell begins the moment I found out Dana was pregnant.

When she shared the news with me, I couldn't have been more excited, but I immediately counted the months to see if the birth would fit into the *American Idol* show schedule.

Let's see . . . it's August now, so that means . . . one month, two months, three. . . . That makes the due date around May 4th. Not ideal . . . but, at least it's not the week of the Finale.

My wife is very much into the natural thing. I was supportive of whatever she wanted, but I was quite squeamish about the thought of being at the birth. Some people are afraid of flying or spiders. I had this huge fear of losing her and the baby. The thought constantly haunted me.

The pregnancy went well until she became ill a few weeks before the due date. She had severe nausea and a horrible headache. When we called the doctor's office, they said it sounded like food poisoning, but I was nervous. As the day wore on, her symptoms were getting worse, not better. When I called the doctor again, he realized it might be more serious and said to get her to the hospital immediately. He was afraid it might be a potentially fatal condition called HELPP syndrome, a pregnancy complication usually characterized by convulsions. However, sometimes its symptoms aren't recognized until it becomes life-threatening.

Looking back, I probably should have called an ambulance.

However, I tried to pull it all together myself; I put her in the car and began racing to the hospital. The traffic seemed heavier than usual as Dana started to go into labor. For some reason, every corner I turned down led me into monstrous congestion. Then I realized that it was 10:00 PM, on a Friday night and the Van Morrison concert at the Hollywood Bowl had just let out. I was totally freaked but experiencing an eerie calm at the same time. As I tried to dodge the traffic going through red light after red light, it felt like something was preventing me from getting to the hospital.

When we finally arrived, they rushed Dana in. Just as she was about to give birth, her face lost all its color and she started to have the feared seizure. Two teams came rushing into her room—the blue team to work on her and the yellow team to work on the baby. Then she went unconscious. I had to help pull Reilly out with forceps. They took him upstairs to the neonatal intensive care unit.

It wasn't until later that they explained to me the details of what had happened. During the delivery, Reilly had about the same chance of survival as a kid who had been pulled out of a swimming pool—which is almost nil—and that he was given a one-in-ten chance of living.

For the next few days, I divided my time between the intensive care and neonatal intensive care units. Dana, who was lapsing in and out of consciousness, was hooked up to every possible machine. Brain, blood, and heart specialists were constantly in and out of her room.

The only thing that took my mind off all of this was the day when I walked into Dana's room and there, next to her bed, was one of the largest displays of flowers I had ever seen. It seemed that when I was upstairs with Reilly, Jessica—one of the *American Idol* segment producers—had dropped them off. They were truly gorgeous.

And as all this was going on, *American Idol* was in the final stages of preparation for that week's show. The guest coach was Andréa Bocelli.

So Tuesday night arrived and there I was, sitting with my wife in the hospital room, and I turned on the TV like a regular viewer. I realized at that moment that I had never had the experience that the rest of America has on Tuesday nights—that feeling of comfort and normalcy, when their favorite TV show comes on like clockwork, and they sit back with their families and watch this phenomenon called *American Idol*.

As the *American Idol* theme began, Dana opened her eyes and had a lucid moment, which was so thrilling for me—and then, the funniest thing happened. They started running the segments of Andréa Bocelli coaching the *Idols*. At the same moment, Dana and I noticed that the big display of flowers, now sitting next to Dana's bed, was on the TV in Andréa's music room! Almost simultaneously, we said, "They stole the flowers from Andréa Bocelli!" That was the first time I had heard the sound of Dana's beautiful laughter in four days. It felt so perfect: our *American Idol* family thinking, *Let's steal these flowers and take them to Dana,* and us sitting there and seeing them, while we're trying to be normal people watching *American Idol* together. That moment, and knowing that our *American Idol* family was looking out for us, made me feel safe and secure—like everything was going to be okay.

And everything has been okay. Dana and Reilly both pulled through. She is doing so well that we're expecting our next son this summer, and Reilly is a healthy nine-month-old who is so happy that we call him Smiley Reilly. But there's more.

If you believe in miracles, it seems that if we had gotten to the hospital even fifteen minutes sooner, they would have given Dana a C-section; they know now that she wouldn't have survived. But because they had no time to prepare her, and they had to get the baby out immediately, they both survived. So it was all perfect, Hollywood Bowl and all.

And now we're eagerly anticipating the birth of Reilly's brother. We're thinking of calling him Ryan. Reilly and Ryan—cute, huh? But I don't know if I can work with a Ryan all day, and then go home and be with another one—who needs even more attention. We'll have to see.

Some Things Are Priceless

Charles Grigsby with Ramona Grigsby
Top 12, Season 2

It was a cold and snowy November night, and my family had gathered to celebrate my sister's wedding. As the snowfall increased and some guests had not yet arrived, we all grew nervous.

My cousin raised her glass in a toast. "May nobody in our family have any car accidents!"

Everyone remained safe that night, but one week later, my sister and I were involved in a serious crash. Though our lives were spared, our vehicle was totaled, and we were badly bruised and in great pain. My mom took us to her house, and family members came to give us support and see for themselves that we were okay.

That evening, my mom handed me a FedEx envelope that had arrived from *American Idol*. I held my breath, hoping the envelope would not hold bad news. My hands shook as I tore it open and pulled out a letter. It confirmed that I was definitely headed for Hollywood, and I needed to be there by the end of the week: I was going to be on *American Idol!*

It should have been one of the happiest days of my life, but the news was bittersweet. My heart soared at the same time that it broke because I couldn't share my joy with Ceasar.

Ceasar was my best friend. We had been through thick and thin together—fun times, crazy times—he was like a brother to me. When I transferred schools in sixth grade (middle school is awkward enough without being the new kid in town), Ceasar was the first one who offered friendship to me. We clicked right away, like we had known each other forever. When we entered high school, we shared a dream of becoming successful musicians. We'd write lyrics, beat-box, and drum on the desks in study hall.

And we always kept our eyes open, looking for a shot at stardom. Coming from a small Ohio town, these dreams seemed unreachable. But as long as we stuck together, we felt there was nothing we couldn't do.

When I announced that I was going to try out for *American Idol*, Ceasar was my biggest supporter. Along with our friends Gerves and John, he helped me work on my rap, harmony, and melody. He was as excited as I was when I made it through the first rounds of the auditions.

That August, I was at the beach trying to catch a break from the stifling Midwest heat and humidity when my cell phone rang. It was my sister who worked as a police dispatcher.

"Charlie, we got a call from Ceasar's house. You better get to the hospital right away."

By the time I got there, Ceasar was gone. He had suffered a fatal asthma attack. When I walked into the ER, Ceasar's family and friends reached out to me. Tears ran through me like waterfalls, but nothing surfaced.

I was in shock for days. I wondered, *How could this happen, just when my dream and the dream Ceasar held for me was in sight? How do I carry on when I feel so devastated?*

Although Ceasar was no longer in physical form, I felt his spirit encouraging me to pursue our dream. Throughout the challenges I met during the *American Idol* competition and the amazing experiences in Hollywood, I knew my best friend was sharing the ride. And how he would have loved it! During all the red carpet treatment—first-class flights, limousines, fancy restaurants, trips to the Beverly Hills mall, I pictured him grinning and saying, "Boy, you think you're all that, don't you!"

And when the judging got tough, I felt him tell me, "Keep going, Charlie, you can do this."

I had filled the void that Ceasar left by spending more time with John and Gerves. They live and breathe music, too, and we helped each other deal with Ceasar's death. When I left for Hollywood, I felt so connected to John and Gerves that it made it easier for me to deal with the loneliness I felt being thousands of miles away from my family and friends.

Making it to the Top 12 of Season 2 was undoubtedly the biggest thrill of my life. But after singing before millions on TV, and thousands of fans live on tour, interviewed countless times, and smiling through television appearances and meet and greets, my formal *Idol* experience was over.

What next? I thought.

People connected to the music industry advised me to stay on the West Coast "where the action is." It sounded like good advice, so I started planning my life in Los Angeles. I was negotiating with a potential agent when I received a call from home that changed my plans.

As my friends on *Idol* prepared to go their separate ways, we shared farewell handshakes and hugs. "Where are you headed, Charlie?" they asked.

"I need to go back home to take care of something," I

answered quietly. "I'll try to get back out here as soon as I can."

The red-eye flight home provided a few hours to reflect on the roller-coaster ride my life had taken over the last year: I had survived a serious car crash. I had lost my best friend—but found strength to continue pursuing our dream of stardom. I had become a part of the biggest phenomenon in television history.

Now I was going home to bury another friend. John's fatal motorcycle accident brought the harsh reality of life back into the midst of the glamorous world I had lived in. Sometimes life teaches you painful lessons, but you become stronger because of them. Dreams cost. Friendship is priceless. And young people can come to unexpected and untimely ends. Singing at John's service was much harder than performing at the Kodak.

It hasn't been easy for me to reconstruct the West Coast music connections, but I have a dream, and I'm going to make it come true. I have to. Now I have two voices telling me, "Keep going, Charlie, you can do it!"

Finally Home

Jordin Sparks
American Idol *Season 6*

If you asked me to tell a story, any story, about my life, I couldn't do it if I couldn't talk about God. God gave me the gift of my voice, and I intend to never forget that.

It was the last night of camp in the summer of 2005, and we were all a little sad that camp was ending. Every summer for the last seven years I'd gone to a Christian Athletics camp called Kanakuk, in Durango, Colorado, and every summer, on the last night of camp, I had the opportunity to sing. The mountain air was crisp and chilly, but as we gathered in the warming hut, our hearts were warmed by love. That night, I had an experience that changed my life forever.

Although we usually spent our days water-skiing, mountain biking, and riding the rapids, on the last day of camp we always talked about what God had done in our lives during the time we spent there.

Everyone at camp knew that I loved to perform and was always asking me to sing for them—and to be honest, I loved the attention and the praise.

So once again everyone was saying, "Sing, Jordin. Sing, Jordin," when one of the camp directors came up to me and said, "Jordin, if you sing, you should do it not because you want the attention but because it's a gift that God has given you."

I had to stop for a minute and take that in. Then it hit me how much I needed to hear those words. It was like, *Yeah, I've been thinking it's me who can sing, and I'm the one who has the gift, and I'm so special.* And for a moment I didn't know what to do because it was the last night and everyone was expecting me to sing, but I didn't know how to find that place to sing from that wasn't about wanting the attention and admiration.

The only thing I could do at that moment was pray. So I prayed and prayed. My heart was pounding, and in my prayer I said, "I know that I've been taking all the credit, but I do know it's You who has given me this gift, and I realize that this whole time I've been thinking it was me. What do I do now?" Suddenly a wave of peace washed over me, and I knew that I was ready to sing, and although the year before I had sung an upbeat song, I knew that on that night an upbeat song would not have shown what I was feeling.

So I got up in front of the camp and I sang "Finally Home" by Natalie Grant. It was the first time in my life that I felt like the Holy Spirit came through me. I had chills, and I cried, and I said silently, *I'm so sorry that I've taken all the credit, and I'm so sorry that I kept thinking it was me.* It was the most amazing moment I've ever had, and since then whenever I get really proud, I think of that moment and I'm completely humbled.

Once during Hollywood week, after my performance, I thought, *Wow, that was the best thing ever!* and I heard the voice over my shoulder say, "Hel-lo. It's not you. It's me." So after that, every time before I began to sing, I prayed that I'd be just a vessel for God to work through, so that I'd remember I wasn't doing it for myself.

And it's funny—I usually never get nervous when I sing, but the situation on *Idol* was extreme. I'd be shaking before I was about to walk out, but as soon as I stepped onto the stage and started to sing, I became oddly serene. Everything just came together and I felt at peace.

I believe it's because I knew it wasn't me, and I knew everything was in His hands, so whatever happened was okay. Even if I forgot the words, it would be totally okay. He just helps me through so much—I knew when I was out there, I wasn't alone.

More Chicken Soup?

Many of the stories you have read in this book were submitted by readers like you who had read earlier Chicken Soup for the Soul books. We publish many Chicken Soup for the Soul books every year. We invite you to contribute a story to one of these future volumes.

Stories may be up to 1,200 words and must uplift or inspire. You may submit an original piece, something you have read, or your favorite quotation on your refrigerator door.

To obtain a copy of our submission guidelines and a listing of upcoming Chicken Soup for the Soul books, please write, fax, or visit our website.

Please submit your submissions through our website:

www.chickensoup.com

or via mail to:

Chicken Soup for the Soul
P.O. Box 30880, Santa Barbara, CA 93130
fax: 805-563-2945

Supporting Others

In the spirit of fulfilling dreams and giving back, a portion of the profits from *Chicken Soup for the American Idol Soul* will be donated to the following charities:

Idol Gives Back

American Idol, FremantleMedia, 19 Entertainment, and FOX TV have teamed up with Charity Projects Entertainment Fund (CPEF) to raise money and awareness to benefit children and young people living in poverty in the United States and Africa. The money raised from *Idol Gives Back* will go to organizations that focus on assisting with basic life needs, including food and health care.

In the U.S., the money will be distributed to organizations such as Save the Children, America's Second Harvest—The Nation's Food Bank Network, Boys & Girls Clubs of America, and Children's Health Fund, to deliver food, medical care, and other assistance programs to children living in some of the most disadvantaged areas of the United States.

In Africa, the money will be focused on delivering health and education programs and will be distributed via CPEF to a number of organizations, including U.S. Fund for UNICEF; the Global Fund to Fight AIDS, Tuberculosis, and Malaria; Save the Children; NothingButNets.net; and Malaria No More.

CPEF's mission is to use the power of entertainment to drive positive change and achieve its vision of creating a just world, free from poverty. To learn more about where your dollars will go, visit: www.cpefund.org.

Idol Gives Back
c/o Citizens Bank
P.O. Box 4365
Woburn, MA 01888-4365

The Bubel/Aiken Foundation

The Bubel/Aiken Foundation grew out of the relationship between Clay Aiken, Diane Bubel, and Diane's then thirteen-year-old son, Mike, who had been diagnosed with autism. Clay met the Bubel family while pursuing a career in special education.

The bond between Clay and the Bubel family grew strong as they shared a vision of a world where children like Mike could be fully immersed in society. Both Clay and Diane had witnessed children with disabilities repeatedly turned away from activities accessible only to typical children. They knew with the right support system, doors could be opened that had been closed in the past. This shared goal grew into a reality on July 28, 2003, when the Bubel/Aiken Foundation was founded.

The mission of the Bubel/Aiken Foundation is to raise awareness and to create communities where all children can learn, live, and play together. The Foundation serves to bridge the gap between young people with special needs and the world around them, and to create an environment for children with disabilities where barriers break, doors open, and inclusion is embraced.

To learn more about the Bubel/Aiken Foundation, please visit www.bubelaiken.org.

The Bubel / Aiken Foundation
8601 Six Forks Road, Suite 400
Raleigh, NC 27615
Tel 919-882-2152

Highrollers with Heart

Highrollers with Heart is a fan-based effort administered by fans of Ace Young to raise money for the Children's Hospital of Denver. Ace and his Highrollers are helping Children's Hospital raise $1.5 million to construct the Family Amenities Area, which will be added to their new state-of-the-art anchor facility on its Fitzsimons campus, scheduled to open in Fall 2007.

When a child is admitted to the Children's Hospital in Denver, he or she will stay an average of seven days. Some children, especially those cared for in the neonatal and pediatric intensive care units, stay much longer. The current hospital has only four sleeping rooms for family members who don't want to be far from their sick children—and these are only for families with kids in the intensive care unit. Due to the overall lack of space in the current hospital, families have few close and affordable places to stay when their child requires a long-term hospital stay. The new Family Amenities Area will provide comfortable, temporary living quarters for patients' family members during this difficult time in their lives.

To learn more please visit: www.highrollerswithheart.org.

The Children's Hospital Foundation
P.O. Box 5585
Denver, CO 80217-5585
Tel 720-917-1700

Who Is Jack Canfield?

Jack Canfield is the cocreator and editor of the *Chicken Soup for the Soul* series, which *Time* magazine has called "the publishing phenomenon of the decade." The series now more than 140 titles with over 100 million copies in print in forty-seven languages. Jack is also the coauthor of eight other bestselling books including *The Success Principles™: How to Get from Where You Are to Where You Want to Be, Dare to Win, The Aladdin Factor, You've Got to Read This Book,* and *The Power of Focus: How to Hit Your Business, Personal and Financial Targets with Absolute Certainty.*

Jack has recently developed a telephone coaching program and an online coaching program based on his most recent book *The Success Principles.* He also offers a seven-day *Breakthrough to Success* seminar every summer, which attracts 400 people from about fifteen countries around the world.

Jack is the CEO of Chicken Soup for the Soul Enterprises and the Canfield Training Group in Santa Barbara, California, and founder of the Foundation for Self-Esteem in Culver City, California. He has conducted intensive personal and professional development seminars on the principles of success for more than a million people in twenty-nine countries around the world. Jack is a dynamic keynote speaker and he has spoken to hundreds of thousands of others at more than 1000 corporations, universities, professional conferences and conventions, and has been seen by millions more on national television shows such as *Oprah, Montel, The Today Show, Larry King Live, Fox and Friends, Inside Edition, Hard Copy,* CNN's *Talk Back Live, 20/20, Eye to Eye,* the NBC *Nightly News,* and the CBS *Evening News.* Jack was also a featured teacher on the hit movie *The Secret.*

Jack is the recipient of many awards and honors, including three honorary doctorates and a Guinness World Records Certificate for having seven books from the *Chicken Soup for the Soul* series appearing on the *New York Times* bestseller list on May 24, 1998.

To write to Jack or for inquiries about Jack as a speaker, his coaching programs, trainings, or seminars, use the following contact information:

Jack Canfield
The Canfield Companies
P.O. Box 30880 • Santa Barbara, CA 93130
phone: 805-563-2935 • fax: 805-563-2945
E-mail: info4jack@jackcanfield.com
www.jackcanfield.com

Who Is Mark Victor Hansen?

In the area of human potential, no one is more respected than Mark Victor Hansen. For more than thirty years, Mark has focused solely on helping people from all walks of life reshape their personal vision of what's possible. His powerful messages of possibility, opportunity, and action have created powerful change in thousands of organizations and millions of individuals worldwide.

He is a sought-after keynote speaker, bestselling author, and marketing maven. Mark's credentials include a lifetime of entrepreneurial success and an extensive academic background. He is a prolific writer with many bestselling books, such as *The One Minute Millionaire, Cracking the Millionaire Code, How to Make the Rest of Your Life the Best of Your Life, The Power of Focus, The Aladdin Factor,* and *Dare to Win,* in addition to the Chicken Soup for the Soul series. Mark has had a profound influence on many people through his library of audios, videos, and articles in the areas of big thinking, sales achievement, wealth building, publishing success, and personal and professional development.

Mark is the founder of the *MEGA Seminar Series. MEGA Book Marketing University* and *Building Your MEGA Speaking Empire* are annual conferences where Mark coaches and teaches new and aspiring authors, speakers, and experts on building lucrative publishing and speaking careers. Other MEGA events include *MEGA Info-Marketing* and *My MEGA Life.*

He has appeared on *Oprah,* CNN, and *The Today Show.* He has been quoted in *Time, U.S. News & World Report, USA Today, New York Times,* and *Entrepreneur.* In countless radio interviews, he has assured our planet's people that "you can easily create the life you deserve."

As a philanthropist and humanitarian, Mark works tirelessly for organizations such as Habitat for Humanity, American Red Cross, March of Dimes, Childhelp USA, and many others. He is the recipient of numerous awards that honor his entrepreneurial spirit, philanthropic heart, and business acumen. He is a lifetime member of the Horatio Alger Association of Distinguished Americans, an organization that honored Mark with the prestigious Horatio Alger Award for his extraordinary life achievements.

Mark Victor Hansen is an enthusiastic crusader of what's possible and is driven to make the world a better place.

Mark Victor Hansen & Associates, Inc.
P.O. Box 7665 • Newport Beach, CA 92658
phone: 949-764-2640 • fax: 949-722-6912
website: www.markvictorhansen.com

Who Is Debra Halperin Poneman?

Debra Halperin Poneman is the founder and president of Yes to Success, Inc., an international seminar company dedicated to the transformation of people's lives in the direction of greater happiness, success, and fulfillment. Since founding Yes to Success in 1981, Debra has given hundreds of keynote speeches for businesses, associations, and professional organizations across the country. Her seminar has been taught in most major U.S. cities and seven countries internationally. She has also written a syndicated newspaper column on the principles of true success and how to achieve it.

After the births of her two beautiful children, Deanna and Daniel, Debra temporarily "retired" to be a stay-at-home mom. For Debra, retirement meant being the go-to parent for all of her children's school and extracurricular activities, being an active civic leader, running a multimillion-dollar home-based business with her wonderful husband Fred, coauthoring *What No Meat?!? What to Do When Your Kid Becomes a Vegetarian*, writing a screenplay, contributing to Chicken Soup and other anthologies, and speaking at conventions and seminars—but only if she was sure there were no basketball games, birthdays, or recitals on the schedule!

Now that her daughter is off to college and her son can chauffeur himself, Debra is coming out of "retirement" and resuming her career, once again speaking around the country on the principles of achieving true success and lasting happiness.

Debra has been a die-hard *American Idol* fan since Season 1 and says that *Chicken Soup for the American Idol Soul* is proof positive that what she has taught in her seminars over the last twenty-five years really works: what we put our attention on will manifest in our lives in perfect timing. Many years ago she set the goal to write a bestselling book that would transform people's lives while working with people she loves. Her goal became a reality when she had the opportunity to coauthor this powerfully transformational book and spend her days talking and writing with the *Idols*—because next to her family and friends, there is no one Debra loves more than her *Idols*!

For more information about Debra, please contact her at:

Debra Poneman
1555 Sherman Ave., Box 155
Evanston, IL 60201
Phone: 847-492-0077
americanidolsoul@iglide.net
Website: www.yestosuccess.com or www.100DaystoHappiness.com

Writers and Editors

We wish to extend our deepest thanks to the following writers and editors whose contributions were vital to the success of this book.

Cindy Buck happily switched from writing software user guides to crafting inspirational stories when she became coauthor of *Chicken Soup for the Gardener's Soul.* She has gone on to contribute her writing and editing talents to many other Chicken Soup for the Soul titles and other inspirational books, including *The Soul of Success, Living Reality, You've Got to Read This Book,* and *Happy for No Reason.* Currently writing lots of press releases as a public relations consultant and giving occasional talks and workshops on writing, Cindy also enjoys performing with the Iowa Theater Company and cohosting a weekly radio program called *That Pet Show.* You can reach her at cbuck@lisco.com.

Lise Hintze, prior to embarking on her writing career, headed up her New York–based agency, LHM, Inc., representing top commercial photographers. While her account list spanned the world of entertainment and fashion, Lise took a leap of faith and focused all efforts into her passion for writing. With the support of her husband, Steven, a retired FDNY captain, and daughters Vienna and Sophie, Lise hit her stride as she teamed up with *American Idol Magazine* as their senior writer. Writing from her charming, historic home on Long Island, Lise touches her readers with a palpable sense of honesty and humor. Whether she is writing about the bright lights of Hollywood or the tranquil beauty of her country garden, her storytelling radiates a genuine love of her work. Lise was a contributing writer on many of the *Chicken Soup for the American Idol Soul* stories, including "The Ace of Hearts," "'My Guardian Angel," "The Body Shop," "Never Over," "Taking a Chance," and "The Great Coin Caper." More on Lise can be found at www.lisehintze.com.

Carol McAdoo Rehme is an active freelance writer who has found her niche in the inspirational market. Besides coauthoring several gift books, Carol writes for magazines and children's publications and teaches writing workshops. A busy editor for the Chicken Soup series, Carol is also one of its most prolific contributors. In addition, her award-winning work appears widely in other anthologies. *Chicken Soup for the Soul: Book of Christmas Virtues* was the first project she coauthored for Chicken Soup Enterprises. *Chicken Soup for the Empty Nester's Soul* will be released in 2008. She can be reached at carol@rehme.com or www.rehme.com.

Josh Murray is a New York–based writer and editor who watches way too much television—or at least his mother thinks so. He is the author of *American Idol: The Journey to Stardom*, a behind-the-scenes peek at what it takes to win the show and was the senior editor of *American Idol Magazine* for two seasons. He contributes regularly to magazines in both Canada and the United States and runs the entertainment blog ohmyjosh.ca, where he provides daily news and gossip updates. He was a contributing writer on several *American Idol Soul* stories, including "Fourth Time's a Charm," "Now I Know," "Meeting Life Head-On," "My Superstar, and "Pens, Anyone?" Contact him at josh@joshmurray.ca.

Contributors

Clay Aiken, multi-platinum recording artist and *American Idol* Season 2 runner-up, has enjoyed enormous success since *Idol*. His debut album, *Measure of a Man*, sold over 600,000 copies in the United States in its first week and has since gone double platinum. His single, "This Is the Night," went platinum in the United States, and six times platinum in Canada. In addition to his successful sold-out concerts, TV appearances, and a *New York Times* bestselling book, Clay is a Goodwill Ambassador for UNICEF, co-founder of the Bubel/Aiken Foundation, and was appointed to the President's Committee for Persons with Intellectual Disabilities. For more about Clay, go to www.clayonline.com or www.clayaiken.com.

Bryan Aubrey is a freelance writer and editor who lives in Fairfield, Iowa. He has contributed stories to several Chicken Soup for the Soul books and has edited many Chicken Soup for the Soul stories. He can be reached at wotan@lisco.com.

Dean Banowetz, the Hollywood Hair Guy, joined the nationally syndicated television series *Extra* in 2000 as hairstylist to the show's talent, including Leeza Gibbons and Dayna Devon. Dean has been the hairstylist for all six seasons of *Idol*. He continues to serve as personal hairstylist for Leeza Gibbons, Tony Robbins, Kelly Clarkson, Ryan Seacrest, Simon Cowell, Sanjaya, and many others. Dean and his work have been featured on *Oprah, The Today Show, Entertainment Tonight,* and *Access Hollywood,* and in *People, U.S. Weekly, TV Guide, Glamour,* and *Spa Magazine*. Visit Dean at www.hollywoodhairguy.com.

Mary Baust holds a degree in Speech Pathology and enjoys playing with her grandchildren, reading, making jewelry, and going to Clay Aiken concerts. Clay's interest in special-needs children has also been an inspiration to her. This is her first piece of published writing. She can be reached via e-mail at mysterybroad427@hotmail.com.

Paris Bennett, also known as "Princess P," sailed to #5 on Season 5 of *American Idol*. Known for her tiny presence but powerful singing voice, she just released her first album, *Princess P,* with label 306 Entertainment and TVT Records. Paris continues to wow crowds of all ages and can be found at www.myspace.com/parisbennett.

Cynthia Borris is the award-winning author of the humorous novel, *No More Bobs,* a quirky misadventure. She resides in California and is a frequent *Chicken*

Soup for the Soul contributor. A humor columnist and inspirational speaker, she is working on her next novel, *To Serve Duck*. Please contact Cynthia at cynthi-aborris@juno.com or www.cynthiaborris.com.

Charles Boyd has been an *American Idol* producer since Season 1. His producing credits also include *World Idol, American Juniors, Making Sense of the Sixties*, and numerous other shows. He is currently the Co-Executive Producer of *America's Got Talent*.

Natalie Burge was only seventeen years old when she became a Top 15 finalist on the first season of *American Idol*. She is currently a music business management/music production major at Columbia College in Chicago. You can keep up on Natalie and her music or contact her at www.natalieburge.com.

Debra Byrd has been the vocal coach and arranger at *American Idol* for all six seasons and *Canadian Idol* for Seasons 2 through 5, as well as for the 2006 tour of *High School Musical: The Concert, The 49th Annual GRAMMY Awards*, and *My GRAMMY Moment Contest with Justin Timberlake*. Byrd has recorded duets with Barry Manilow and Bob Dylan, and has been featured in five Broadway shows. Her DVD, *Vocal Help Now!* offers important advice on how to improve and protect your voice. For more about Byrd, visit www.debrabyrd.com.

Kimberly Caldwell is best known for being a Top 10 finalist on *American Idol* Season 2. She has been an on-camera personality for the TV Guide Channel for the past four years as an entertainment correspondent and host. She continues to make personal appearances nationwide and is a frequent guest on television news and talk shows. She appears in her first movie role in *Wrong Turn* and is currently recording a country/rock album. More about Kimberly can be found at www.kimberlycaldwell.com and www.myspace.com/kimberly caldwellofficial.

Kevin Covais began singing at the age of ten. In August 2005, he successfully auditioned for Season 5 of *American Idol*, eventually making it to the Top 12. Kevin was diagnosed with type 1 diabetes at age eleven and devotes significant time to raising the level of awareness of diabetes and the challenges facing diabetics. More information about Kevin can be found at www.kevincovais.com.

Bucky Covington, since his Top 10 finish in Season 5, has gone on to release his self-titled debut CD on Disney's Lyric Street Records. The album was met with rave reviews and debuted at number one on the country chart with the best first-week sales for any new male country artist in fifteen years. His various media appearances include *Good Morning America, Live!* with *Regis & Kelly, Jimmy Kimmel Live, FOX & Friends,* and *Larry King Live.* To learn more about Bucky Covington, log on to www.buckycovingtonmusic.com.

Jennifer Lee "Jennah" Crain is a third-grade teacher and resident of Washington Parish, Louisiana. She dreams of one day becoming a professional actress, singer, and dancer. Her passion is inspiring her love for performing in each and every student who walks through her classroom door.

Melinda Doolittle, an *American Idol* Season 6, Top 3 finalist, worked as a professional back-up singer for, among others, Aaron Neville, Alabama, and BeBe and CeCe Winans. On the night of her elimination, Melinda was referred to as one of the greatest singers in the history of the show by the judges as well as Ryan Seacrest. You can visit Melinda at www.myspace.com/melindadoolittle.

Kim Estep is the proud mother of Kendall, Shelby, and Weston. Her oldest daughter, Kendall Phillips, went to Hollywood with *Idol* in Season 4. Kendall is an up-and-coming musical artist and is currently working on her first CD release. To find out more about Kendall and hear her music, go to www.myspace.com/kendallphillipsmusic or visit www.kendallphillips.com.

Anthony Fedorov, an *American Idol* Season 4, Top 4 finalist, was not only a fan favorite on the show, but was always very popular on the *American Idols Live!* 2005 tour. Anthony appeared as a celebrity judge in MTV's *Little Talent Show Triple Threat,* and as a celebrity contestant on FOX's *Fear Factor.* In May 2007, Anthony joined the cast of Broadway's *The Fantasticks.* Since the loss of his brother, Denis, Anthony has become a devoted advocate for the Sarcoma Foundation. Anthony is currently working on his solo album. For more about Anthony, visit www.anthonyfanclub.com or www.curesarcoma.org.

Cecile Frot-Coutaz, Executive Producer of *American Idol,* is also CEO of FremantleMedia North America where she oversees the development, production, and business operations of over 400 hours of programming distributed over eleven network and cable platforms. FremantleMedia is the production arm of the RTL Group, Europe's largest television and radio broadcast company. Born and raised in France, Frot-Coutaz earned her MBA from the prestigious INSEAD, Paris in 1994. For further information, visit www.fremantlemedia.com.

Gina Glocksen, *American Idol*'s Season 6 "resident rocker" (or so they called her), apparently doesn't like to take no for an answer. She made the Top 10 after her fourth audition. Although she was the rocker of the season, she also has a softer side as she showed in her rendition of "Smile" by Charlie Chaplin. She has no regrets for the season and wouldn't redo *anything*—except maybe winning! More Gina can be found at www.rocktheglock.com.

Bruce Gowers, director of *American Idol*, has been with the show all six seasons. After creating and directing some of the most original music videos, including Queen's "Bohemian Rhapsody," Bruce's career brought him from the United Kingdom to the United States. Here, he has directed many award shows, from the MTV Awards to the Emmys, and numerous specials for artists including Prince, The Rolling Stones, Paul McCartney, and Eddie Murphy. Bruce's trophy case is home to a GRAMMY, an Emmy, and a Directors Guild of America Award.

Tamyra Gray captured America's heart with her standout performance on the inaugural season of *American Idol*. Her television credits include *Boston Public, Las Vegas, Half and Half, What I Like About You*, and *Tru Calling*. She's appeared on Broadway in *Bombay Dreams* and *RENT*. She even has a movie credit for a role in the 2005 release *The Gospel*. As a song writer, she cowrote the #1 hit "I Believe" by Fantasia and "You Thought Wrong" by Kelly Clarkson. For more Tamyra, go to www.tamyra-gray.com.

Charles Grigsby, an Ohio native and 2003 *American Idol* Top 10 finalist, has performed in venues across the country. In addition to singing and coproducing his first CD, *Charles Grigsby*, Charlie has spoken words of encouragement to youth audiences in public and alternative schools and faith-based organizations. Contact Charlie at cnote440@yahoo.com or www.myspace.com/cnote440.

Dena Harris is a national humor writer with several books about living with cats to her credit. She also writes young adult novels and ghostwrites humor and nonfiction books, but still hasn't learned to cook. Visit her website at www.denaharris.com or e-mail her at WriteForYou@triad.rr.com.

Dorian Holley is a multi-talented vocal coach, songwriter, and singer who has toured with Michael Jackson, Queen Latifah, Rod Stewart, and many others. His voice can be heard in *Happy Feet, Ice Age 2, American Gangster*, and on *Dancing with the Stars*. He teaches at the Los Angeles Music Academy, and coached both Taylor Hicks and Jordin Sparks to the top prize on *American Idol*. His solo CD will be found in the winter of 2007 at www.dorianholley.com.

George Huff is the New Orleans native who captured the hearts of America with his brilliant smile and urban style on Season 3 of *American Idol*, where fans around the country voted him into the Top 5. Today, with nationwide appearances including *Live! with Regis & Kelly*, *NBA All-Star Jam*, and Billy Graham crusades, George is gaining a reputation as "the nicest man in showbiz" as he shares his sensational vocal gift and delivers energetic performances from his debut Word/WB release *Miracles*. For more on George, go to www.myspace. com/georgehuff.

Mezhgan Hussainy has become one of the most respected makeup artists in Hollywood. In addition to doing makeup for *American Idol* since Season 2, she has worked with some of the biggest television shows and hottest names in the entertainment industry. She is currently creating her own makeup line, a portion of the profits of which will go to her charity, The FARAWAY Foundation, which helps women and children from her homeland, Afghanistan. More on Mezhgan can be found at www.mezhgan.com. E-mail her at mezhgan@mezhgan.com.

Amy Johnson has been a neonatal intensive care nurse for fifteen years. She and her husband, Steve, have five daughters and live in the Midwest. Amy's nursing expertise and deep faith helped care for daughters, Lindsay, who endured multiple surgeries to correct heart defects, and Mackenzie, who is undergoing treatments for leukemia. Amy enjoys the outdoors and being with her family. For more about their inspiring journey, visit www.myspace.com/acesgirlfriend or www.caringbridge.org/il/mackenzie.

LaKisha Jones, Season 6, Top 10 finalist, began singing at the Mount Zion Missionary Baptist Church at age five. She was formally trained in classical music, although her favorite genre is gospel. As part of the Top 24, she gave an outstanding performance when she sang the Jennifer Holliday hit, "And I Am Telling You I'm Not Going."

Cynthia Lane, M.A., has been a freelance writer, ghostwriter, and editor for twenty years. She has also been a teacher and guide for personal and spiritual transformation for more than three decades. Cynthia loves hiking, gardening, meeting new people, and sharing life with good friends. Her website is www.firstlighttransformations.com.

Blake Lewis, Season 6 Runner-Up, is from Seattle, Washington, and has been beat-boxing and singing professionally for eight years. Blake also plays the guitar, piano, and drums, and is a prolific song writer. He's looking forward to touring the United States and Canada, sharing his music and working on his solo album. Find out what's up with Blake at www.myspace.com/blakelewis.

Jon Peter Lewis, affectionately known as JPL, was a fan favorite and Top 10 finalist in Season 3. An exceptional singer and songwriter, he was known on *Idol* not only for his voice, but also for his high-energy performances. Jon went on to form a band and create his own record label. He released his debut album, *Stories from Hollywood*, in November 2006. Jon is currently performing-with his band throughout the country. For updates, visit his website at www.jonpeterlewis.com.

Heather Cook Lindsay lives in Bangor, Maine. She is currently writing a memoir about her unusual life, including the years she spent living in an oxygen tent and her ongoing battle with chronic illness. She graduated from Mount Holyoke College and Harvard University. Please e-mail her at hclindsay@aol.com.

Kimberley Locke, *American Idol* Season 2, Top 3 finalist, has scored five Top 10 *Billboard* hits and has been number one on various *Billboard* charts with songs such as "8th World Wonder," "Change," and her holiday hits "Jingle Bells" and "Up on the Housetop." Kimberley records for Nashville-based Curb Records, which has released her two solo albums, *One Love* and *Based on a True Story*. She had been a plus-sized model for Lane Bryant but then shed weight by participating in "Celebrity Fit Club 5," and is a spokesperson for Jenny Craig. You can find more about Kimberley at www.kimberleylockeweb.com.

LaToya London was thought to be the early front runner to win Season 3 of *American Idol*. LaToya, now known simply as "London," finished at #4. She released an album in 2005 entitled, *Love & Life*. Now playing the role of "Nettie" on tour with the Broadway Musical *The Color Purple*, London is a bona fide star! In sharing her gift with the world, London's mission is "to spread love." Visit LaToya at www.myspace.com/latoyalondon.

Patrick Lynn works in both television and feature film, and has an eye for spotting early talent in both fields. He is the Senior Producer for *American Idol* and has been with the show since its debut here in the United States. Visit Patrick at www.myspace.com/patricklynn.

Nigel Lythgoe, President of 19 Television, joined 19 as Chief Executive in 2001 from London Weekend Television. One of the United Kingdom's most respected TV talents, Lythgoe choreographed over 500 television shows around the world before he became a household name as a tough judge on the series *Popstars*, leading him to be dubbed "Nasty Nigel." He has produced shows, including *Gladiator, Pop Idol,* and the British version of *Survivor*, and is currently the Executive Producer of all six seasons of *American Idol*, as well as all three seasons of *So You Think You Can Dance*.

Sanjaya Malakar practically stole the show during Season 6 with his dare-to-be-different personality, sweet melodic voice, and ever-changing style. This seventeen-year-old Top 10 finalist was the first person in *Idol* history to sing a song in Spanish. Throughout the season he held his head high and kept a smile on his face in spite of a continuous onslaught of negative press and feedback from the judges. Watch for the release of Sanjaya's own album! More about Sanjaya can be found at www.sanjayamalakar.com.

Mandisa became a stand-out contestant as soon as she stepped into the spotlight on Season 5 of *American Idol*. "I'm such a fan already," Barry Manilow exclaimed after Mandisa's rehearsal session of "I Don't Hurt Anymore." Manilow added, "Mandisa is one of a kind." Since *Idol*, Mandisa released her debut album, *True Beauty* (EMI/Sparrow) and book, *Idoleyes* (Tyndale House). She also served as a spokesmodel for Ashley Stewart Stores, the fashion retailer that outfitted a number of her performances on *American Idol*. For more Mandisa, visit www.mandisaofficial.com.

Constantine Maroulis contributed to *American Idol's* exceptional fourth season with his delivery of Queen's "Bohemian Rhapsody." Constantine's accomplishments since Idol include starring in Broadway's *The Wedding Singer* and singing in Off-Broadway's acclaimed *Jacques Brell*. Constantine also cohosted *Idol Chatter* on FOX's *Good Day New York*. In May 2007, Constantine became a featured performer on *The Bold and the Beautiful,* and the show incorporates music from Constantine's upcoming album, which hit stores in August 2007 on Sixth Place Records/Sony RED. Contact management at Passick@dpent.net.

Jayne Marquit lives on Cape Cod in Brewster, MA, with her elderly mother, Marjorie, and teenage daughter, Megan. Jayne graduated from Central Connecticut State University with a degree in French. She has been an educational assistant in Special Needs at Nauset Regional High School for seventeen years. She is a single mom who dreams of one day writing a book. Please e-mail her at pandapals2@verizon.net.

Lexie Matthew's son is her daily inspiration and sunshine. She is grateful for the loving support of her family and "Clay" friends. A creative spark bequeathed to her by her father is one of her many blessings from God.

Melissa McGhee, Top 12 finalist from Season 5, is remembered for her sultry, raspy voice. Melissa was forced to take time off for vocal surgery following her departure from the show. She has kept herself busy working with numerous charitable organizations, including the World Sailfish Championship, which benefits Camp Boggy Creek, and the Don Shula Foundation. She is currently writing and recording her debut album. Check out her website for the latest at www.officialmelissamcghee.com.

Nikki McKibbin, a Grand Prairie, Texas, resident and the original "rebel rocker" on *Idol*, came in at #3 on Season 1. Nikki is currently working with the Dallas band Rivethead. Their CD was released in May 2007 and has received amazing reveiws. She married Craig Sadler on July 13, 2007—Friday the 13th. Her baby boy, Tristen, has a new older stepsister, Carlie Sadler. For more on Nikki, go to www.nikkimckibbin.com.

Nicole Merchut has no experience in writing except what she has learned in school. She is currently a sophomore in high school and enjoys listening to Katharine McPhee and Carrie Underwood, watching her favorite shows, and skateboarding. She plans to become a graphic designer, photographer, or model in the future.

Rickey Minor, Emmy-nominated music director, bassist, and producer, has worked with various artists, including Whitney Houston, Sting, Christina Aguilera, Carlos Santana, Alicia Keys, and Stevie Wonder. His work can be heard in television, films, and numerous recordings. Selected performance highlights include: *Genius: A Night for Ray Charles, The 49th Annual GRAMMY Awards, VH1 Divas, BET Awards, Superbowls XXV–XXXIII,* and *American Idol* since Season 4. More about Rickey can be found at www.rickeyminor.com.

Michael Orland resides in Studio City, California, where he relaxes with his dogs, Harry and Maxie, when he's not sitting at a piano or in a recording studio. He's currently working on a CD including some of his original songs featuring vocals with some of the amazing people he's worked with. Besides looking forward to coaching and accompanying the *Idols* each season, Michael musical directs an annual touring company of *The Radio City Music Spectacular*. For more information, go to www.michaelorland.com.

Allison Pittman left a seventeen-year teaching career at Judson High School in Converse, Texas, to pursue a dream of being a Christian novelist. She is the author of *Ten Thousand Charms* and *Speak Through the Wind* from the *Crossroads of Grace* series. She and her husband Mike have three sons. Find out more about Allison at www.allisonpittman.com or e-mail her at pittman66@hotmail.com.

Sherman Pore is best known for being, at sixty-four, the oldest person to ever audition for *American Idol*. He says, "I never thought that I would ever get all this attention. As I promised Melissa, I will keep on singing. I got a chance to record a CD called *For My Lady Love* with a forty-five-piece orchestra, and you can find it at all the stores. I am now a spokesperson for City of Hope for Cancer Research. It's all amazing to me." Sherman can be found at www.shermanporeidol.com.

Nicky Pratt is married and the mother of a twenty-one year old daughter, Corey. She has been a medical secretary for nine years in western New York. Nicky enjoys scrapbooking, camping, reading, and bowling. She has always loved the Chicken Soup for the Soul books. Nicky is both proud and excited to now be part of them.

Carmen Rasmusen, born in Edmonton, Canada, is a Season 2, Top 10 finalist and has been singing country music since she was seven years old. Her first single, "Nothin' Like the Summer," was released in May 2007, and her full album was released in August 2007. You can get more information about Carmen at www.carmenrasmusen.com and www.myspace.com/carmenrasmusen.

Chris Richardson, Top 10, Season 6, hails from Chesapeake, Virginia. After his initial *Idol* audition, Randy Jackson commented that he was reminiscent of Justin Timberlake in looks and style. Chris is now working on an album that he says will be a combination of rock, soul, and R&B. "It'll be a mixture of a Maroon 5 sound with a little bit of Jason Mraz," he says. Chris also plays guitar, drums, and piano.

Anwar Robinson recognizes that his dream of sharing music with countless people wouldn't be possible without God, his family, and all of the other supporters of his dream. Since being a Top 10 finalist in Season 4, Anwar has completed a collection of cover songs for an album entitled, *The Truth About Love*. He has taken his music education background and parlayed it into a unique brand of artistry that not only entertains, but also inspires. To stay updated on Anwar, visit www.anwarmusic.com or www.myspace.com/anwarrobinson.

Sallie A. Rodman is an award-winning author whose work has appeared in many *Chicken Soup* anthologies, as well as magazines such as *Angels on Earth, Mystery Review,* and *ByLine*. She lives with her husband, a cat, and a dog in Los Alamitos, California. Sallie loves to write about the inspiration that occurs from everyday events and is very proud of her daughter, a military wife with two children. The closeness that she feels for her is due in part to their diehard weekly viewing of *American Idol*. You may reach her at sa.rodman@verizon.net.

Matt Rohde is an accomplished musical director, keyboardist, and composer who has toured and/or recorded with a long list of popular artists, including

Alanis Morissette, Jane's Addiction, Maxwell, Jennifer Lopez, and Queen Latifah. He has been an Associate Music Director for *American Idol* since Season 5. Find out more about Matt by visiting www.mattrohde.com.

Tanesha Yvonne Ross, Top 24, Season 1, holds a Bachelor's Degree in Music from Cornish College of the Arts in Seattle, Washington. She is a professional performer, with a focus on live theater. She is also a licensed Kindermusik® educator, and loves volunteering this service at Children's Hospitals. This is her first go at writing professionally.

Michelle (White) Rossi received her Bachelor of Science degree, with honors, from Oakland University, Rochester, Michigan, in 2004. She has devised her own self-esteem program for today's youth, which is being implemented throughout many communities. More on Michelle can be found at www.lulu.com/allaboutme and www.marrossproductions.com.

Scott Savol has loved to sing his whole life. *American Idol* offered him his big break. Currently married and living in Nashville, he is working on his debut album. For updates, please visit www.scottsavol.com.

Haley Scarnato is best known as one of the Top 10 finalists on Season 6 of *American Idol*. In addition to her *Idol* appearance, Haley has performed at venues ranging from musical theater to appearances with live bands. After joining the other Top 10 finalists from Season 6 on the *American Idols Live!* tour, Haley continues to perform and record. Visit Haley at www.haleysscarnato.com.

Radhika Schwartz has a Bachelor of Arts degree from the University of Iowa and is a certified facilitator for *The Work of Byron Katie*. She spent nearly two decades living in India, immersing herself into the culture and rich spiritual atmosphere. She is currently a Breema® Bodywork practitioner and hospice volunteer. She loves to travel and read good books. Radhika can be reached at radhika@lisco.com.

Melissa Shown is nineteen years old and has cerebral palsy. She lives in Middle River, Maryland, and is Clay Aiken's biggest fan. She lives with her mother, Sharon; father, Rick; two sisters, Allie and Victoria; and brother-in-law, Ben.

Miles Siggins, along with a colleague, launched iconic streetwear label Scussy in the United Kingdom in 1990 with great success. He moved to the States in 1994 to start a career in styling and became the *American Idol* stylist in Season 2. Married to Kirsten, a Canadian, they have an *über*-cool son, Alfie, who joined them in 2006. You can find more about Miles at www.mrmiles.com.

Chris Sligh is a vocalist, guitarist, composer, and producer best known for his stint on Season 6 of *American Idol*. The curly-haired, pudgy singer shot to fame with hilarious quips to the *Idol* judges and the voice to back up the fun. He is currently set to release his label debut. Chris can be found at www.myspace.com/chrissligh or his blog at www.frommymindtoyoureyes.blogspot.com.

Sabrina Sloan is best known for displaying her vocal talent as an early front-runner and judge favorite on Season 6 of *American Idol*. Fans say Sabrina's departure from the show was one of the biggest upsets in *Idol* history. A Northwestern University graduate, her Broadway credits include the original cast of the Tony award-winning show *Hairspray*. Sabrina is currently working on an album under Universal Music Group. Check her out at www.myspace.com/sabrinasloan.

Nikko Smith, Season 4, Top 10 finalist, was labeled by Paula as "The Comeback Kid," and said to be one of the most consistent performers in his season. This gifted singer and songwriter performed his own rendition of "The Star-Spangled Banner" before his home crowd of St. Louis during the 2006 World Series. Son of legendary shortstop, Ozzie Smith, Nikko started his own record label, The N Music Group, and is currently working on his album entitled *The Revolution*, due out in late 2007. Nikko can be found at www.Nikkostl.com or www.myspace.com/Nikkostl.

Vonzell Solomon, Season 4, Top 3 finalist, says, "I would like to thank all of my fans—without you none of this would be possible! I love you all." Since *American Idol*, she's been on two national tours, recorded songs on compilation albums with singers such as Chaka Khan and Alicia Keys, and made an appearance in an independent film. She's also started an independent label, Melodic Records, with an album set to be released this year, on which she wrote, arranged, and produced! She feels so blessed to be on this great journey! To stay updated, please visit www.officialbabyv.com.

Jordin Sparks, Season 6's *American Idol*, was the youngest contestant ever to win the title. As a child Jordin was active in theater and singing competitions, recording her first album at age thirteen. She was named "Overall Spotlight Winner" at the Gospel Music Association Academy, appeared in the Tournament of Champions on *America's Most Talented Kids*, and won the title "Arizona Idol." Jordin is signed with 19 Entertainment and Creative Artists Agency. For more, visit www.jordinsparks.com.

Phil Stacey, an *American Idol* Season 6, Top 10 finalist and U.S. sailor, has a passion for people. Everything he does is motivated by the idea that someone's life can be touched. Although he is primarily a singer/songwriter, he also enjoys writing and encouraging others to follow their dreams. For more information on Phil, please visit www.philstacey.com or www.myspace.com/joelphilip.

John Stevens finished at #6 in Season 3 and says that *American Idol* paved the way for him to pursue his dreams. June 2005 brought the release of his first CD, *RED*, a five-day appearance at the prestigious Feinstein's Jazz Club at The Regency Hotel in New York City, and graduation from high school. Now, the underaged but old-fashioned crooner will settle for the development of his craft at the Berklee College of Music in Boston, Massachusetts, where he is a student. Visit John at www.johnstevensmusic.com.

Ruben Studdard, Season 2 *American Idol* winner, earned a scholarship to Alabama A & M University for both football and music. Ruben received a GRAMMY nomination in December 2003 for Best Male R&B Vocal Performance, and in 2004, he won the NAACP Outstanding New Artist award. He also started The Ruben Studdard Foundation for the Advancement of Children in the Music Arts to provide scholarship opportunities for Birmingham-area high-school seniors interested in pursuing degrees in the music arts. Ruben was given the nickname "Velvet Teddy Bear" by music legend Gladys Knight. Find out more about Ruben at www.myspace.com/RubenStuddard.

Jasmine Trias, Season 3 *American Idol* Top 10, was raised in Oahu, Hawaii. Her trademark was wearing a flower in her hair. She would like to thank her fans for voting her all the way to #3. Her U.S. debut album from 2005, self-titled, *Jasmine Trias*, went platinum in Asia. Watch for another release in 2008. Jasmine plans to branch out into a lot of other areas—acting, singing on Broadway, designing clothing, and putting her name on a perfume line. Visit her official fan site at www.allthatjas.net or find personal updates on www.myspace.com/jasminetrias.

Lisa Tucker, Top 10, Season 5 finalist, was praised by Simon as the best sixteen-year-old to ever be on the show. Prior to *Idol*, this talented singer and actress performed a nine-month run as Young Nala in Disney's Los Angeles production of *The Lion King*, and has a recurring guest role on Nickelodeon's *Zoey 101*. *Variety* magazine voted Lisa as one of the "Top Ten Talents to Watch." Lisa is a songwriter, and plays the piano and guitar. Lisa can be reached at www.lisa-tucker.com or www.myspace.com/8874212.

Carrie Underwood, 2005's *American Idol,* has won every award imaginable, including two GRAMMYs for Best Female Country Vocal Performance, one for "Jesus, Take the Wheel," and the other for Best New Artist. Her other awards include two CMAs, five ACMs, four CMTs, eight *Billboard* Music Awards, and many more! Her debut album, *Some Hearts,* has sold over 6 million copies and placed four songs in the top spot on the country singles charts. Carrie would like to thank her fans for all their support and the people of South Africa for changing her life. Visit Carrie's official fansite at www.carrieunderwood.fm.

Jim Verraros was a Top 10 finalist on the first season of *American Idol.* Since his appearance on the show, he's released a CD entitled, *Rollercoaster,* and two films, *Eating Out* and *Eating Out Two.* Jim resides in Chicago and is working on his second album and two more films. For more information, visit www.jimverraros.com.

Emily Weaver writes books for children and lives in Springfield, Missouri, with her husband and two children. When she isn't writing, she spends time gardening, traveling and, of course, watching *American Idol.* She can be reached by e-mail at emily-weaver@sbcglobal.net.

Debra Williams began her show-business performing career at the age of two when she started skating in her family act on ice. She went on to perform for fifteen years of ice skating, musical theater, commercials, voice-overs, and dancing on TV variety shows. For the last thirty-two years, she has worked behind the camera in live variety television. Deb can be contacted at debkwilliams@gmail.com.

Ace Young, Season 6, Top 10 finalist, is a published songwriter and recording artist. As a teen, Ace worked his way onto stages with some of the industry's top artists. He has been a guest star on a television sitcom and has made numerous other TV appearances. Since appearing on *American Idol,* he co-wrote Daughtry's #1 hit single "It's Not Over," has toured the United States with his band, and has developed his foundation for children's hospitals, Highrollers with Heart. His debut album was released in fall 2007. You can see what Ace is up to by visiting www.acemusic.com.

Go to www.chickensoup.com

to enter the

Chicken Soup for the American Idol Soul

CONTEST!

Who Is Your Favorite *American Idol* and Why?

You could be our **Grand Prize Winner** and receive two tickets to the *American Idol* Finale in May 2008, plus two round-trip coach tickets from your hometown to Los Angeles, a three-night stay in Los Angeles, and ground transportation to and from the show!*

The **First Prize Winner** will receive two tickets to the *American Idol* Finale plus a check for $350.*

Be one of **10 Second Prize Winners** and receive an autographed copy of *Chicken Soup for the American Idol Soul.**

**See the Official Rules on pages 310–313
in this book for details.**

Good Luck!

*Some restrictions apply. Void where prohibited.

Who Is Your Favorite
American Idol and Why?

OFFICIAL RULES

1. **Eligibility.** NO PURCHASE NECESSARY. Contest is open to all legal residents of the fifty United States, the District of Columbia and Canada (excluding Quebec) who are thirteen (13) years of age or older. Officers, directors, representatives, and employees of Chicken Soup for the Soul Enterprises, Inc., M.V. Hansen and Associates, Inc., Self Esteem Seminars, Inc., FremantleMedia North America, Inc., American Idol Productions, Inc., 19 TV Limited, 19 Merchandising Ltd., CKX, Inc., and/or Health Communications, Inc., and their respective affiliates or subsidiaries, their respective advertising, promotion, publicity, production, and judging agencies, and members of their immediate families and households, are not eligible to enter. The Contest is not open to residents of the Province of Quebec, Canada.

2. **To Enter.** Contest begins May 15, 2007 and ends March 1, 2008. Contestants may enter as many times as desired either by submitting their Entry online at www.chickensoup.com, or by mailing their Entry to: *Chicken Soup for the American Idol Soul* Contest, Chicken Soup for the Soul Enterprises, Inc., P.O. Box 30880, Santa Barbara, California 93130. Each Entry must be accompanied by a fully completed Official Entry Form which may be obtained online at www.chickensoup.com and must comply with the Requirements. Entries submitted will not be acknowledged or returned. Chicken Soup for the Soul Enterprises, Inc. (the "Sponsor") and those working for the Sponsor or on its behalf, will not be responsible for lost, late, misdirected, damaged, destroyed, misaddressed, garbled, scrambled or incomplete Entries or any incomplete or illegible contestant identifying information. **All Entries submitted online must be received by Chicken Soup for the Soul Enterprises' server no later than 5:00 PM Eastern Standard Time on March 1, 2008. Entries submitted via U.S. mail must be postmarked no later than March 1, 2008, and received by Chicken Soup for the Soul Enterprises, Inc. no later than March 7, 2008.**

3. **Requirements.** Each submitted Entry must be no more than 200 words and authored by the Contestant. The subject matter must address the question, **"Who is Your Favorite *American Idol* and Why?"** Contestants can write about any *American Idol* contestant from any season, starting from the inception of the *American Idol* show. Each entry must be typed or handwritten in legible print. Each Entry must be wholly original and must not incorporate or include material owned by a third party, or that violates any proprietary or privacy rights of any third party, or contains any defamatory, obscene, threatening, or illegal content. Failure to meet the terms of this paragraph, as determined by Sponsor in its sole discretion, will render the Entry ineligible,

and may subject the Contestant to liability in accordance with the indemnification obligations below. If Contestant is under the age of majority in the state or province in which Contestant resides, the Entry and the Official Entry Form must be accompanied by a written authorization from Contestant's parent/guardian in order to complete eligibility and to participate in the Contest.

4. **Odds.** Odds of winning depend on the number of entries and the skill and talent of the entrants.

5. **Winner Selection.** Between April 1st and April 7th of 2008, twelve (12) Entries (1 Grand, 1 First Place and 10 Second Place) will be selected as potential Winners by a panel of judges consisting of book editors, marketers and authors, based upon the following criteria: (i) originality and creativity, (ii) adherence to the *Chicken Soup for the American Idol Soul* Contest guidelines, and (iii) ability to involve and impact the panel of judges. The decision of the judges is final and binding in all regards.

6. **Winner Notification and Validation.** Contestants who are the potential Winners will be notified by email and/or telephone, at the address and phone number identified in their Entry on or about April 8, 2008. In order for the Contestants who have submitted the selected Entries to become validated Winners, each Contestant who has submitted the selected Entries (or parent/guardian of Contestant if Contestant is under the age of majority in the state or province in which Contestant resides) must sign and return the Chicken Soup for the Soul Enterprises, Inc. standard Contributing Author Release within ten (10) days after date notification of winning is sent to potential Winner. Failure of any potential Winner (or parent or guardian of potential Winner if potential Winner is under the age of majority in the state or province in which potential Winner resides) to complete, sign, and return any requested documents within such period; or the return to the Sponsor of any Winner notification; or Winner notification remaining undeliverable for seven (7) days from the first attempt, will result in disqualification of such potential winner and an alternate potential Winner will be selected by the judges. The Contestants who have submitted the selected Entries do not become Winners until the validation process is complete.

7. **Grand Prize; First Prize; Second Prize.** One Grand Prize, one First Prize and ten (10) Second Prizes will be awarded. The Grand Prize Winner will receive two (2) tickets to the *American Idol* Finale show for the seventh season (May 2008) plus two (2) round-trip coach airline tickets from the airport closest to Winner's hometown and Los Angeles, three (3) nights stay at a hotel in Los Angeles (one (1) room) and ground transportation to and from the Finale.* (The value of the Grand Prize is dependent on the location of the winner. The range of possible values of the Grand Prize is approximately $1500.00 U.S. Funds to $4000.00 U.S. Funds. In no event shall the value of the Grand Prize exceed $4000.00 U.S. Funds.) The First Prize Winner will receive two (2) tickets to the *American Idol* Finale show for the seventh season (May 2008)

and a check for $350.00 U.S. Dollars (Three Hundred and Fifty U.S. Dollars). (The total value of the First Prize is $350.00 U.S. Dollars.) The ten (10) Second Prize Winners will each receive one (1) autographed *Chicken Soup for the American Idol Soul* book (approximate retail value of the book: $14.95 U.S. Dollars; Ten (10) Second Prizes total approximate retail value: $149.50 U.S. Dollars). If a Grand Prize Winner's guest is under the age of majority in the state or province in which such guest of the Winner resides, guest/minor must be 8 years of age or older at time of travel and the Grand Prize Winner must be the minor's parent/legal guardian.   Winners may not substitute, assign or transfer prize(s) for cash or to another party. All federal, state, provincial and local taxes, and all prize-related expenses not expressly noted above, are each Winner's sole responsibility. All prizes will be awarded. Sponsors reserve the right to substitute a prize of equal or greater value. In the event the American Idol Finale Show is cancelled or postponed for any reason, Sponsor will have no obligation to award compensation in lieu thereof but the remainder of the trip prize will be awarded. Prizes will be sent to Winners no later than thirty (30) days after each Winner's validation is complete. Total of all prizes will not exceed $4499.50 U.S. Dollars.

8. **Use of submission.** By accepting a prize, each Winner (or parent/guardian of Winner if Winner is under the age of majority in the state or province in which Winner resides) grants to Chicken Soup for the Soul Enterprises, Inc., a non-exclusive, perpetual license to print, re-print, translate, publish, sell and otherwise exploit his/her entry in any Chicken Soup for the Soul book, or other product displaying the Chicken Soup for the Soul trademark, and in any marketing and publicity in connection therewith; and consents to the use of his/her name, photograph, and likeness for such marketing and publicity purposes and for publicity purposes in connection with this Contest without any claim to further compensation, except where prohibited.

9. **Restrictions.** By submitting an Entry to the Contest, each Contestant (or parent/guardian of Contestant if Contestant is under the age of majority in the state which Contestant resides) agrees to (a) be bound by the decisions of the judges and these Official Rules; (b) comply with all federal, state, provincial, and local laws and regulations; and (c) indemnify, release and hold harmless the Sponsor, FremantleMedia North America, Inc., *American Idol* Productions, Inc., 19 TV Limited, 19 Merchandising Ltd., CKX, Inc., Health Communications, Inc., and their respective directors, officers, employees, representatives, agents, successors, assigns, subsidiaries and affiliates from any liability (including legal and attorneys' fees) from any claims, injuries, losses, damages, deaths, causes of action, actions, suits, debts, sums of money, or other liabilities, either at law or equity, whether known or unknown, asserted or non-asserted, arising from or in any way relating to the Winner's or any Contestant's participation in the Contest, the awarding, acceptance, use, or misuse of any prize, or the use of any submission. Any Winner under the age of majority in the state in which such Winner resides, such Winner must be accompanied by a parent or guardian

for all travel. Sponsors reserve the right to utilize Winner's name for promotional and/or publicity materials and Contest Entries will be deemed automatically approved of such utilization. Contestant also agrees that he/she shall have no claim (including, without limitation, claims based on invasion of privacy, defamation, or right of publicity) arising out of any use of his/her name, address (city and state or province only) and approved biographical information by Sponsor. Contestant represents and warrants that Contestant has the full right and authority to enter the Contest and to grant the rights granted herein and that Contestant's agreement to the terms hereof does not conflict with any existing commitment on Contestant's part. By participating in the Contest, each Contestant agrees that California law will apply to the Contest, and that any dispute with respect to the Contest will be resolved in either the federal or state courts located in the State of California. Sponsor is under no obligation to use submitted Entries for any purpose. Sponsor is not responsible and shall not be liable for: any human error or electronic, hardware, software, browser, network, Internet or computer error, failure, malfunction, congestion or incompatibility or difficulties of any kind or any condition caused by events beyond the control of Sponsor which may cause the contest to be disrupted or corrupted. Sponsor reserves the right in its sole discretion to cancel or suspend the contest or any portion thereof should any cause beyond Sponsor's control disrupt, corrupt and/or compromise the administration, security or proper play of the contest.

10. **Official Rules/Winners List.** Copies of these Official Rules and the Contributing Author Release form can be obtained at www.chickensoup. com, or by sending a self-addressed stamped envelope to: *Chicken Soup for the American Idol Soul* Contest Official Rules, c/o Chicken Soup for the Soul Enterprises, Inc. P.O. Box 30880, Santa Barbara, CA 93130. VT residents may omit return postage. Written requests for Official Rules must be received no later than February 28, 2008. To obtain the names of the prize winners, send a self-addressed stamped envelope no later than May 30, 2008, to: *Chicken Soup for the American Idol Soul* Contest Winners List, c/o Chicken Soup for the Soul Enterprises, Inc., P.O. Box 30880, Santa Barbara, CA 93130.

11. **Sponsor.** The Sponsor of the Contest is Chicken Soup for the Soul Enterprises, Inc., P.O. Box 30880, Santa Barbara, CA 93130.

12. **Contest is void where prohibited, taxed, or otherwise restricted.**

*The Sponsor will coordinate with the Grand Prize Winner to select airline flights that are mutually agreeable and such flights will be booked by the Sponsor as E tickets. If the Grand Prize winner resides in the Southern California area, airline tickets will not be applicable; however, in place of airline tickets, in addition to the round-trip ground transportation between the Finale and the hotel, Winner will also be awarded round-trip ground transportation from their home and the hotel. Choice of hotel and ground transportation provider will be at the sole discretion of the Sponsor.

More in the series

To order direct: Telephone (800) 441-5569 • www.hcibooks.com
Prices do not include shipping and handling. Your response code is CCS.